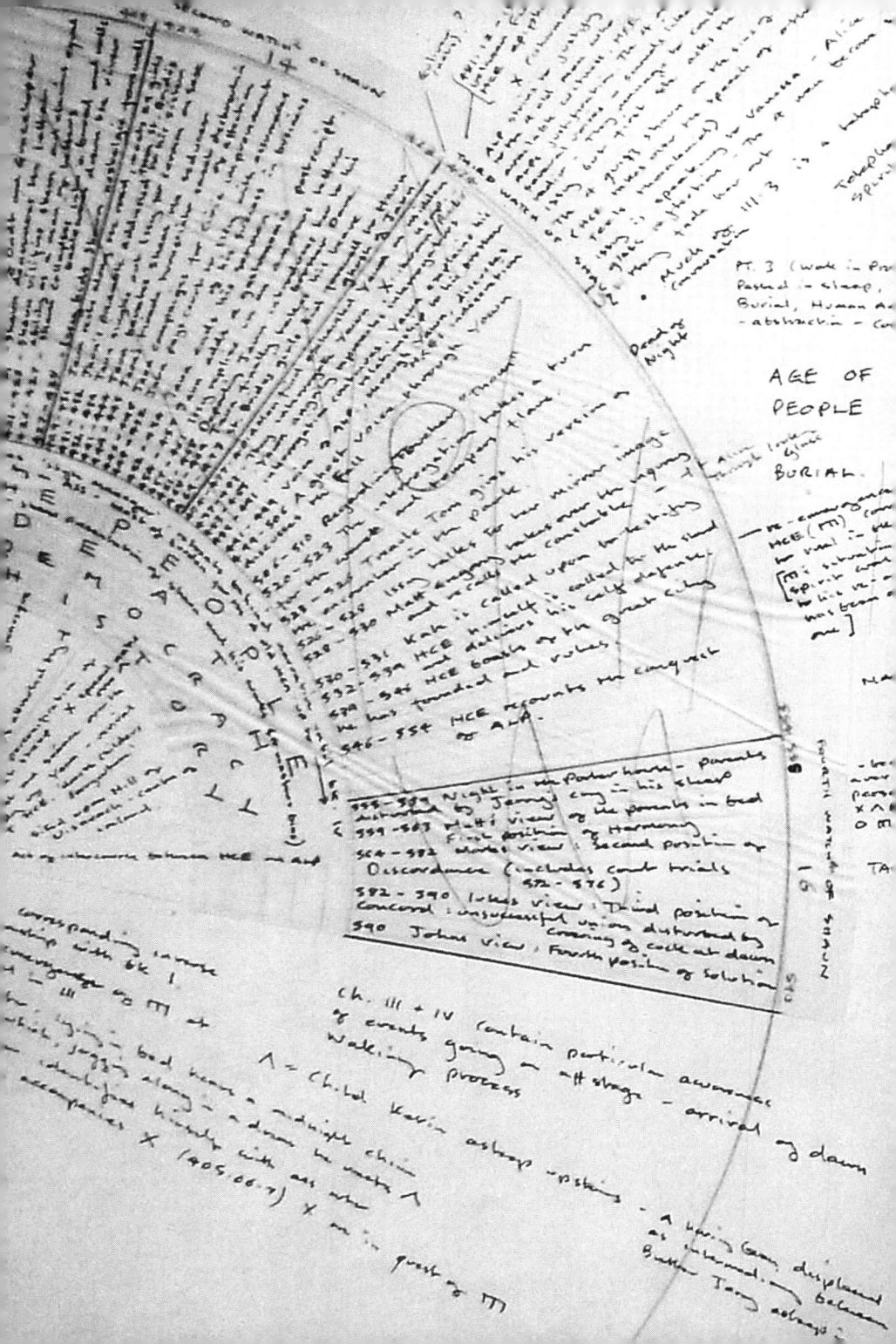

PT. 3 (work in Pr...
Passed in sleep,
Burial, Human A...
- abstraction - C...

AGE OF
PEOPLE
BURIAL.

520-523 Raphael performed "Muta" ...
524-526 Treacle Tom Jive his version ...
526-528 Issy walks to her mirror image ...
528-530 Mark enjoys one comfortable ...
528-530 Kate herself is called for the thud
530-531 HCE himself delivers his self defence
532-554 HCE extols the greats of the great cities
54x he has founded and rules.
546-555 HCE recounts the conquest
of ALP.

555-559 Night in the Porter house - parents
disturbed by Jerry's cry in his sleep
559-563 Matt's view of the parents in bed
First position of Harmony
564-582 Mark's view: Second position or
Discordance (includes court trials
572-576)
582-590 Luke's view: Third position or
Concord : unsuccessful union disturbed by
crowing of cock at dawn
590 Johns view: Fourth position of Solution

ch. III + IV contain particular awareness
of events going on at stage - arrival of dawn
Walking Process
Λ = Child Kevin asleep upstairs

The Giant's Grave

chaos without form, seeds of ... + Wicklow mountains + Wake cycle.

Finnegans Wake
Dead Giant eaten. Cannibalism

Ballads 'Epic of Earwicker' composing, disappear.
Rumours about Archaeological
Archaeology back in his
Return of King Arthur

Description of Earwicker
stories of fraternal
Mid Catholics conflict — Protestants

Hen
— 3 pages of alternative mythology
Finnskey — Interior
... mine ... 'The Ring' ...
... terms of clothing ...
... envelope of words?
Document to be interpreted
dunghill. Analysis ...
Authorship + Forgery

'Questions and answers.'
interpolated chapter

Narrator becomes Male
omnipresent
Central on Father / hero

1.1 Primeval hill country enduring recurrent violation

Fraternal quarrels
James and Stanislaus.
'Work in Progress'

ALP ... 1001 Sons ...

'Shem'
Joyce autobiography

buried monolith
fertile, this landscape.

hypermedia joyce

edited by
DAVID VICHNAR
LOUIS ARMAND

Prague 2010

Litteraria Pragensia Books
www.litterariapragensia.com

 Published 2009/2010 by Univerzita Karlova v Praze
Filozofická Fakulta

Litteraria Pragensia Books
Centre for Critical & Cultural Theory, DALC
Náměstí Jana Palacha 2
116 38 Praha 1, Czech Republic

The publication of this book has been partly supported by research grant
MSM0021620824 "Foundations of the Modern World as Reflected in Literature and
Philosophy" awarded to the Faculty of Philosophy, Charles University, Prague, by the
Czech Ministry of Education.

Cataloguing in Publication Data

Hypermedia Joyce, edited by David Vichnar & Louis Armand. — 1st ed.
p. cm.
ISBN 978-80-7308-314-4 (pb)
1. James Joyce. 2. Literary Theory. 3. Cultural Studies. 4. New Media.
I. Vichnar, David. II. Armand, Louis. III. Title

Printed in the Czech Republic by PB Tisk
Typesetting & design by lazarus

Cover images: Ian Hays
Frontispiece: Clinton Cahill

Contents

INTRODUCTION
Hypermnēsis | Hypertext | Text | Mnēsis

1. The perhaps defining peculiarity of Joycean scholarship is its awareness of its own presence *already in the text*, of its coming not from the outside, but somehow generated from, solicited by, the Joyce text which always already includes, as it were, its own theory.

One finds evidence of this critical double-bind in many different places. To take but a few examples: In his analysis of the opening of the "Sisters" story, Colin MacCabe insists that Joyce's insertion of the famed triad of the floating signifiers is a gesture by which the writing subject imposes severe limitation of the positions to be taken up by the reading subject, and thus prevents the text's analysis from being "constructed in terms of some external truth which the text represents or embodies," but rather in terms of the lines of force constitutive of the text, which engage with those same forces in our own discourse—in MacCabe's words, "truth is no longer correspondence but struggle."[1] At the 1984 Frankfurt symposium, in many respects a watershed for Joycean scholarship of the past quarter-century, Derek Attridge's opening address of the panel on "Deconstructive Criticism of Joyce" entitled "Criticism's Wake" points out that, just as Stephen's *amor matris* in *Ulysses*, the name of the panel contains both a subjective and an objective genitive—and that any notion of "applied deconstruction" is impossible especially regarding Joyce's writing.[2] The more rigorous psychoanalytical criticism *of* Joyce—undertaken in the wake of Jacques Lacan's engagement with Joyce's texts in the 1970's—also found the preposition ambiguous and in need of reconceptualisation; for instance, Luke Thurston dismisses any notion of "applied" psychoanalysis by referring to Lacan's notion of *pas-à-lire* as the only possible attitude to a "*writing* practice that exceeded [Lacan's] theoretical discourse" by "touch[ing] on a problem irreducible to the psychoanalytic representation of the subject."[3] Pitting against one another the early feminist critic of

---

[1] Colin MacCabe, *James Joyce and the Revolution of the Word* (New York: Palgrave, 1978) 38.

[2] Derek Attridge, "Deconstructive Criticism of Joyce," *Joyce Effects: On Language, Theory, and History* (Cambridge: Cambridge University Press, 2000).

[3] Luke Thurston, *James Joyce and the Problem of Psychoanalysis* (Cambridge: Cambridge University Press, 2004) 9.

the Anglo-American tradition, Susan Gilbert, and the later French feminist thinker, Julia Kristeva, and confronting their widely different views
on Joyce's treatment of female characters, Jeri Johnson concludes the
survey claiming that both positions represent a spliut within feminist
readings of Joyce that is generated in and by Joyce's text—or, "both
Gilbert and Kristeva have been right for both have identified operations
which do occur in *Ulysses*."[4] The ease with which Joyce's writing lends
itself to the various vawes of critical fashion has been also noted within
the framework of postcolonial studies; surveying the vogue, particularly
prominent in the late 1990's, of the "semi-colonial" Joyce, Mark Wollaeger comments on how "specific qualities of Joyce's work" enabled
critics "to re-dress a familiar modernist or poststructuralist Joyce in the
vestments of postcoloniality without seriously engaging Irish history or
substantially revising longstanding perspectives on Joyce as a high-
modernist innovator."[5] In view of these several examples, one can regard the criticism of Joyce as a discourse centered around a few
governing notions and operations already "at work" in Joyce's text, the
"truth" of its meta-discourse being, to borrow from Nietzsche, "a mov-
able host of metaphors, metonymies, and anthropomorphisms."[6]

2. This uncanny property of Joyce's writing was given its perhaps most
fitting expression in Jacques Derrida's plenary address at the 1984
Frankfurt symposium, "*Ulysses* Gramophone: Hear say yes in Joyce," as
well as in his essay on *Finnegans Wake*, "Two Words for Joyce."[7] Here,
the operations of Joyce's texts are likened to that of a "1000th generation computer" or "hypermnesis machine," and their effects

> are admirable and terrifying, and sometimes of intolerable violence. One of
> them has the following form: nothing can be invented *on the subject* of
> Joyce. Everything we can say about *Ulysses*, for example, has already
> been anticipated, including, as we have seen, the scene about academic
> competence and the ingenuity of metadiscourse.[8]

This all-inclusiveness is amusingly played out on how Derrida intervea-
wes his lecture with a seemingly digressive story about his purchase of
postcards in a Tokyo Hotel, only in order to demonstrate that

[4] Jeri Johnson, "Beyond the Veil": *Ulysses*, Feminism, and the Figure of Woman," *Joyce and the Art of Mediation*, ed. Christine van Boheemen (Amsterdam: Rodopi, 1989) 227.
[5] Mark Wollaeger, "Joyce and Postcolonial Theory: Analytic and Tropical Modes," *A Companion to James Joyce*, ed. Richard Brown (Oxford: Blackwell, 2008) 174.
[6] Friedrich Nietzsche, "On Truth and Lie in an Extra-Moral Sense," *The Continental Aesthetics Reader*, ed. Clive Cazeaux (London: Routledge, 2000) 55.
[7] Jacques Derrida, "Ulysses Gramophone: Hear Say Yes in Joyce," *James Joyce—The Augmented Ninth*, ed. Bernard Benstock (New York: Syracuse University Press, 1988); "Two Words for Joyce," *Poststructuralist Joyce*, ed. Derek Attridge & Daniel Ferrer (Cambridge: Cambridge University Press, 1984).
[8] Derrida, "Ulysses Gramophone," 48.

[e]verything that happened to me, including the narrative that would attempt to make of it, was already foretold and forenarrated, this
unusualness being dated, prescribed in a sequence of knowledge and narration: within *Ulysses*, to say nothing of *Finnegans Wake*, by a
hypermnesis machine capable of storing in an immense epic work, within
the Western memory and virtually all the languages in the world *including
traces of the future*. Yes, everything has already happened to us with
Ulysses and has been signed in advance by Joyce.[9]

This textual machine that somehow "includ[es] traces of the future,"
thereby exposing "the ingenuity of metadiscourse" yet to come, is what
drives the operations of the Joycean "yes." Joyce's preemptive inclusion
of the other, a *yes in advance* that, while seeming to affirm, paradoxically bespeaks a certain denial of the other. For this affirmation is
revealed to reflect the human awareness of being in the world as always
already aimed toward some other. Derrida's quasi-Heideggerian "being-
at-the-telephone" — paralleling Heidegger's *Dasein* as *der Angerufene* (the
called one)[10] — bears withnes to this denial through affirmation, as manifested by a whole series of technological means of communication
which Derrida follows throughout *Ulysses*: including the phonograph, the
gramophone, the telephone, the photographic camera, or indeed, the
rudimentary technology of writing itself.

3. The present volume, then, strives to conceptualize and think through
the whole of the Joycean canon by means of the metaphor of the *hypertext*. In 1965, Theodor H. Nelson coined the term "hypertext" to denote
"non-sequential writing — text that branches and allows choices to the
reader, best read at an interactive screen. As popularly conceived, this is
a series of text chunks connected by links which offer the reader different pathways."[11] In hypertext, one finds the Joycean programme of
machinic hypermnesis technologically transformed into the very ontological condition of text; text which devolves upon "affiliation,
correspondence, and resonance" and thus, presents a mere "temporally
extended network of relations which successive generations of readers
and writers perpetually make and unmake."[12] The bearings this technological transformation has upon the operations and functioning of
literature and writing can (and, particularly in the period right after its
advent, did) appear momentous. Especially as long as the literary canon
continues to be conceived of as an archive of written texts, which according to Jay D. Bolter function as "stable record[s] of thought" whose
stability resides precisely in the text's "physical medium: clay, papyrus

---

[9] Derrida, "Ulysses Gramophone," 48.
[10] Derrida, "Ulysses Gramophone," 40.
[11] Theodor H. Nelson, *Literary Machines* (Swarthmore, PA: Self-published, 1981) 2.
[12] Stuart Moulthrop, "You Say You Want a Revolution? Hypertext and the Laws of Media,"
      Postmodern Culture 1.3 (May 1991) 19.

or paper; tablet, scroll or book."[13] In this view, the potentially liberating instability of hypertext lies in its ontologically unstable *writing space*, where "the space is the computer's videoscreen where text is displayed as well as the electronic memory in which text is stored"—its conceptual innovation consists in what Bolter terms *topography*, referring to "mapping or charting—that is, to a visual and mathematical rather than verbal description," in which "electronic writing is [...] not the writing of a place, but rather a writing *with* places, spatially realized topics."[14] Similarly, George P. Landow has claimed that "one great advantage of digitalisation lies in the ease with which that form permits manipulation, searching, and [...] re-purposing."[15] Thus, both Bolter and Landow engage in establishing a binary opposition between an essentially solidifying and rigidifying print technology of the book, on the one hand, and the unfixing, destabilising technology of electronic textuality, on the other.

However, in both arguments, this division becomes blurred by occasional hints that the celebrated innovation has come as none other than an updated version of, and not a radical departure from, its predecessor. For Bolter, hypertext comes to cast light on the (already discovered) nature of textuality, of writing as such:

> Like all other forms of writing, electronic writing is an act of postponement or deferral. As writers, we defer our words by setting them down on a writing surface for later reading by ourselves or by others. [...] In the case of writing as elsewhere, it is not possible to put away technology. Writing with pen and paper is no more natural, no less technological than writing at a computer screen.[16]

According to Landow, electronic writing becomes a vantage testing ground on which to evaluate theories of textuality developed independently thereof:

> Electronic linking, which provides one of the defining features of hypertext, also embodies Julia Kristeva's notions of intertextuality, Mikhail Bakhtin's emphasis upon multivocality, Michel Foucault's conceptions of networks of power, and Gilles Deleuze and Félix Guattari's ideas of rhizomatic, "nomad thought."[17]

---

[13] Jay D. Bolter, "Hypertext, Hypermedia and Literary Studies: The State of the Art," *Hypermedia and Literary Stu*dies, eds. George P. Landow & Paul Delaney (Cambridge, MA: The MIT Press, 1994) 3.

[14] Jay D. Bolter, *Writing Space: The Computer, Hypertext, and the History of Writing* (Fairlawn, NJ: Lawrence Erlbaum Associates, 1990) 11; 25.

[15] George P. Landow, "What's a Critic To Do?: Critical Theory in the Age of Hypertext," *Hyper/Text/Theory*, ed. George P. Landow (Baltimore: Johns Hopkins University Press, 1994) 27.

[16] Bolter, "Hypertext, Hypermedia and Literary Studies," 30; 37.

[17] Landow, "What's a Critic To Do?" 1.

Hence, as Nelson himself never tired of emphasising, hypertext is such stuff as modern literature and its postmodern theory are made on—and the advent of hypertext, together with the ensuing establishment of hypertext theory, seem to confirm Walter J. Ong's assertion that despite occasioning a change in cognition, new media only transform, never eradicate their precursors.[18] An indeed convenient yardstick against which to measure the either relative or radical newness of the hypertext medium is the famed McLuhanesque tetrad of "laws of media,"[19] formulated as proceeding from four basic questions to be asked about any medium: 1. What does it enhance? 2. What does it render obsolete? 3. What does it retrieve that was previously obsolete? 4. What does it flip into when pushed to its extremes? In this light, the obvious answer to the question of obsolescence, i.e., "the book" or "literacy," are insufficient. For, as many have argued,[20] the principal enemy of the print culture, which carries to the extreme its tendency to privilege the visual, the homogeneous, and the global, is not so much the PC as the TV. Thus, a possible answer would employ another of Ong/McLuhan's notions, claiming that what the advent of hypertext renders obsolete is "secondary orality," a term denoting a recursion to non-print forms of language as enabled by the telephone and television. Electronic writing, and especially what Nelson termed *hypermedia*, interactive multimedia texts that involve music, animation, and video together with the text, presents a recursion of literacy, or in Bolter's words: "Hypermedia is the revenge of text upon television. In television, text is absorbed into the video image, but in hypermedia the televised image becomes part of the text."[21]

What bearing media and hypertextual theory has on Joyce's texts (and hypertexts) will remain for the collection essays to estimate, each in its own fashion and with different emphasis. Here, suffice it to point out how, coincidentally, the time in which Bolter and Landow pioneered hypertextual theory by thinking through the causes and consequences of hypertext as a new medium for literature and communication overlapped with the first attempts undertaken in the field of the Joycean hypertext. In 1990 the bulk of Joyce's work moved out of copyright for what was to be an unexpectedly brief period of a mere three years, as in 1993 Britain and the United States aligned their copyright laws with the broader EU standards and retrospectively extended the term of copyright protection from fifty to seventy years from the author's death. The period between 1990 and 1993 saw a flurry of activity on the part of Joycean scholars devoted to hypertextual adaptation and application of Joyce's texts: Donald Theall at the Canadian Trent University estab-

---

[18] Walter J. Ong, *Interfaces of the Word* (Ithaca: Cornell University Press, 1977) 82.
[19] Marshall McLuhan, *Laws of Media: The New Science* (Toronto: University of Toronto Press, 1988).
[20] See, e.g., Alvin Kernan, *The Death of Literature* (New Haven: Yale University Press, 1990).
[21] Bolter, "Hypertext, Hypermedia and Literary Studies," 26.

lished online versions of *Ulysses* and *Finnegans Wake*, followed by online texts of *A Portrait*, *Dubliners* and transcriptions of various notebooks and concordances; Fritz Senn and the Zurich Joyce Foundation undertook a computer presentation of the work of James Joyce, the so-called *HyperWake*, a computer-based hypermedia presentation of a paragraph from *Finnegans Wake*, which was first put on public display at a Joyce exhibition in 1991; in the early 1990's, Michael Groden, of the University of Western Ontario, one of the editors of the monumental *James Joyce Archive*, got involved in a project focused on engineering a hypermedia resource for *Ulysses* called *James Joyce's Ulysses: A Hypermedia Presentation*, to become *Digital Ulysses* — a project he was, for copyright reasons mentioned above, forced to abandon by the James Joyce Estate, and which therefore could be presented only in fragments.[22] In view of the increasing importance of the internet in everyday life, and in keeping with the nature of the projects above, the time was ripe for launching a first online magazine devoted to Joycean hypertextual theory and scholarship.

4. This collection sets out to commemorate the 10th volume of the *Hypermedia Joyce Studies* (*HJS*) magazine (issued in February 2010), the first electronic journal of Joycean scholarship, whose inaugural issue saw the light of day in December 1995 under the joint editorship of Louis Armand, Rob Callaghan, Alan Roughley and Julian Crofts. The following issue appeared in mid-1999, edited by Sheldon Brivic, Rob Callahan, Michael Groden, Cheryl Herr, Brandon Kershner and Thomas Rice, with another hiatus before its third issue in 2002, under the sole editorship of Armand, which established it as a regular bi-annual journal henceforth. By the appearance of its 10th volume in January 2010, the fifteen issues that comprise the history of *HJS* had brought to the public well over a hundred essays covering both the topic of its original intention, i.e. Joycean hypertext as a practical tool and a theoretical issue, and the whole gamut of traditional forms of more strictly text-based, exegetical Joycean scholarship. This volume seeks to preserve the twofold focus by dividing the presented material into two halves, each comprising seven essays, the former based on theoretical conceptualizations of hypertextuality within Joyce's writing, the latter mapping the variously undertaken "hypertextual" approaches to the whole of the Joycean canon, from the earliest epiphanies via *Stephen Hero* and *A Portrait* to *Ulysses* and *Finnegans Wake*.

5. The backbone of the first half of the book consists in four essays by Donald F. Theall, one of the most significant scholars of the historico-

---

[22] For a more detailed account, see Louis Armand, "Introduction: Literary Machines," *JoyceMedia: James Joyce, Hypermedia & Textual Genetics*, ed. Louis Armand (Prague: Litteraria Pragensia, 2006).

cultural-technological conditioning of Joyce's poetics, whose work is yet to given its due within the Joycean scholarship. The collection opens with Theall's seminal "Beyond the Orality/Literacy Dichotomy: James Joyce & the Prehistory of Cyberspace," which is involved with demonstrating how "the road to VR and MIT's Media Lab begins with poetic and artistic experimentation in the late nineteenth and early twentieth century." Surveying the breakneck pace, in the time of the writing of *Finnegans Wake*, of the development of communication media, such as the telegraph, telephone, cable, or television, Theall comes to view Joyce's poetic practice as a mode of resituating the medium of the book within the new communicative environment within which "the very nature of the word, the image, and the icon also changes," and consequently both writing and speech "are subsumed into entirely new relationships with non-phonemic sound, image, gesture, movement, rhythm, and all modes of sensory input, especially the tactile." The influence of electric media, in accordance with McLuhan's tetrad mentioned above, come to undermine the orality/literacy dichotomy in ways similar to how communication operated in its earliest stages where "objects, gestures and movements apparently intermingled with verbal and non-verbal sounds." Theall concludes by listing six reasons why Joyce's *Wake*an linguistic experimentation is of significance and interest for communication history and theory: first, Joyce's new language, designed as an investigation of the new modes of semiotic production; second, Joyce's critique of the historical role played by communication in the production of culture; third, his work as the first thorough exploration of the complexities of reading, writing, rewriting, speaking, aurality, orality, and so on; fourth, the accent on the "poetic" as a concept in communication, generating new communicative potentials between medium and message; fifth, Joyce's discussion of the contemporary transformation of our media of communication; and finally, Joyce's work as an exemplum of the socio-ecological role of the poetic in human communication.

This broad historical outline is supplemented, in Theall's next essay, "Joyce's Practice of Hypertextuality: The Anticipation of Hypermedia & Its Implications for Textual Analysis of *Finnegans Wake*," by a practical application of computer-based textual analysis onto various interpretive issues in Joyce's text. Derrida's computer-metaphor is invoked to corroborate that "computers exponentially increase the capability to investigate the *Wake* not only by their use in concordancing, searching and linking or their statistical power, but also because their hypermediac encyclopaedism is complementary to the *Wake*'s proto-hypermnesiac-encyclopaedism." Theall's example of a fruitful hypertextual "raiding" of *Finnegans Wake* is the use of a textual search engine:

> While the *Wake* is often described as a book about death. dream, sleep, trees and rivers, one of the more statistically significant words in it is

"old"—there are 463 occurrences of "old" alone (about three times as many as would likely be anticipated). When this is supplemented by the use of "old" as an initial syllable in compounds, the count rises to 539. If a dominant variant of old, "auld" together with its initial appearance in compounds is added, the count increases to 555. ... such analysis may reveal challenging, counter-intuitive views of the thematics of the *Wake*. Primarily, though, I am using it here to illustrate the potentialities for producing readings of the *Wake*, perhaps even reading the *Wake* in a manner closer to its conception.

Theall's third essay, "From the Cyberglobal Chaosmos to the Gutenberg Galaxy: The Prehistory of Cyberelectronic Language(s)," links the work of the pioneers of media & communication studies, Marshall McLuhan and Walter J. Ong, to the advances on the field of linguistic experimentation undertaken by the literary avant-gardists with Joyce as their taciturn patron saint. Theall terms the avant-garde aesthetico-political investment in language as "linguistic alchemy" and goes on to show how it lays the groundwork for not only "the ongoing transformations of media, since it underlines the fluidity of modes of communication, linking them with transitions in science and technology," but also "a growing acceptance of the quest for hypermedia, since it presents the probes which provide the linguistic fluidity and the synaesthetic consciousness that are requisite to understand the accelerating convergence of modes of statement." Ultimately, insists Theall, to appreciate the roots of electric media and hypetextual writing in the avant-garde movements entails both retrospection and prospection, for it means to return to them for "a deeper understanding of the problems of media ecology," but also to become aware of "the need to attend to and study the mature contemporary artists and poets" as a guide to comprehending "the ecological implications of the future of the twenty-first century."

This avant-garde context is further elaborated upon in Theall's fourth and last text, "Transformations Of The Book in Joyce's Dream Vision of Digiculture," which departs from the contention that Joyce's radical experimentation was not achieved "ex nihilo, for that historic Dadaist moment in Zürich during World War I was coupled shortly after with Dadaistic movements in New York, Berlin and Paris, later supplemented by Surrealism." However, more than with any other writer, to speak of "influence" is precarious with Joyce, who steadfastly refused any affiliation with the artistic groups or movements of his time. Instead, it was what Theall terms a multi-logical, polysemic "context of situation" that "opened up new ways of perceiving and thinking about events and phenomena that Joyce jointly shared with a contemporary community of artists and intellectuals." Joyce's "Dream Vision," then, consists in how his literary experiment not only embraced and exhausted its day and age (Theall mentions the noteworthy affinity of Joycean interests with the techno-scientific forays of the likes of Klee, Duchamp, Picabia, or Ernst), but also—and here Theall analyses a late (1938) insertion of a paragraph linking Anna Livia's letter with the Patrick/Berkeley debate—to mark its summation and forebode its future:

> What Joyce is able to dramatically demonstrate at the conclusion of the seventeen year process of writing the *Wake* is that through his transformations of poetic language he has moved writing and speech into that new post-electric world which was rapidly moving beyond media to a hypermedia and virtual reality.

As before, Joyce's investment in the contemporary and to-come is always simultaneously retrospective, as well as prospective: the many references, throughout the *Wake*, to ready-mades, mobiles, optical experimentation, along with other terms associated with the avant-garde artistic movements, function as the sundry exemplars of the semiotic, dialectical and rhetorical in the aesthetics of Joyce's time, for "[l]ike the Dadaists, their immediate progenitors and their successors, Joyce commingled in print what they had commingled in their performances and presentations." Still, one major aspect of the Dadaist aesthetics— represented, for Theall, primarily by Apollinaire—could be traced back to the beginnings of the printed book: the so-called "pattern" or "figured poetry." Therefore, concludes Theall, it must be noted that "Joyce's vision of the book is one that recognises its past historic transformations and its potentialities for a near infinite set of possibilities for future transformations."

Theall's broadly historico-cultural-technological forays into Joyce's literary experiment are punctuated by three essays, two by Darren Tofts and one by Louis Armand, which deal with the more specifically theoretical aspects of Joycean hypertextuality. Tofts' "'A Retrospective Sort of Arrangement': *Ulysses* & the Poetics of Hypertextuality," presents perhaps the most sustained attempt, in the present collection, at thinking hypertextuality as a condition underwriting Joyce's literary experimentation, and thus also present in its critical metadiscourse. Analogously to Theall's treatment to Joyce as a hypertextual writer *avant la lettre*, Tofts treats David Hayman's *Ulysses: The Mechanics of Meaning* (1970) and Hugh Kenner's *The Stoic Comedians* (1974) as critical works which expounded Joyce's "discontinuous textual poetics" that for Tofts "clearly anticipated the paradigmatic non-linearity of hypertext theory." Hypertextuality is conceived of as

> a way of characterising textual behaviour: in other words, as a form of poetics. In this respect, the idea of a textual poetics, which we can call hypertextuality, is a more useful device for thinking about the relationship between *Ulysses* and hypertext culture. That said, it is nonetheless a term to be applied to *Ulysses* with great care. Hypertextuality can be defined as a timely formulation of a more general, theoretical approach to understanding the way certain kinds of texts work.

Hayman's work serves as an illustration of literary meaning arising from a disjunctive structure, whereas Kenner's focuses on the operations of dissemination—both well before the hyper-vogue during which these notions became highly fashionable, thus re-enacting Joyce's hypertextual project *avant la lettre* by a similar pioneering of hitherto uncharted ground of hypertext theory, in whose examination *Ulysses* appears "as a kind of machinic assemblage that is built up, bit by bit, to and fro, from elaborate arrangements of its constituent parts, foregrounds a creative tension between the synchronic particularity of individual detail and the diachronic linking of details into systems of cross-reference." In turn, by surveying the hypertext theory of the 1990's, Tofts shows how "interactivity, non-linearity, and retrospective backtracking" all have their origin in "a fundamental, vectoral configuration of textual behaviour," which in Joyce's case grew out of his strategy of "applied Aquinas" - in particular, the principle of *consonantia*, "the exact interrelation of parts within the whole," is what "motivated the momentous potential in the text for cross-reference, incidence and coincidence." Echoing Aarseth's criticism of the binary schemata upheld by Bolder or Landow, Tofts calls for moving "beyond the clichés of linear book and non-linear hypertext" and coins the term "cybertext," as a "perspective on all forms of textuality" that require an "interactive, combinative approach to reading."

Tofts's second collected piece, "Where Are We at All? & Whenabouts in the Name of Space?", follows the theoretical framework built up in the former piece by a more closely exegetical essay that looks at the ways modern media technologies, both present (television) and future (the internet) vis-à-vis Joyce's time, illuminate from within, or cast light back on, the complex mimetic operations of the *Wake*. Chapter three of Book two, features the most prominent appearance of the television, and Tofts's analysis shows that not only is Joyce's "interest in its historical formation as a mode of communication" closely connected with his "familiarity with contemporary understandings on the nature of time and space," but also that his treatment of this medium shows Joyce's conviction that "television would become the dominant form of popular culture in this century." As regards the internet, Tofts links Nelson's famous axiom, "everything is deeply intertwingled," to the *Wake*an "nightmaze" (*FW* 411.8) and, indeed, to the exclamation that forms the title of his essay (*FW* 558.33). To place the text of the *Wake* within the lineage of hypertext and hypermedia, for Tofts, is to, once again, abolish the simplistic binary within (hyper)textual (non-)linearity and to regard writing as a technology in need of constant extension of itself in response to cultural evolution from paperspace to cyberspace:

> He was, as the vanguard saying goes, ahead of his time in making the jump from paperspace to cyberspace. However it is a mistake to think that with the *Wake* he simply wrote a book that *looks like* hypertext. In fact he didn't write a book at all. He provided a complex system of prompting, the primary node in an interface to be activated by the reader.

Emblematic of both Joyce's investment in the technological interest of the arts of his time and his importance as a clairvoyante for experimentation yet to come are the parallels Tofts draws between his writing and the projects of Duchamp and Cage, respectively. What these three artists from across disciplines, eras, and programmes do share is their enhancement and transgression of the respective media to which their art forms have been traditionally reduced: "Joyce didn't write books. Duchamp didn't create works of art. Cage didn't compose music. They created interfaces, instances into which someone intervened to make choices and judgements that they were not willing to make." Tofts, thus, recontextualizes Joyce, in the company of Duchamp and Cage, under the banner of "interactive media," defined by their sustainment of the creative act, the act of engagement, and "the pleasure of feeling that you don't have to go somewhere, but are simply going," a pleasure with which "you are as much interested in what you are doing as any reason you might be doing it for."

Louis Armand's piece, "From Symptom to Machine," holds up Humberto Maturana and Francesco Varela's cybernetic notion of *autopoietic machine* as a parallel to what in philosophical discourse Gilles Deleuze and Félix Guattari have termed "desiring machines" whose operations bring about "transverse communications" which, for Armand, emerge in the *Wake* in terms of "an overall apparatus, underwriting a general thematics of identity, autopoiesis, alchemy, duplicity, copyright, historicity and so on." Another (pre-)cybernetic notion, the Turing 'grid," a means of "organising language as a whole in terms of material combination and recombination," provides a metaphor for how some of the key Joycean intertexts come to structure his own works: "In this way the cyclical notions of Giambattista Vico or Friedrich Nietzsche, or the structural repetitions of Homer's *Odyssey* and the Bible, can equally be thought of in acrostic terms." However, one of the key questions posed by Joyce's writing, for Armand, goes beyond such parallels and is one of "how to account for the possibility of this acrostic grid exceeding its own rules." A structural analysis of the overall setup of the *Wake* and its three-plus-one logic with the impossible postulate of three equaling four, reveals the relevance of Jacques Lacan's comment that *Finnegans Wake* should not be viewed as circular but as knotted, instead. From here, Armand plunges deeper into Lacan's late seminars on Joyce, where the figure of the Borromean knots is deployed to demonstrate the entanglement within the three-plus-one structure of the three orders and their link (the symptom): "It is necessary to posit the Borromean knot in a doubly four-fold manner: as the symptomatic *topos* of the encounter of the imaginary, symbolic and real, and as their *tropological* linkage. It is this tropological counterpart of the symptom that Lacan refers to as *le sinthome*." The gist of Armand's essay, then, consists in demonstrating that this entanglement can indeed be "regarded as describing (by a process of metonymy) the basic condition of Joyce's language in *Finnegans Wake*."

6. The first seven pieces by Donald Theall, Darren Tofts and Louis Armand, who have employed, in their own various ways and for their own various needs, the metaphor of *hypertext* in order to grasp some of the defining features of Joyce's techno-poetics, are followed by seven essays by seven different authors, each of whom creatively reimagines the technology of writing at work in Joyce's *oeuvre* by means of a conceptual metaphor of its own: writing as a dance (Milesi), as the product of epiphany (Norris), as recyclation (Bénéjam), as the impossible origin (Deppman), as bootstrapping (Dumitrescu), as a boundary-blurring force of unification (Marvin), and as linguistic inscription (Roughley).

In "Joyce's Choreo-graphies in *Stephen Hero* & *A Portrait of the Artist as a Yong Man*," Laurent Milesi departs from the following question:

> how does Joyce the *poète manqué* who, via several evolving artistic personae (Stephen Dedalus(es), Shem the Penman), never abandoned his interest in theories of language and the place these allocate to the poetic, feature among a range of practitioners who foregrounded the mechanics of writing, using as an analogical touchstone similes with rhythm, dance, gesture, e-motion, etc, in order (ultimately) to work out alternative genealogies for the practice of writing?

Milesi examines this question by mapping the gradual development of Joyce's aesthetics of the epiphany into a more full-blown "choreography of writing" in *Stephen Hero* and *A Portrait*. Epiphany itself becomes "a gesture recording kinetically [...] the intrusion of the vivid external reality of lived experience into the realm of artistic expression, the successful embodiment of something real and objective into something linguistic and subjective." Milesi's comparative treatment of *A Portrait* and its Urtext, then, shows a regression of the former's kinetic treatment of epiphany into the latter's static understanding of "beauty." Once the raw material of *Stephen Hero* has become subjected to the modernist rewriting in *A Portrait of the Artist as a Young Man*, "the more straightforwardly kinetic dimension of the epiphanic experience will modulate into the stasis of dramatic equipoise at the heart of the 'rhythm of beauty.'" There is, however, a retrograde movement within *A Portrait* alone, since Milesi interprets Joyce's decision to turn the end of *A Portrait* into a series of shorthand entries from a first-person diary "as a retrograde "doubling backwards into the past" for strategic compositional purposes, an overall choreography of writing of which there will be many numerous examples in *Ulysses* and *Finnegans Wake*." Thus, even though epiphany in *A Portrait* no longer occupies a place as central as it did in *Stephen Hero*, the text exhibits a gesture of retrospection and return by means of which "this crucial difference between religion and aesthetics" recasts more effectively "the still predominantly rhythmical-gestural, quasi-mythical foundation of art." The further revisitation of these topics in *Ulysses* and *Finnegans Wake* will, for Milesi, ultimately entail "a fuller coming to terms with the necessity of compromising with polar opposites [...] and with what the younger fictional artist had despised about the President in *Stephen Hero*: the 'hermaphroditic gesture' (*SH* 90)."

Andrew Norris's essay "Joyce & the Post-Epiphanic" departs from the observation that "Joyce's epiphanies and the accounts of the epiphany he stages in his work, lack claritas" and furthermore that entailed within them is "a confusion of agency: we are not sure who or what does what to what or whom." Norris's focus here is not only on the hesitation between consonantia and claritas or the destabilised subject-object relation, but also on the process through which epiphanic revelation of singularity enters the plurality of language, giving rise to what he terms "post-epiphanic style." As in Milesi's view, Norris regards this style as marked by a peculiar duality of stasis and kinesis:

> As the thing enters the presence of its whatness, the sequential thought which characterises the kinesis of consciousness is arrested. Beauty is neither in the eye of the beholder nor in the thing beheld, but in the perceptual moment of stasis in which both are clearly involved [...] Stephen says that the true "produces a stasis of the mind," but we might prefer to suppress the kinesis of the verb and say simply that stasis is truth. The epiphany, whatever else it is, is certainly a form of truth; and the post-epiphanic, whatever else it is, is a problematisation of this singular form of truth.

Also in accordance with Milesi's chart of development is Norris's belief that this problematisation of singularity becomes fully articulated as Joyce's writing evolves through *Ulysses* to *Finnegans Wake*, where kinesis becomes surpassed by polykinesis (Norris's example is Bloom's variations on his name in the "Ithaca" chapter) and style encroaches upon the structures that render kinesis susceptible to epiphany in the first place. Hand in hand with the post-epiphanic comes a revision of the Aristotelian logic of non-contradiction, where the multiplication of the properties of the subject and object leads to a collapse of absence into presence and vice versa, "juxtaposing a logic of representation submissive to the conventions of sequential narrative and its "one great goal of revelation" with a permissive violation of these conventions conceivably inspired by the example of claritas." Eventually, the medium of writing delegates the presence of the epiphanic moment always already to the past, or, in Norris's conclusion: "After the epiphany, whatness is also its own wasness."

Valérie Bénéjam's essay on "The Reprocessing of Trash in *Ulysses*: Recycling & (Post)Creation" focuses on the thematisation, throughout *Ulysses*, of writing as a production of marks upon a material surface, and uses the topics of trashing and recycling to illuminate some of

Joyce's own creative methods. The complementary modes of recycling found in the two protagonists—Bloom's "careful husbandry" of objects others have discarded and Stephen's "prodigious memory" that recycles the words of others—are found mirrored in Joyce's own creative method:

> The notebooks, manuscripts and proofs, thus deciphered and fitted with commentary, stand as so many witnesses to the formidable reprocessing that produced Joyce's text. For when genetic critics look at the *Notebooks*, they consider in turn the origin and the finality: on one hand, they are concerned with finding the sources Joyce borrowed from, and on the other, with discovering where the quotes have been transferred in Joyce's text.

Again, this metaphor of recycling is brought onto yet another level in Joyce's final work, where "the recycling comes close to nuclear reprocessing, given the thoroughness and the meticulousness of the transformations completed, at the atomic level almost, when the structure of words may be altered beyond recognition."

In "The Problem of Genesis," Jed Deppman looks at the theme of "origin" as presented in three important scenes of character's writing in *Ulysses*, which "in particular seem to form an important local economy or nodal network." The scenes are the following ones: first, "the scene toward the end of "Proteus" in which Stephen searches for paper to write down a poem"; next, the scene in which Bloom "composes in his mind a poem about a seagull and then revises it, with purposeful irony, later in the same chapter"; and finally, the scene where Buck Mulligan "begins scribbling down some humorously-intended ideas for a play" and later on "reads from his "tablet." Stephen's poem, then, is "best understood as a failed genesis expressed through a poetics of excretion"; Bloom's "postulates not automatic writing [...] but the furthest possible radicalization of the idea of the passive artist"; and Mulligan's "presents the limit point of a prestidigitative artist and an artistry without any art: the opposite, then, of the Bloomian genesis." Deppman's sensitive reading suggests the potential use of looking "more synoptically and simultaneously at the poetics of genesis in play in different units of [Joyce's] texts and avant-textes."

Alexandra Dumitrescu's "Mapping Networking Universes, or, Bootstrapping *Finnegans Wake* in Search of Truth," offers "bootstrapping" as a metaphor for some of the semantic operations of the *Wake*, referring to "a conception of the material world as an interconnected web of relations." In a text thusly construed, "bootstrapping refers to the dynamics of the network," its defining function being "the emergence of meaning as a result of this dynamism." This cybernetic networking implies not just a reversal of hierarchies as evinced in e.g. Blake, but their thorough cancellation which adumbrates the ethos of postmodernism. Or, in Dumitrescu's words:

Finnegans Wake, with its unhierarchical textual organization affords a vision of the world crystallized alongside principles of interconnectivity: a universe perceived as made up of networks whose cultural, political, economical, historical or human nodes or hubs determine and explain each other. [...] Joyce never tires of reinforcing the idea that the kosmos he creates, as the world he sees (and listens to), defies ranking not only when it comes to the sounds and words used to describe it and its dynamism, but also in terms of the non-linguistic constitutive elements it evokes.

What the bootstrapping model requires of the critic is fairly evident: it presupposes that one should "consider the text, the manuscripts and biographical anecdotes as making up a whole that allows for a plurality of interpretations, none of which can be deemed to be 'false' or 'the only true.'" In an epistemological context, "bootstrapping means the negation of a single absolute truth in favour of truths that interrelate and thus define themselves in the process."

John Marvin in his *"Finnegans Wake* III.3 & the Third Millennium: The Ghost of Modernisms Yet to Come" revisits Joyce's final masterpiece in its own day and age, drawing parallels between Joyce's advances in poetics with that of contemporary physics: while Joyce was writing, "Einstein was grappling with the relationship between the world of things we sense, and the uncertain, chaotic world view that emerges from quantum mechanics and the inexorable laws of chance." Joyce's aesthetic achievement, for Marvin, lied in precisely what physics of his time—split in between the irreconcilable relativity theory and quantum mechanics—sought to achieve: the unification of disparate force fields.

Finally, Alan R. Roughley's "Feigning Dublin: Joyce's Repositioning of His Readers" provides a commodius vicus of recirculation in that it surveys, one by one, Joyce's three mature texts, providing a bird's-eye view on a substantial part of the corpus from the vantage point of the author-reader relationship. The philosophical starting point, for Roughley, is the work of Jacques Derrida, which for a critic of a work of a writer like Joyce, who "interrogates the nature and the roles of the reader from a philosophical as well as a literary perspective [...] offers a valuable, alternative way of opening up an engagement with these relationships." Roughley's transverse reading of the three Joyce texts reveals the following: *A Portrait* seems governed by "both realist and symbolist modes of representation," its narrative structure "sustained by metaphors like the table, the net, the bird, the tower, the old sow and a variety of religious symbols," which metaphors are all supported by "the chain of metonymy that supports the metaphors and provides the reader with an alternative network of paths for traversing the text." In *Ulysses*, Joyce's writing is structured "in part by the paronomasian link between representing Dublin and a writing that is continually "doubling" its subject," a writing which, together with the withdrawal from mimetic representation to linguistic inscription, "allows the reader to experience the "sublime relation between the presentable and the unpresentable" (Roughley's example here is the famous "Plumtree ad"). Eventually, the *Wake* is a democratic text that "invites its readers to share in a recreation which is, literally, a re-creation, and there is little evidence to suggest that it en- snares its readers or draws them into its dense textual thickets only to leave them wandering lost in the middle of its woods." The creation of such reader positions is still only "one of the numerous strategies by which the *Wake* assists its readers, and its use of pronouns for the interpellation of its readers is inscribed in a writing that identifies itself as "prepronominal" (*FW* 120.9).

7. This volume as a whole, then, moves in the double movement best described in the French phrase *reculer pour mieux sauter*, drawing back in order to jump better. It regresses from hypertext to text by putting back into the print medium texts originally conceived and written to be viewed on the computer screen, some of which are of their time and quite distant in ethos from our present moment. As with any commemo- rative (*mnēsis*) volume of this scope, there must be a sense of a certain belatedness, even outdateness.

However, the circumstances of the present moment make this belat- edness into an expectation of the future, for this collection comes on the eve of what will hopefully be a resuscitation of long-abandoned projects that saw the light of day in that brief period between 1990 and 1993; in 2011, the term of copyright protection for Joyce's works will be termi- nated, and so in 2012, they will at last be allowed to enter the public (cyber)sphere. Joycean scholarship has certainly much to fall back on as regards both the practical applications of hypertext from twenty years ago and the discourse aimed at reconceptualising textuality through engagement with Joyce's writing, but also much work to do in pursuit of blending these two together in a new synthesis, especially within the potentially highly productive fusion of hypertext with textual genetics. It is to both these aspects of its present moment that *Hypermedia Joyce* seeks to bear witness.

David Vichnar
Prague, June 2010

DONALD F. THEALL
Beyond the Orality / Literacy Dichotomy: James Joyce & the Pre-History of Cyberspace

The Gutenberg Galaxy, a book which redirected the way that artists, critics, scholars and communicators viewed the role of technological mediation in communication and expression, had its origin in Marshall McLuhan's desire to write a book called "The Road to *Finnegans Wake*." It has not been widely recognized just how important James Joyce's major writings were to McLuhan, or to other major figures (such as Jorge Luis Borges, John Cage, Jacques Derrida, Umberto Eco, and Jacques Lacan) who have written about aspects of communication involving technological mediation, speech, writing, and electronics. While all of these connections should be explored, the most enthusiastic Joycean of them all, McLuhan, provides the most specific bridge linking the work of Joyce and his modernist contemporaries to the development of electric communication and to the prehistory of cyberspace and virtual reality. McLuhan's scouting of "the Road to *Finnegans Wake*" established him as the first major disseminator of those Joycean insights which have become the unacknowledged basis for our thinking about technoculture, just as the pervasive McLuhanesque vocabulary has become a part, often an unconscious one, of our verbal heritage.

In the mid-80s, William Gibson first identified the emergence of cyberspace as the most recent moment in the development of electromechanical communications, telematics and virtual reality. Cyberspace, as Gibson saw it, is the simultaneous experience of time, space, and the flow of multi-dimensional, pan-sensory data:

> All the data in the world stacked up like one big neon city, so you could cruise around and have a kind of grip on it, visually anyway, because if you didn't, it was too complicated, trying to find your way to the particular piece of data you needed. Iconics, Gentry called that.[1]

This "consensual hallucination" produced by "data abstracted from the banks of every computer in the human system" creates an "unthinkable complexity. Lines of light ranged in the nonspace of the mind, clusters

[1] William Gibson, *Mona Lisa Overdrive* (New York: Bantam Paperback, 1989) 16.

and constellations of data. Like city lights receding."[2] Almost a decade earlier, McLuhan's remarks about computers (dating from the late 70s) display some striking similarities:[3]

> It steps up the velocity of logical sequential calculations to the speed of light reducing numbers to body count by touch... . It brings back the Pythagorean occult embodied in the idea that "numbers are all"; and at the same time it dissolves hierarchy in favor of decentralization. When applied to new forms of electronic-messaging such as teletext and videotext, it quickly converts sequential alphanumeric texts into multi-level signs and aphorisms, encouraging ideographic summation, like hieroglyphs.[4]

McLuhan's *hieroglyphs* certainly more than anticipate Gibson's *iconics* and McLuhan's particular use of hieroglyph or iconology, like that of mosaic, primarily derives from Joyce and Giambattista Vico.

It is not surprising then that McLuhan's works, side by side with those of Gibson, have been avidly read by early researchers in MIT's Media Lab,[5] for these researchers also conceive of a VR composed, like the tribal and collective "global village," of "tactile, haptic, proprioceptive and acoustic spaces and involvements."[6] The experiments of the artistic avant-garde movements (such as the Dadaists, the Bauhaus and the Surrealists) and of individuals (such as Marcel Duchamp, Paul Klee, Sergei Eisenstein or Luis Bunuel) generated the exploration of the semiotics and technical effects of such spaces and involvements. Duchamp, for example, became an early leading figure in splitting apart the presumed generic boundaries of painting and sculpture to explore arts of motion, light, movement, gesture, and concept, exemplified in his *Large Glass*[7] and the serial publication of his accompanying notes from *The Box of 1914* through *The Green Box* to *A l'infinitif*. His interest in the notes as part of the total work echo Joyce's own interest in the publication of *Work in Progress* and commentaries he organized upon it (e.g., *Our Exagmination Round his Factification for Incamination of Work in Progress*). Joyce also explores similar aspects of motion, light, movement, gesture and concept. So the road to VR and MIT's Media Lab begins with poetic and artistic experimentation in the late nineteenth and

---

[2] William Gibson, *Neuromancer* (New York: Ace, 1984) 51.

[3] This quotation is taken from the posthumously published Marshall McLuhan and Bruce R. Powers, *The Global Village: Transformations in World Life and Media in the 21st Century* (New York: Oxford University Press, 1989). It was edited and rewritten from McLuhan's working notes, which had to date from the late 70s, since he died in 1981. McLuhan's words were written more than a decade before their posthumous publication in 1989.

[4] Marshall McLuhan and Bruce R. Powers, *The Global Village: Transformations in World Life and Media in the 21st Century* (New York: Oxford University Press, 1989) 103.

[5] Stuart Brand, *The Media Lab: Inventing the Future at MIT* (New York: Viking, 1987).

[6] Marshall McLuhan, *The Letters of Marshall McLuhan*, ed. Matie Molinaro, Corinne McLuhan and William Toye (Toronto: Oxford University Press, 1987) 385.

[7] Craig E. Adcock, *Marcel Duchamp's Notes from the Large Glass: An N-Dimensional Analysis* (Ann Arbor, Michigan: UMI, 1983), 28: "The *Large Glass* is an illuminated manuscript consisting of 476 documents; the illumination consists of almost every work that Duchamp did."

early twentieth century; later, as Stuart Brand notes, many of the Media Lab researchers of the 60s and 70s placed great importance on collaboration with artists involved in exploring the nature and art of motion and in investigating new relationships between sight, hearing, and the other senses.[8]

Understanding the social and cultural implications of VR and cyberspace requires a radical reassessment of the inter-relationships between Gibson's now commonplace description of cyberspace, McLuhan's modernist-influenced vision of the development of electric media, and the particular impact that Joyce had both on McLuhan's writings about electrically mediated communication and on the views of Borges, Cage, Derrida, Eco and Lacan regarding problems of mediation and communication. Such a reassessment requires that two central issues be discussed: (i) the crucial nature of VR's challenge to the privileging of language through the orality/literacy dichotomization used by many theorists of language and communication; (ii) the idea of VR's presence as *the* supermedium that encompasses and transcends all media. The cluster of critics who have addressed orality and literacy, following the lead of Walter Ong, H.A. Innis and Eric Havelock, have—like them—failed to comprehend the fact that McLuhan was disseminating a Joycean view which grounded communication in tactility, gesture and CNS processes, rather than promulgating the emergence of a new oral/aural age, a secondary orality. This emphasis on the tactile, the gestural and the play of the CNS in communication is a key to Joyce's literary exploration of a theme he shared with his radical modernist colleagues in other arts who envisioned the eventual development of a coenaesthetic medium[9] that would

---

8 Stuart Brand, The Media Lab: Inventing the Future at MIT (New York: Vik ng, 1987).
9 A further paper needs to be written on the way in which synaesthesia as well as coenesthesia participate in the pre- history of cyberspace. The unfolding history of poets and artists confronting electromechanical technoculture, which begins in the 1850s, reveals a growing interest in synesthesia and coenesthesia and parallels a gradually accelerating yearning for artistic works which are syntheses or orchestrations of the arts. By 1857 Charles Baudelaire intuited the future transformational power of the coming of electro-communication when he established his concept of synaesthesia and the trend toward a synthesis of all the arts as central aspects of *symbolisme*. The transformational matrices involved in synaesthesia and the synthesis of the arts unconsciously respond to that digitalization implicit in Morse code and telegraphy, anticipating how one of the major characteristics of cyberspace will be the capability of all modes of expression to be transformed into minimal discrete contrastive units-bits.

This assertion concerning Baudelaire's use of synesthesia is developed from Benjamin's discussions of Baudelaire. The role of shock in Baudelaire's poetry, which links the "Correspondances" with "La Vie Anterieur," also reflects how the modern fragmentation involved in "Le Crepuscle du Soir" and "Le Crepuscle du Matin" is reassembled poetically through the verbal transformation of sensorial modes. This is the beginning of a period in which the strategy of using shock to deal with fragmentation is transformed into seeing the multiplicity of codifications of municipal (or urban) reality. So when the metamorphic sensory effects of nature's temple are applied to the splenetic here and now, in the background is the emergence of the new codifications of reality, such as the photography which so preoccupied Baudelaire, and telegraphy, which had an important impact in his lifetime.

integrate and harmonize the effects of sensory and neurological information in currently existing and newly emerging art forms.

Joyce's work should be recognized as pioneering the artistic exploration of two sets of differences—orality/literacy and print/[tele-] electric
media—that have since become dominant themes in the discussion of
these questions. *Finnegans Wake* is one of the first major poetic encounters with the challenge that electronic media present to the traditionally
accepted relationships between speech, script and print. (*Ulysses* also
involves such an encounter, but at an earlier stage in the historic development of mediated communication.) Imagine Joyce around 1930 asking
the question: what is the role of the book in a culture which has discovered photography, phonography, radio, film, television, telegraph, cable,
and telephone and has developed newspapers, magazines, advertising,
Hollywood, and sales promotion? What people once read, they will now
go to see in film and on television; everyday life will appear in greater
detail and more up-to-date fashion in the press, on radio and in television; oral poetry will be reanimated by the potentialities of sound
recording.[10]

The "counter-poetic," *Finnegans Wake*, provides one of *the* key texts
regarding the problem presented by the dichotomization of the oral and
the written and by its frequent corollary, a privileging of either speech or
language. This enigmatic work is not only a polysemic, encyclopedic
book designed to be read with the simultaneous involvement of ear and
eye: it is also a self-reflexive book about the role of the book in the elec-
tro-machinic world of the new technology.[11] The *Wake* is the most
comprehensive exploration, prior to the 1960s or 70s, of the ways in
which these new modes created a dramatic crisis for the arts of language and the privileged position of the printed book. The *Wake*
dramatizes the necessary deconstruction and reconstruction of language
in a world where multi-semic grammars and rhetorics, combined with
entirely new modes for organizing and transmitting information and
knowledge, eventually would impose a variety of new, highly specialized
roles on speech, print and writing. Joyce's selection of Vico's *New Science*[12] as the structural scaffolding for the *Wake*—the equivalent of
Homer's *Odyssey* in *Ulysses*— underscores how his interest in the contemporary transformation of the book requires grounding the evolution of

---

[10] See D.F. Theall, "The Hieroglyphs of Engined Egypsians: Machines, Media and Modes of
Communication in *Finnegans Wake*," *Joyce Studies Annual 1991*, ed. Thomas F. Staley
(Austin: Texas University Press, 1991) 129-52. This publication provides major source mate-
rial for the present article.

[11] "Machinic" is used here very deliberately as distinct from mechanical. See Gilles Deleuze,
Dialogues, trans. Hugh Tomlinson & Barbara Haberjam (New York: Columbia University Press,
1987) 70-1, where he discusses the difference between the machine and the "machinic" in
contradistinction to the mechanical.

[12] Giambattista Vico, *The New Science*, ed. T.G. Bergen and M. Fisch (Ithaca, New York:
Cornell University Press, 1948).

civilization in the poetics of communication, especially gesture and language and the "prophetic" role of the poetic in shaping the future.

As the world awakens to the full potentialities for the construction of artifacts and processes of communication in the new electric cosmos, Joyce foresees the transformation (not the death) of the book—going beyond the book as it had historically evolved. Confronted with this situation, Joyce seeks to develop a poetic language which will resituate the book within this new communicative cosmos, while simultaneously recognizing the drive toward the development of a theoretically all-inclusive, all-encompassing medium, "virtual reality." Since the action takes place in a dreamworld, Joyce can produce an impressively prophetic imaginary prototype for the virtual worlds of the future. His dreamworld envelops the reader within an aural sphere, accompanied by kinetic and gestural components that arise from effects of rhythm and intonation realized through the visual act of reading; but it also reproduces imaginarily the most complex multi-media forms and envisions how they will utilize his present, which will have become the past, to transform the future.[13]

The hero(ine)[14] in the *Wake*, "Here Comes Everybody." is a communicating machine, "This harmonic condenser enginium (the Mole)" (*FW* 310.1), an electric transmission-receiver system, an ear, the human sensorium, a presence "eclectrically filtered for all irish earths and ohmes" (*FW* 309.24). Joyce envisions the person as embodied within an electro-machinopolis (an electric, pan-global, machinic environment), which becomes an extension of the human body, an interior presence, indicated by a stress on the playfulness of the whole person and on tactility as calling attention to the interplay of sensory information within the electro-chemical neurological system. This medley of elements and concerns, focussed on questioning the place of oral and written language in an electro-mechanical technoculture that engenders more and more comprehensive modes of communication biased towards the dramatic, marks Joyce as a key figure in the pre-history of virtual reality.

Acutely sensitive to the inseparable involvement of speech, script, and print with the visual, the auditory, the kinesthetic and other modes

---

[13] For fuller discussion of Joyce and these themes see Donald Theall, "James Joyce: Literary Engineer," in *Literature and Ethics: Essays Presented to A.E. Malloch*, ed. Gary Wihl & David Williams (Montreal: McGill-Queen's University Press, 1988) 111-27; Donald and Joan Theall, "James Joyce and Marshall McLuhan," *Canadian Journal of Communication* 14:4/5 (Fall 1989): 60-1; and Donald Theall, "The Hieroglyphs of Engined Egypsians: Machines, Media and Modes of Communication in *Finnegans Wake*," *Joyce Studies Annual 1991*, ed. Thomas F. Staley (Austin: Texas University Press, 1991) 129-152. A number of subsequent passages are adapted with minor modifications from parts of the last article, which is a fairly comprehensive coverage of Joyce and technology.

[14] While in one sense the dreamer is identified as the male HCE, the book opens and closes with the feminine voice of ALP. It is her dream of his dreaming, or his dream of her dreaming? Essentially, it is androgynous, with a mingling of male and female voices throughout. For another treatment of the male- female theme in the *Wake*, see Suzette Henke, *James Joyce and the Politics of Desire* (New York: RKP, 1989).

of expression, Joyce roots all communication in gesture: "In the beginning was the gest he jousstly says" (*FW* 468.5-6). Here the originary nature of gesture (gest, F. *geste* = gesture)[15] is linked with the mechanics of humor (i.e., jest) and to telling a tale (gest as a feat and a tale or romance). Gestures, like signals and flashing lights that provide elementary mechanical systems for communications, are "words of silent power" (*FW* 345.19). A traffic crossing sign, "Belisha beacon, beckon bright" (*FW* 267.12), exemplifies such situations "Where flash becomes word and silents selfloud" (*FW* 267.16). Since gestures, and ultimately all acts of communication, are generated from the body, the "gest" as "flesh without word" (*FW* 468.5-6) is "a flash" that becomes word and "communicake[s] with the original sinse" (originary sense + the temporal, "since" + original sin [*FW* 239.1]). "Communicake" parallels eating to speaking, and speaking is linked in turn to the act of communion as participation in, and consumption of, the Word—an observation adumbrated in the title of one of Marcel Jousse's groundbreaking books on gesture as the origin of language, *La Manducation de la Parole* ("The Mastication of the Word"). By treating the "gest" as a bit (a bite), orality and the written word as projections of gesture can be seen to spring from the body as a communicating machine.[16] The historical processes that contribute to the development of cyberspace augment the growing emphasis, in theories such as Kenneth Burke's, on the idea that the goal of the symbolic action called communication is *secular, paramodern communion*.[17]

The *Wake* provides a self-reflexive explanation of the communicative process of encoding and decoding required to interpret an encoded text, which itself is characteristically mechanical:

> The prouts who will invent a writing there ultimately is the poeta, still more learned, who discovered the raiding there originally. That's the point of eschatology our book of kills reaches for now in soandso many counterpoint words. What can't be coded can be decorded if an ear aye seize what no eye ere grieved for. Now, the doctrine obtains, we have occasioning cause causing effects and affects occasionally recausing altereffects. Or I will let me take it upon myself to suggest to twist the penman's tale posterwise. The gist is the gist of Shaum but the hand is the hand of Sameas. [*FW* 482.31-483.4]

[15] "Jousstly" refers to Marcel Jousse's important work on communication and the semiotics of gesture, with which Joyce was familiar. See especially Lorraine Weir, "The Choreography of Gesture: Marcel Jousse and *Finnegans Wake*," *James Joyce Quarterly* 14:3 (Spring 1977): 313-25.

[16] This motif will be developed further below. It relates to Joyce's interest in Lewis Carroll. Gilles Deleuze comments extensively on manducation in *The Logic of Sense*, trans. Mark Lester with Charles Stivale, ed. Constantin V. Boundas (New York: Columbia University Press, 1990).

[17] See Dewey, *Art As Experience* (New York: G.P. Futnam, 1958) and Kenneth Burke, *Permanence and Change: An Anatomy of Purpose* (Indianapolis, IN: Bobbs-Merrill, 1965).

The dreamer as a poet, a Hermetic thief, an "outlex" (FW 169.3)—i.e., an outlaw, lawless, beyond the word and, therefore, the law—"invents" the writing by originally discovering the reading of the book and does so by "raiding" (i.e., "plundering" [reading + raiding]).[18] Th s reading encompasses both the idealistic "eschatology" and the excrementitious-materialistic (pun on scatology) within the designing of this "book of kills" (deaths, deletions, drinking sessions, flows of water—a counterpoint of continuity and discontinuity),[19] a book as carefully crafted or machined as the illuminations of the *Book of Kells* are. Seeing and hearing are intricately involved in this process, so the reader of this nightbook also becomes a "raider" of the original "reading-writing" through the machinery of writing. It is a production "in soandso many counterpoint words" that can be read only through the machinery of decoding, for "What can't be coded can be decorded, if an ear aye seize what no eye ere grieved for" (FW 482.34). The tale that the pen writes is transmitted by the post, and the whole process of communication and its interpretation is an extension of the hand and of bodily gesture-language: "The gist is the gist of Shaum but the hand is the hand of Sameas" (FW 483.3-4).

Orality, particularly song, is grounded in the machinery of the body's organs: "Singalingalying. Storiella as she is syung. Whence followeup with endspeaking nots for yestures" (FW 267.7-9).[20] The link is rhythm, for "Soonjemmijohns will cudgel some a rhythmatick or other over Browne and Nolan's divisional tables" (FW 268.7-9). Gesture, with its affiliation with all of the neuro-muscular movements of the body, is a natural script or originary writing, for the word "has been reconstricted out of oral style into verbal for all time with ritual rhythm cs" (FW 36.8-9). Since the oral is "reconstricted" (reconstructed + constricted or limited) into the verbal, words also are crafted in relation to sound, a natural development of which is "wordcraft": for example, hieroglyphs and primitive script based on drawings or mnemonic devices.[21] Runes and ogham are literally "woodwordings," so pre- or proto-writing (i.e., syllabic writing) is already "a mechanization of the word," which is itself implicit in the body's use of gesture.

---

[18] Cf. T.S. Eliot, *Selected Essays* (New York: Harcourt, Brace, 1932) 182: "One of the surest of tests is the way in which a poet borrows. Immature poets imitate; mature poets steal..."; see also "Old stone to new building, old timber to new fires" ("East Coker," *Four Quartets* I.5). Joyce's use of "outlex" relates to Jim the Penman, for Joyce analyzing Shem in the *Wake* is aware of how the traditions of the artist as liar, counterfeiter, con man, and thief could all coalesce about the role of the artist as an outlaw.

[19] "Kills" in the sense of "to kill a bottle"; "kills" also as a stream or channel of water.

[20] See Walter Ong's remarks about Marcel Jousse in *The Presence of the Word* (New Haven, CT: Yale University Press, 1967) 146-7, and Lorraine Weir's more extensive development of the theme in the aforementioned "The Choreography of Gesture," and in *Writing Joyce: A Semiotics of the Joyce System* (Bloomington and Indianapolis: Indiana University Press, 1989).

[21] I.J. Gelb, *A Study of Writing* (Chicago: University of Chicago Press, 1963).

Joyce's practice and his theoretical orientation imply that as the road to cyberspace unfolds, the very nature of the word, the image, and the icon also changes. Under the impact of electric communication, it is once again clear that the concept of the word must embrace artifacts and events as well.[22] Writing and speech are subsumed into entirely new relationships with non-phonemic sound, image, gesture, movement, rhythm, and all modes of sensory input, especially the tactile. To continue to speak about a dichotomy of orality versus literacy is a misleading over-simplification of the role that electric media play in this transformation, a role best comprehended through historical knowledge of the earliest stages of human communication where objects, gestures and movements apparently intermingled with verbal and non-verbal sounds. Marschak's study of early cultural artifacts, the Aschers' discussion of the quipu, and Levi- Strauss's discussions of the kinship system demonstrate the relative complexity of some ancient, non-linguistic systems of communication.[23] Adapting Vico's speculation that human communication begins with the gestures and material symbols of the "mute," Joyce early in the *Wake* presents an encounter between two characters whose names deliberately echo Mutt and Jeff of comic strip fame. Mutt (until recently a mute) and Jute (a nomadic invader) "excheck a few strong verbs weak oach eather" (*FW* 16.8-9).

Beginning with gesture, hieroglyph and rune, Joyce traces human communication through its complex, labyrinthine development, right down to the TV and what it bodes for the future. For example, an entire episode of the *Wake* (I,v)[24] is devoted to the technology of manuscripts and the theory of their interpretation—textual hermeneutics—in which the *Wake* as a book is interpreted as if it were a manuscript, "the proteiform graph is a polyhedron of all scripture" (*FW* 107.8). At each stage, Joyce recognizes how the machinery of codification is implicit in the history of communication, for discussing this manuscript, he observes that

> on holding the verso against a lit rush this new book of Morses responded most remarkably to the silent query of our world's oldest light and its recto let out the piquant fact that it was but pierced but not punctured (in the university sense of the term) by numerous stabs and foliated gashes made by a pronged instrument... [*FW* 123.34-124.3]

[22] Marshall McLuhan and Bruce R. Powers, The Global Village: Transformations in World Life and Media in the 21st Century (New York: Oxford University Press, 1989) 182.
[23] Alexander Marschak, *The Roots of Civilization* (New York: McGraw-Hill, 1982); Marcia Ascher and Robert Ascher, *Code of the Quipu: A Study in Media, mathematics and Culture* (Ann Arbor: University of Michigan Press, 1981); Claude Levi-Strauss, *The Elementary Structures of Kinship*, trans. James Harle Bell and John Richard von Sturmer, ed. Rodney Needham (Boston: Beacon Press, 1969).
[24] The usual way to indicate sections of the *Wake* is by part and episode. Hence I,v is Part I episode 5. There are four parts, the first consisting of eight episodes, the second and the third of four episodes each and the fourth of a single episode.

This illustrates how the beginning of electric media (the telegraph) is a transformation of the potentialities of the early manuscript, just as any manuscript is a transformation of the "wordcraft" of "woodwordings." "Morse code" is indicative of the mechanics of codification, for while code is essential to all communication (thus prior to the moment when the mechanical is electrified), the role of codification is radically transformed by mechanization.

The appearance of the printing press demonstrates the effect of this radical transformation:

> Gutenmorg with his cromagnon charter, tintingfast and great primer must once for omniboss step rubrickredd out of the wordpress else is there no virtue more in alcohoran. For that (the rapt one warns) is what papyr is meed of, made of, hides and hints and misses in prints. T ll ye finally (though not yet endlike) meet with the acquaintance of Mister Typus, Mistress Tope and all the little typtopies. Fillstup. So you need hardly spell me how every word will be bound over to carry three score and ten toptypsical readings throughout the book of Doublends Jined. [FW 20.7-16]

As "Gutenmorg with his cromagnon charter, tintingfast and great primer" steps "rubrickredd out of the wordpress," the dream reminds us that "papyr is meed of, made of, hides and hints and misses in prints." Topics (L. *topos*) and types (L. *typus*) as figures, forms, images, topics and commonplaces, the elemental bits of writing and rhetoric, are now realized through typesetting. Implicit in the technology of print is the complex intertextuality of verbal ambivalence, for "every word will be bound over to carry three score and ten toptypsical readings throughout the book of Doublends Jined." Printing sets in place the 'root language" (*FW* 424.17) residing in the types and topes of the world and potentially eliminates a multitude of alternate codes such as actual sounds, visual images, real objects, movements, and gestures that will re-emerge with the electromechanical march towards VR and cyberspace.

By the 1930s, in a pub scene in the *Wake*, Joyce playfully anticipated how central sporting events or political debates would be for television when he described the TV projection of a fight being viewed by the pub's "regulars" (possibly the first fictional TV bar room scene in literary history). Joyce's presentation of this image of the battle of Butt and Taff, which is peppered with complex puns involving terminology associated with the technical details of TV transmission, has its own metamorphic quality, underscored by the "viseversion" (vice versa imaging) of Butt and Taff's images on "the bairdboard bombardment screen" ("bairdboard" because John Logie Baird developed TV in 1925). Joyce explains how "the bairdboard bombardment screen," the TV as receiver, receives the composite video signal "in syncopanc pulses" (the synchronization pulses that form part of the composite video signal), that come down the "photoslope" on the "carnier walve" (i.e., the carrier wave which carries the composite video signal) "with the bits bugtwug their teffs." Joyce imagines this receiver to be a "light barricade" against which the charge of the light brigade (the video signal) is directed, re-producing the "bitts" (FW 345.5-12). Although (at least to my knowledge) bit was not used as a technical term in communication tech-nology at the time, Joyce is still able, on analogy with the telegraph, to think of the electrons or photons as bits of information creating the TV picture.

Speech, print and writing are interwoven with electromechanical technologies of communication throughout the *Wake*. References to the manufacture of books, newspapers and other products of the printing press abound. Machineries and technological organizations accompany this development: reporters, editors, interviewers, newsboys, ad men who produce "Abortisements" (FW 181.33). Since complex communica-tion technology is characteristic of the later stages, in addition to newspapers, radio, "dupenny" magazines, comics (contemporary cave drawing), there is "a phantom city phaked by philm pholk," by those who would "roll away the reel world." Telecommunications materialize again and again throughout the night of the *Wake*, where "television kills telephony."

The "tele-" prefix, betraying an element of futurology in the dream, appears in well over a dozen words including in addition to the familiar forms terms such as "teleframe," "telekinesis," "telesmell," "telespho-rously," "televisible," "televox," or "telewisher," while familiar forms also appear in a variety of transformed "messes of mottage," such as "velivision" and "dullaphone." This complex verbal play all hinges on the inter-translatability of the emerging forms of technologically mediated communication. In the opening episode of the second part, the "Feen-icht's Playhouse," an imaginary play produced by HCE's children in their nursery is "wordloosed over seven seas crowdblast in cellellenneteu-toslavzendlatinsoundscript. In four tubbloids" (FW 219.28-9). Like the cinema, "wordloosed" (wirelessed but also let loose) transglobally, all such media are engaged in a "crowdblast" of existing languages and cultures, producing an interplay between local cultures and a pan-international hyperculture.

In the concluding moments of the *Wake*, Joyce generalizes his pre-cybernetic vision in one long intricate performance that not only con-cerns the book itself, but also anticipates by twenty years some major discussions of culture, communication, and technology. A brief scene setting: this is the moment in the closing episode just as the HCE is awakening. In the background he hears noises from the machines in the laundry next door. It is breakfast time and there are sounds of food be-ing prepared; eggs are being cooked and will be eaten, so there is anticipation of the process of digestion that is about to take place.[25] At

---

[25] Danis Rose and John O'Hanlon, *Understanding Finnegans Wake* (New York: Garland Publishing, 1982) 308-09.

this moment a key passage, inviting interminable interpretation, presents in very abstract language a generalized model of production and consumption, which is also the ricorso of the schema of this nocturnal poem, that consumes and produces, just as the digestive system itself digests and produces new cells and excrement—how else could one be a poet of "litters" as well as letters and be "litterery" *FW* 114.17; 422.35) as well as literary?

The passage begins by speaking about "our wholemole millwheeling vicociclometer, a tetradomational gazebocroticon" (*FW* 614.27-8), which may be the book, a letter to be written, the digestive system assimilating the eggs, the sexual process, the mechanical "mannormillor clipperclappers" (*FW* 614.13) of the nearby Mannor Millo⁻ laundry, the temporal movement of history, or a theory of engineering, for essentially it relates the production of cultural artifacts or the consumption of matter (like reading a book, seeing a film or eating eggs; the text mentions a "farmer, his son and their homely codes, known as eggburst, eggblend, eggburial, and hatch-as-hatch-can" [*FW* 614.31-3]). The passage concludes, "as sure as herself pits hen to paper and there's scribings scrawled on eggs" (*FW* 615.9-10). Here the frequent pairing of speaking (writing) with eating is brought to a climax in which it is related to all the abstract machines which shape the life of nature, decomposing into "bits" and recombining.

These bits, described as "the dialytically [dialectic + dialysis] separated elements of precedent decomposition," may be eggs, or other "homely codes" such as the "heroticisms, catastrophes and eccentricities" (the stuff of history or the dreamers stuttering speech or his staggering movements) transmitted elementally, "type by tope, letter from litter, word at ward, sendence of sundance" (*FW* 614.33-615.2). All of these bits—matter, eggs, words, TV signals, concepts, what you will—are "anastomosically assimilated and preteri-dentified paraidiotically," producing "the sameold gamebold adomic structure... as highly charged with electrons as hophazards can effective it" (*FW* 615.5-8). In anticipation of the contemporary electronic definition of the "bit," Joyce associates the structure of communication (ranging from TV and telegraphic signals to morphophonemic information and kinesthesia) with bits of signals, "data" and information. He presents it as essentially an assemblage of multiplicities, different from a synthesizing or totalizing moment, for it occurs by the crossing of pluralistic branches of differing motifs, through a process of transmission involving flows, particularly the flowing of blood, water and speech, and breaks such as the discontinuous charges of electrical energy, telegraphy, and punctuation—those "endspeaking nots for yestures" (*FW* 267.8).

Here Joyce's entire prophetic, schizoid vision of cyberspace seems somewhat Deleuzian. It is an ambivalent and critical vision, for the "ambiviolence" of the "langdwage" throughout the *Wake* implies critique as it unfolds this history, since Joyce still situates parody within satire. He does not free it from socio-political reference, as a free-floating "post-modernist" play with the surface of signifiers would. This can be noted in the way that Joyce first probes what came to be one of the key-stones of McLuhanism. Joyce plays throughout the work with spheres and circles, some of which parody one of the mystical definitions of God frequently attributed to Alan of Lille (Alanus de Insulis), but sometimes referred to as Pascal's sphere. Speaking of a daughter-goddess figure, he says:

> our Frivulteeny Sexuagesima to expense herselfs as sphere as possible, paradismic perimutter, in all directions on the bend of the unbridalled, the infinisissimalls of her facets becoming manier and manier as the calicolum of her umdescribables (one has thoughts of that eternal Rome). [*FW* 298.27-33]

Here a sphere is imagined whose center is everywhere and circumference nowhere, since it is infinitesimal and undescribable (though apparently the paradigmic perimeter is sexual), as the paradisal mother communicates herself without apparent limit. This is both an embodied and a disembodied sphere, polarizing and decentering the image so as to impede any closure. The same spherical principle is applied more widely to the presentation of the sense of hearing. The reception of messages by the hero/ine of the *Wake*, "(Hear! Calls! Everywhair!)" (*FW* 108.23), is accomplished by "bawling the whowle hamshack and wobble down in an eliminium sounds pound so as to serve him up a melegoturny mary-goraumd" (*FW* 309.22-4), a sphere for it requires "a gain control of circumcentric megacycles" (*FW* 310.7-8). It can truly be said of HCE, "Ear! Ear! Weakear! An allness eversides!" (*FW* 568.26),[26] precisely because he is "*h*uman, *e*rring and *c*ondonable"(*FW* 58.19), yet "humile, commune and ensectuous" (*FW* 29.30), suffering many deprivations his "*h*ardest *c*rux *e*ver" (*FW* 623.33) [italics mine]. Though "humbly to fall and cheaply to rise, [this] exposition of failures" (*FW* 589.17) living with "*H*einz *c*ans *e*verywhere"(*FW* 581.5), still protests his fate "making use of sacrilegious languages to the defect that he would *c*hallenge their *h*emosphores to *e*xterminate them" (*FW* 81.25) by decentering or dislo-cating any attempts to enclose him.

This discussion of sphere and hearing critically anticipates what McLuhan later called "acoustic space"—a fundamental cyberspatial con-ception with its creation of multi-dimensional environments, a spherical environment within which aural information is received by the CNS—that also embodies a transformation of the hermetic poetic insight that "the universe (or nature) [or in earlier versions, God] is an infinite sphere, the

---

26 For detailed discussion of the treatment of the ear and hearing in *Finnegans Wake*, see John Bishop, *Joyce's book of the Dark: Finnegans Wake* (Madison, WI: University of Wisconsin Press, 1986), chapter 9 "Earwickerwork," 264-304.

center of which is everywhere, the circumference nowhere."[27] Today, VR, as Borges' treatment of Pascal's sphere seems to imply, is coming to be our contemporary pre-millennial epitome of this symbol, a place where each participant (rather than *the* deity), as microcosm, is potentially the enigmatic center. People englobed within virtual worlds find themselves interacting within complex, transverse, intertextual multimedia forms that are interlinked globally through complex, rhizomic (rootlike) networks.

All of this must necessarily relate back to the way Joyce treats the subject of and produces the artifact that is *the book*. While, beginning with Mallarme, the themes of the book and the death of literature resound through modernism, Joyce's transformation of the book filtered through the "mcluhanitic" reaction to "mcluhanism" becomes, in the usual interpretation of McLuhan, the annunciation of the death of the book, *not* its transformation, as with Joyce. Joyce is important, for following Marcel Jousse and Vico,[28] he situates speech and writing as modes of communication within a far richer and more complex bodily and gestural theory of communication than that represented by the reductive dichotomy of the oral and the literate. As the predominance of print declines, the *Wake* explores the history of communication by comically assimilating the method of Vico's *The New Science*—which, as one of the first systematic and empirical studies of the place of poetic action in the history of how people develop systems of signs and symbols, attributes people's ability for constructing their society to the poetic function.

Joyce avoids that facile over-simplification of the complexities of print, arising from the orality/literacy dichotomy, which attributes a privileged role to language as verbal—a privilege based on theological and metaphysical claims. The same dichotomy creates problems in discussing technological and other non-verbal forms of mediated communication, including VR and TV. At one point in the *Wake* "Television kills telephony in brothers' broil. Our eyes demand their turn. Let them be seen!" (*FW* 52.18-9), for TV also comprehends the visual and the kinesthetic. Yet most McLuhanites who have opted for the orality/literacy split still call it an oral medium in opposition to print. The same problem occurs when mime, with its dependence on gesture and rhythm, is analyzed as an oral medium. As the *Wake* jocularly observes:

> seein as ow his thoughts consisted chiefly of the cheerio, he aptly sketched for our soontobe second parents... the touching seene. The solence of that stilling! Here one might a fin fell. Boomster rombombonant! It scenes like a landscape from Wildu Picturescu or some seem on some

[27] Jorge Luis Borges, *Other Inquisitions: 1937- 1952*, trans. Ruth R. Sims (New York: Simon and Schuster, 1968) 6-9.
[28] Lorraine Weir, *Writing Joyce: A Semiotics of the Joyce System* (Bloomington and Indianapolis: Indiana University Press, 1989).

dimb Arras, dumb as Mum's mutyness, this mimage... is odable to os across the wineless Ere no dor nor mere eerie nor liss potent of suggestion than in the tales of the tingmount. [*FW* 52.34-53.6]

The mime plays with silence, sight, touch and movement seeming like a landscape or a movie.

Facile over-simplification also overlooks that long before the beginnings of the trend towards cyberspace, print had not been strictly oriented towards linearity and writing, for the print medium was supplemented by its encyclopedic, multi-media nature, absorbing other media such as illustrations, charts, graphs, maps, diagrams, and tables, not all aspects of which are precisely linear. While writing may have had a predominantly linear tendency, its history is far more complex, as Elizabeth Eisenstein has established.[29] The orality/literacy distinction does not provide an adequately rich concept for dealing with print, any more than it does for the most complex and comprehensive images of virtual reality and participatory hyperspace (e.g., sophisticated extensions of the datagloves or the Aspen map), which, to adapt a Joycean phrase, directly transmit "feelful thinkamalinks." Since VR should enable a person to feel the bodily set of another person or place, while simultaneously receiving multiple intersensory messages, understanding the role of the body in communication is crucial for understanding VR. When McLuhan and Edward Carpenter first spoke about their concept of orality (linked to aurality, mouth to ear, as line of print to eye scan), it entailed recognizing the priority and primacy of tactility and inter-sensory activity in communication, for "In the beginning there was the gest."

As Kenneth Burke realized in the 30s, Joyce's grounding communication and language in gesture is distinctly different from an approach which privileges language, for it involves a complete embodying of communication. While the oral only embodies the speech organs, the entire CNS is necessarily involved in all communication, including speech. As John Bishop has shown in *Joyce's Book of the Dark*, the sleeper primarily receives sensations with his ear, but these are tranformed within the body into the world of signs that permeate the dream and which constitute the *Wake*.[30] Joyce views language as "gest," as an imaginary means of embodying intellectual-emotional complexes, his "feelful thinkamalinks." From this perspective, the semic units of the *Wake* (integrated complexes constructed from the interaction of speech and print involving, rhythm, orthography as sign and gesture and visual image) assume the role of dialogue with other modes of mediated communication, exploiting their limitations and differences. Joyce crafts a new *lingua* for a world where the poetic book will deal with those aspects of the imaginary that cannot be encompassed within

---

[29] Elizabeth Eisenstein, *The Printing Revolution in Early Modern Europe* (New York: Cambridge University Press, 1983).
[30] Bishop, *Joyce's book of the Dark*, 264-304.

technologically mediated communication. Simultaneously, he recognizes that a trend towards virtual reality is characteristic of the electro-mechanically or technologically mediated modes of communication. This process posits a continuous dialogue in which *Ulysses* and the *Wake* were designed to play key roles.

As Joyce—who quipped that "some of the means I use are trivial—and some are quadrivial"[31]—was aware, ancient rhetorical theory (which he parodied both in the Aeolus episode of *Ulysses* and in the "Triv and Quad" section (II, 2) of the *Wake*) also included those interactive contexts where the body was an intrinsic part of communication. Delivery involved controlling the body, and the context within which it was presented, as well as the voice. The actual rhetorical action (particularly in judicial oratory) also frequently involved demonstration and witnesses. This analysis, closer to the pre-literate, recognized the way actual communication integrated oral, visual, rhythmical, gestural and kinesthetic components. Recent research into the classical and medieval "arts of memory," inspired by Frances Yates,[32] have demonstrated that memory involves the body, a sense of the dramatic and theatrical, visual icons and movement, as well as the associative power of the oral itself. Joyce playfully invokes this memory system familiar to him from his Jesuit education: "After sound, light and heat, memory, will and understanding. Here (the memories framed from walls are minding) till wranglers for wringwrowdy wready are..." (*FW* 266.18-22). A classical world, which recognized such features of the communicative process, could readily speak about the poem as a "speaking picture" and the painting as "silent poetry." Here, there is an inclusiveness of the means available rather than a dependency on a single channel of communication.

Joyce was so intrigued by the potentials of the new culture of time and space for reconstructing and revolutionizing the book that he claimed himself to be "the greatest engineer," as well as a Renaissance man, who was also a "musicmaker, a philosophist and heaps of other things."[33] The mosaic of the *Wake* contributes to understanding the nature of cyberspace by grasping the radical constitution of the electronic cosmos that Joyce called "the chaosmos of Alle" (*FW* 118.21). In this "chaosmos," engineered by a sense of interactive mnemotechnics, he intuits the relation between a nearly infinite quantity of cultural information and the mechanical yet rhizomic organization of a network, "the matrix," which underlies the construction of imagnary and virtual worlds. One crucial reason for raising the historic image of Joyce in a discussion of cyberspace is that he carries out one of the most comprehensive contemporary discussions of virtual recollection (a concept first

[31] Eugene Jolas, "My Friend James Joyce," *James Joyce: Two Decades of Criticism*, ed. Seon Givens (New York: Vanguard, 1948) 24.
[32] E.g., in Frances Yates, *The Art of Memory* (Chicago: University of Chicago Press, 1966).
[33] James Joyce to Harriet Shaw Weaver, *Letters*, ed. Stuart Gilbert (New York: Viking, 1957) 251 [Postcard, 16 April 1927].

articulated by Henri Bergson as virtual memory).[34] In counterpoint to the emerging technological capability to create the "virtual reality" of cyberspace, Joyce turned to dream and hallucination for the creation of virtual worlds within natural language.

That tactile, gestural-based dreamworld has built-in mnemonic systems:

A scene at sight. Or dreamoneire. Which they shall memorise. By her freewritten. Hopely for ear that annalykeses if scares for eye that sumns. Is it in the now woodwordings of our sweet plantation where the branchings then will singingsing tomorrows gone and yesters outcome. [FW 280.01-07]

Joyce's virtual worlds began with the recognition of "everybody" as a poet (each person is co-producer; he quips, "his producers are they not his consumers?" [FW 497.1-2]). All culture becomes the panorama of his dream; the purpose of poetic writing in a post-electric world is the painting of that interior (which is not the psychoanalytic, but the social unconscious) and the providing of new language appropriate to perceiving the complexities of the new world of technologically reproducible media:

What has gone? How it ends? Begin to forget it. It will remember itself from every sides, with all gestures, in each our word. Today's truth, tomorrow's trend. [FW 614.19-21]

Joyce's text is embodied in gesture, enclosed in words, enmeshed in time, and engaged in foretelling "Today's truth. Tomorrow's trend." The poet reproducing his producers is the divining prophet.

If speaking of Joyce and cyberspace seems to imply a kind of futurology, the whole of McLuhan's project was frequently treated as prophesying the emergence of a new tribalized global society—the global village, itself anticipated by Joyce's "international" language of multilingual puns. In fact, in *War and Peace in the Global Village*, McLuhan uses *Wake*se (mostly from Joyce, freely associated) as marginalia. McLuhan flourished in his role as an international guru by casting himself in the role of "*the* prime prophet" announcing the coming of a new era of communication[35] (now talked about as virtual reality or cyberspace,

---

[34] For a discussion of this see Gilles Deleuze, *Bergsonism* (New York: Zone, 1988), chapter 3 "Memory as Virtual Co-existence," 51-72.

[35] Speaking of the all-embracing aspects of VR and cyberspace, the work which Baudrillard has made of "simulation" and "the ecstasy of communication" should be noted. This issue is too complex to engage within an essay specifically focused on Joyce. In approaching it, however, it is important to realize the degree of similarity that Baudrillard's treatment of communication shares with McLuhan's. In many ways, I believe it could be established that what Baudrillard critiques as the "ecstasy of communication" is his understanding of McLuhan's vision of communication divorced from its historical roots in the literature and arts of *symbolisme*, high modernism, and particularly James Joyce.

though he never actually used that word). The prime source of his "prophecies," which he never concealed, is to be found in Joyce and Vico.[36] The entire Joycean dream is prophetic or divinatory in part, for the anticipated awakening (Vico's fourth age of ricorso following birth, marriage, and death) is "providential divining":

> Ere we are! Signifying, if tungs may tolkan, that, primeval conditions hav-ing gradually receded but nevertheless the emplacement of so id and fluid having to a great extent persisted through intermittences of sullemn ful-minance, sollemn nuptialism, sallemn sepulture and providential divining, making possible and even inevitable, after his a time has a tense haves and havenots hesitency, at the place and period under consideration a so-cially organic entity of a millenary military maritory monetary morphological circumformation in a more or less settled state of equonomic ecolube equalobe equilab equilibbrium. [*FW* 599.8-18]

Earlier, it is said of the dreamer that "He caun ne'er be bothered but maun e'er be waked. If there is a future in every past that is present..." (*FW* 496.34-497.1). Joyce, from whom McLuhan derived the idea, is playing with the medieval concept of natural prophecy, making it a fun-damental feature of the epistemology of his dream world, in which the "give and take" of the "mind factory," an "antithesis of ambidual antici-pation," generates auspices, auguries, and divination—for "DIVINITY NOT DEITY [is] THE UNCERTAINTY JUSTIFIED BY OUR CERTITUDE" (*FW* 282.R7-R13).

Natural prophecy, the medieval way of thinking about futurology with which Joyce and McLuhan were naturally familiar from scholasticism and Thomism, occurs through a reading of history and its relation to that virtual, momentary social text (the present), which is dynamic and al-ways undergoing change. Joyce appears to blend this medieval concept with classical sociological ideas—of prophecy as an "intermediation"— quite consistent with his concepts of communication as involving as-pects of participation and communion. It is only through some such reading that the future existent in history can be known and come to be. McLuhan's reading, adapted from Joyce, of the collision of history and the present moment led him to foresee a world emerging where commu-nication would be tactile, post-verbal, fully participatory and pan-sensory.[37]

Why ought communication history and theory to take account of Joyce's poetic project? First, because he designed a new language (later disseminated by McLuhan, Eco, and Derrida) to carry out an in-depth interpretation of complex socio-historical phenomenon, namely new modes of semiotic production. Two brief examples: Hollywood "word-

---

[36] This is a major theme of McLuhan and McLuhan's *The Laws of Media* (Toronto: University of Toronto Press, 1988).
[37] See Donald F. Theall, *The Medium is the Rear View Mirror; Understanding McLuhan* (Montreal: McGill-Queen's University Press, 1971).

loosing celluloid soundscript over seven seas," or the products of the Hollywood dream factory itself as "a rolling away of the reel world," reveal media's potential international domination as well as the problems film form raises for the mutual claims of the imaginary and the real. For example, the term "abortisements" (advertisements) suggests the manipulation of fetishized femininity with its submerged relation of advertisement to butchering—the segmentation of the body as object into an assemblage of parts.

Second, Joyce's work is a critique of communication's historical role in the production of culture, and it constitutes one of the earliest recognitions of the importance of Vico to a contemporary history of communication and culture.[38] Third, his work is itself the first "in- depth" contemporary exploration of the complexities of reading, writing, rewriting, speaking, aurality, and orality. Fourth, developing Vico's earlier insights and anticipating Kenneth Burke, he sees the importance of the "poetic" as a concept in communication, for the poetic is the means of generating new communicative potentials between medium and message. This provides the poetic, the arts, and other modes of cultural production with a crucial role in a semiotic ecology of communication, an ecology of sense, and making sense. Fifth, in the creative project of this practice, Joyce develops one of the most complex discussions of the contemporary transformation of our media of communication. And finally, his own work is itself an exemplum of the socio-ecological role of the poetic in human communication.

VR or cyberspace, as an assemblage of a multiplicity of existing and new media, dramatizes the relativity of our classifications of media and their effects. The newly evolving global metropolis arising in the age of cyberspace is a site where people are intellectual nomads: differentiation, difference, and decentering characterize its structure. Joyce and the arts of high modernism and postmodernism provide a solid appreciation of how people constantly reconstruct or remake reality through the traversing of the multi-sensory fragments of a "virtual world" and of the tremendous powers with which electricity and the analysis of mechanization would endow the paramedia that would eventually emerge.

---

[38] John O'Neill credits Vico with a "wild sociology" in which the philologist is a wild sociologist in *Making Sense Together: An Introduction to Wild Sociology* (New York: Harper & Row, 1974) 28-38. The significance of Vico's emphasis on the body is developed in John O'Neill, *Five Bodies: The Human Sense of Society* (Ithaca, New York: Cornell University Press, 1985).

DARREN TOFTS
A Retrospective Sort of Arrangement:
Ulysses & the Poetics of Hypertextuality*

Hypertextuality is a term that we have come to associate with digital connectivity, hypertext and the computer revolution. It is also a term that has, in retrospect, been applied to James Joyce's *Ulysses*. Indeed, David Gold, in a detailed case study of the text, suggests that *Ulysses* is "the perfect hypertext subject."[1] Such a view assumes some kind of correspondence between *Ulysses* and the emergent electronic architecture of hypertext, an acknowledgment that *Ulysses* is somehow like hypertext. On the basis of this homology, *Ulysses* is seen to be eminently eligible for hypertextualisation. However, the relationship between a literary work such as *Ulysses* and electronic hypertext is a problematic one. While the nomenclature of hypertext and hypertextuality dates back to the late 1960s, it was for many years unknown to literary criticism. Nevertheless, its association with literature as a form of poetics can be traced back to those formative years of hypertext research and development. Ted Nelson, author of *Literary Machines* and originator of the term hypertext, had clearly defined it in 1965 as a literary phenomenon. The importance for *Ulysses* scholarship of thinking of the literary in machinic terms, and the broader logic of hypertextual poetics, will hopefully become apparent in this paper.

Two critical works on *Ulysses* published after 1965 stand out in terms of their sustained attempt to come to terms with qualities of its textuality that would, two decades later, be canonised as generic features of hypertext. These works, David Hayman's *Ulysses: The Mechanics of Meaning* (1970) and Hugh Kenner's *The Stoic Comedians* (1974), developed a number of key concepts that articulate a discontinuous textual poetics that clearly anticipated the paradigmatic non-linearity of hypertext theory in the 1990s. These works can also be said to have laid the foundations of a practice of Joycean hypertext criticism, of which this paper is itself an instance. However it is important to

* A version of this essay was presented at the XVIIth International James Joyce Symposium, Goldsmith's College, London, June, 2000.
1 David Gold, "*Ulysses*: A Case Study in the Problems of Hypertextualisation of Complex Documents," *Computers, Writing, Rhetoric and Literature Ejournal* vol. 3 (1997): http:www.cwrl.utexas.edu.

stress a caveat to do with any association of *Ulysses* with hypertext. It is by no means the case that with the vocabulary of hypertext and the computer network we have found a readymade critical language to apply to *Ulysses*, to reanimate it as an honorary hypertext.

It is actually more constructive to think of hypertextuality as a way of characterising textual behaviour: in other words, as a form of poetics. In this respect, the idea of a textual poetics, which we can call hypertextuality, is a more useful device for thinking about the relationship between *Ulysses* and hypertext culture. That said, it is nonetheless a term to be applied to *Ulysses* with great care. Hypertextuality can be defined as a timely formulation of a more general, theoretical approach to understanding the way certain kinds of texts work. Such texts, whether they be Michael Joyce's *Afternoon*, or James Joyce's *Ulysses*, actively foreground disjunctive structure, thematic multi-layering and a machinic tendency to generate prodigious systems of meaning that are in excess of the sum of its parts. Reading such texts is an indeterminate and highly differential process that frustrates any sense of an ending or closure. It is rather an intransitive sense of unending, the building up of a rich mosaic of understanding that develops over time through many re-readings. On the basis of such a theory it is clear that *Ulysses* is already hypertextual. It is therefore misleading to simply apply the term to it, as if the prefix "hyper" somehow endowed the work with qualities that we didn't think it possessed, or helped us to see more clearly those qualities that we knew about, but didn't have an adequate term for. A theory of the mechanics of disjunctive structure and disseminated meaning can be found in the work of Kenner and Hayman well before hyper-terminology was in vogue. Even if they were aware of its currency in the rarefied circles of computer science, it would not have given them anything more resourceful to work with than they already had at their disposal. It can be argued, therefore, that both Kenner and Hayman had theorised, in advance, what would later be referred to as hypertextuality.

While published in 1974, Hugh Kenner's *The Stoic Comedians* was based on lectures originally presented between 1960 and 1962. Ostensibly a discussion of the work of Flaubert, Joyce and Beckett, the unifying theme in this work is actually the cultural technology of the printed book. Kenner's interest in the theme of "the book as book" stems, initially, from his fascination with the dynamics of encylopae-dism, of what the great book of knowledge makes feasible. A feat of organising, rather than understanding, it assembles thousands and thou-sands of solitary, fragmentary items into an exhaustive inventory of everything that we know.[2] "Nothing," Kenner asserts, "except when a cross-reference is provided, connects with or entails anything else."[3] The cross-reference, as a point of connection between discrete, spatially

---

[2] Hugh Kenner, *The Stoic Comedians. Flaubert, Joyce and Beckett* (Berkeley, University of California Press, 1974) 2.

[3] Kenner, *The Stoic Comedians*, 3.

remote fragments in a large work, is an important figure, to which I will return. It is in *Ulysses* that Kenner finds a profound and extensive exploitation of this mechanism of connection between remote details. The collation and assemblage of specific details is active and dynamic and depends upon the very existence of the book as book, in which the reader can "turn to and fro."[4] The idiomatic simplicity of such a decisive formulation, turning to and fro between different parts of the text, is vital to an understanding of the complexity of *Ulysses'* textuality. It is another key figure to which I shall also return.

Kenner's attention to the book as a means of organising material "discontinuously in space rather than serially in time"[5] was also informed by a number of interrelated disciplines that, integrated in the work of John von Neumann, contributed to the development of the digital computer. Through a variety of direct and indirect invocations, Kenner evidences the aptness of number theory and cybernetics for his anatomy of *Ulysses* as a closed, generative system or feedback loop. In this Kenner is interested in the book as a machinic assemblage.

In *Ulysses: The Mechanics of Meaning* (originally published in 1970), Hayman also focuses on the technical structures of arrangement within the text, the linkages and points of connection between and within its different sections, different styles and overall fragmentary structure. Hayman is sensitive to the strangeness of *Ulysses*, noting that it "still defies definition, remaining open to each new reader and susceptible to new approaches."[6] Wanting to move beyond "stream of consciousness" and Homeric analogies as the epitome of Joyce's innovation, Hayman was interested in the paradoxical features of the text that tended towards systematic fragmentation and "a rage for order."[7] In focussing on this quality of the book as a quality to be properly analysed rather than criticised, Hayman noted that as the book becomes more difficult and fragmented, particular types of control over the material can be identified. His concept of the Arranger is one of the more memorable and decisive formulations of this work. It is, for Hayman, a figure of arrangement and organisation responsible for the forging of connections, cross-references and associations within its overall fragmentary structure.

In his "After Thoughts" to the 1982 reprint of the book, Hayman develops the concept further, referring to the Arranger as "a significant, felt absence in the text, an unstated but inescapable source of control."[8] Its centrality in cohering the disjunctive structure of the text is heightened, but so too is Hayman's sense of the dramatic unprecedented

[4]   Kenner, *The Stoic Comedians*, 34.
[5]   Kenner, *The Stoic Comedians*, 41.
[6]   David Hayman, *Ulysses. The Mechanics of Meaning* (Madison, University of Wisconsin Press, 1982; revised and expanded edition of the original 1970 text) 11.
[7]   Hayman, *Ulysses: The Mechanics of Meaning*, 83.
[8]   Hayman, *Ulysses: The Mechanics of Meaning*, 122.

dynamics of *Ulysses'* mechanics. It is apparent in his observations twelve years down the track that what he had previously referred to as the text's "mechanics of meaning" were even more complex and strange, despite his articulate attempts to name and categorise them, largely through the Arranger. While the Arranger is reassuring to the struggling reader as a force of organisation and control, Hayman was in no doubt that with *Ulysses* we are dealing with a "strange new medium," an "unpredictable narrative space."[9] To attempt to name and describe this strange new medium, Hayman conjoined the grammatical notion of parataxis with textual disjuncture. His "paratactics" became a focal point for his ongoing study of the ways in which *Ulysses* operated dynamically and unstably as a perpetual interplay of disarray and order, in which gaps and absences of connection between remote elements are required to be filled by the reader, who becomes, in Hayman's words, a "necessary and active, if sometimes unwilling, presence."[10]

Like Hayman, Kenner also took the concept of the Arranger further by developing an adjunct concept, the aesthetic of delay. In Joyce's use of the optical concept of parallax, Kenner found a means of explicating the temporal as well as spatial dimension of Joyce's method of cross-referencing, now referred to as a "network of coincidence" or "points of correlation."[11] Kenner sees in Joyce's manner of providing at least two versions of the same detail a parallactic method, in which events are not merely repeated but intensified.[12] Kenner uses his discussion of parallax to account for more extensive points of connection between remote parts of the text to consolidate a radical portrait of the volatility and indeterminacy of *Ulysses'* textuality. The moment of epiphany, when all elements suddenly fit and cohere into a logical system of understanding, may or may not ever occur for any given reader. This is Joyce's aesthetic of delay; an indeterminate interplay of one detail now, one possibly later, one here, one possibly there. Kenner's theory of reading, like Hayman's, had by this stage of inquiry into "Joyce's strange book," located the reader as a collaborator, and the reading process as an unpredictable, Heisenbergian "symbiosis of observer with observed." It was this principle of creative unpredictability that, in Kenner's words, marked the "radiant novelty of *Ulysses*."[13] Hypertextuality is a term that has been appropriated to describe this novelty.

A number of common ideas to do with the textuality of *Ulysses* emerge from this summary of Kenner and Hayman. To recapitulate two central figures signposted earlier, both Kenner and Hayman are interested in the forging of relationships between different parts of the text.

---

[9] Hayman, *Ulysses: The Mechanics of Meaning*, 124.
[10] David Hayman, "Paratactics and the Shape of Joyce's Fiction," *Scripsi* 1.2 (1982): 81.
[11] Kenner, *The Stoic Comedians*, 75; 79.
[12] Kenner, *The Stoic Comedians*, 76.
[13] Kenner, *The Stoic Comedians*, 154.

The notion of *Ulysses* as a kind of machinic assemblage that is built up, bit by bit, to and fro, from elaborate arrangements of its constituent parts, foregrounds a creative tension between the synchronic particularity of individual detail and the diachronic linking of details into systems of cross-reference. *Ulysses* works by systematically arranging a varied but finite lexicon of details into larger systems or networks of contiguity. The effects of recognition and recapitulation, the pleasure and surprise of encountering the same details again and again, contribute to the sense of patterning and orchestration. The concept of the Arranger is grounded in this interplay between local detail (the virtuoso, graphic treatment of individual words and phrases) and remote cross-reference (the self-conscious recollection of earlier parts of the book, often signalled by the repetition of specific words).

In this respect we can describe the synchronic/diachronic patterning between different parts of the book as vectoral. I am invoking the term here as it has been used in recent media theory to describe the effects of technologies of distance, their ability to construct complex and intimate relationships of communication between remote participants. The thematic cross-reference is a vectoral event, an exchange or link between the local and remote, immediate and mediated objects of narration. For example, think of the way in which Bloom's whereabouts are located at the start of "Wandering Rocks." On page 261 of the 1960 Random House edition, our immediate context is Thornton's, where we find Boylan flirting with the assistant and buying fruit for Molly. The Arranger intrudes with a mediated glimpse of a remote "darkbacked figure" scanning books under Merchants' arch (*U* 10.315). Eight pages on, Lenehan and McCoy pass under Merchants' arch, having just referred indirectly to Bloom, before espying him scanning books. The identical phrasing ("A darkbacked figure scanned books") suggests, in turn, that Lenehan and McCoy were also passing under Merchants' arch, but not identified, at the time of the previous sighting of Bloom. So much for the idea of print as a linear medium. Two pages on we are introduced to Bloom on his own terms as an immediate object of narration, turning "over idly pages of *The Awful Disclosures of Maria Monk*, then of Aristotle's Masterpiece" (*U* 10.585-6). It is therefore inappropriate to speak of events occurring one after the other in these episodes, in the linear, concatenated Forsterian manner of "and then, and then." It is more appropriate to describe the vectoral cross-links in terms of syncopation, of "elsewhere and elsewhere." What we experience as synchronicities are non-linear instances of convergence and juxtaposition, links within a discontinuous narrative space.

The idea of *Ulysses* as a kind of "grammar for being elsewhere" (to borrow Porter Abbott's phrase)[14] hopefully demonstrates why it has proven to be so attractive to hypertext theorists as a precursor to a

[14] H.P. Abbott, "A Grammar for Being Elsewhere," *Journal of Modern Literature* 6.1 (1977).

theory of hypertextual poetics. I hope it also reveals how easy it has been to simply endow *Ulysses* with the nomenclature of hypermedia. I have deliberately introduced some of the defining terminology of hypertext theory **into** the preceding discussion of "Wandering Rocks" and "Sirens" to show that while such terms will work in the context of a discussion of *Ulysses*, they work by substitution. The conceptual frameworks of Kenner and Hayman are perfectly adequate for accounting for the unprecedented complexity of *Ulysses*' textuality. While it could be argued that they were, in fact, inventing a theory of hypertextuality, we need to remember that the "hyper" paradigm has a historical context, one largely associated with the last decade of the twentieth century. What is more important to stress is that both Hayman and Kenner intuited that the kind of approach they were taking to *Ulysses* was likely to precipitate new critical approaches to the text. If hypertextuality is an example of such an approach, and it is, it does not follow that it is a superior or more accurate one. In fact, as parallels between the truisms of hypertext theory and their parallactic/paratactic precursor suggests, there is a remarkable degree of conceptual overlap.

In his case study of *Ulysses*, David Gold, in attempting to define hypertext, cites the following quotation:

> A hypertext system is one in which links may be specified between different places in the text. Whereas books do offer a primitive sort of linking process (in that notes may refer to footnotes, which may refer the reader to further texts), a computer-based system, which is what we are interested in for the purposes of this inquiry, takes the reader or user directly to the linked material, or, if you prefer, brings the linked material to the reader.[15]

Gold's "simple working" definition of the mechanics of hypertext, as a spatial environment contoured by links between different places in the text, is indicative, in a fundamental way, of some of the axiomatic descriptions of hypertext:

> George Landow: Hypertext [...] denotes text composed of blocks of text [...] and the electronic links that join them.[16]

> Ben Shneiderman: a database that has active cross-references and allows the reader to 'jump' to other parts of the database as desired.[17]

> Jakob Nielsen: hypertext consists of interlinked pieces of text (or other information).[18]

---

[15] Gold, "*Ulysses*: A Case Study."
[16] George Landow, *Hypertext: The Convergence of Contemporary Critical Theory and Technology* (Baltimore, Johns Hopkins University Press, 1992) 4.
[17] B. Shneiderman, "Reflections on authoring, editing, and managing hypertext," *The Society of Text*, ed. Barrett, (Cambridge, Mass.: MIT Press, 1989) 115.
[18] Jakob Nielsen, *Hypertext and Hypermedia* (Boston, Mass.: Academic Press, 1990) 2.

The vectoral relationship between local detail and remote cross-reference that I have generalised from the work of Hayman and Kenner, is clearly the defining structure of hypertext. Jakob Nielsen's now canonical, diadic structure of node and link encompasses the idea that a network of linked information in a hypertext is based upon a vectoral relationship between an immediate node and ensembles of other nodes elsewhere.[19] The link is the pointer or indicator of cross-reference between local and remote nodes. It is, as Steven Johnson has noted in his *Interface Culture*, "a way of drawing connections between things, a way of forging semantic relationships."[20] In Joycean textuality, it is alterity within thematic and metaphoric systems of reference that constitutes the link that points to connections to be made elsewhere. One example, noted by Kenner in this very context in *The Stoic Comedians*, will suffice to make the general point.[21] Virtually at the commencement of the text, Stephen, prompted by a remark of Mulligan's, recalls the incident of an Oxford ragging:

> Shouts from the open window startling evening in the quadrangle. A deaf gardener, aproned, masked with Matthew Arnold's face, pushes his mower on the sombre lawn watching narrowly the dancing motes of grasshalms. [*U* 1.172-5]

Elsewhere, a full four hundred and eighty-seven pages elsewhere, in the phantasmagoria of 'Circe,' we encounter Philip Drunk and Philip Sober, "two Oxford dons [...] masked with Mathew Arnold's face" (*U* 15.2513-5). Both have lawnmowers that purr "with a rigadoon of grasshalms" (*U* 15.2537).

Issues to do with interactivity, non-linearity, and retrospective backtracking all stem from this fundamental, vectoral configuration of textual behaviour. For Joyce such concepts were implicit in his inventive strategy of "applied Aquinas." In particular, the principle of consonantia, the exact interrelation of parts within the whole, motivated the momentous potential in the text for cross-reference, incidence and coincidence.[22] In electronic hypertexts, such qualities are endemic to connectivity and the fluidity of digital code. What is striking, however, is the degree of conspicuous overlap in relation to the way such texts are read. Kenner, for instance, observes how we "reread in quest of patterns, finding them aplenty, largely created by ourselves from selective observation of cues, often cues planted by Joyce."[23] Jay Bolter, in his *Writing Space*, notes of the hypertext experience: "In general, the reader of an electronic text

[19] Nielsen, *Hypertext and Hypermedia*, 2.
[20] Steven Johnson, *Interface Culture. How New Technology Transforms the Way We Create and Communicate*, (New York, Harper Collins, 1997) 111.
[21] Kenner, *The Stoic Comedians*, 66.
[22] Kenner, *The Stoic Comedians*, 60.
[23] Hugh Kenner, *Ulysses* (London: Allen & Unwin, 1980) 155.

is made aware of the author's simultaneous presence in and absence from the text, because the reader is constantly confronting structural choices established by the author."[24]

We can, perhaps, in retrospect, even credit Kenner with inventing the locutions of interactive criticism most frequently associated with works such as Afternoon. Of *Ulysses* he observes:

> Its universe is Einsteinian, non-simultaneous, internally consistent but never to be grasped in one act of apprehension: not only because the details are so numerous but also because their pertinent interconnections are more numerous still.[25]

What I have hopefully achieved in demonstrating here is that our reading of hypertext, our navigation of hypertextuality, is not so much a novel, but rather a familiar experience. The complex textuality of *Ulysses*, which depends upon the technology of the printed book, has prepared us for the hypertextual poetics of nodal screens. Espen Aarseth, in his *Cybertext: Perspectives on Ergodic Literature* (1997), reinforces the principle that hypertextuality is not a quality endemic to the computer but a form of textual behaviour, a poetics forged out of the tradition of print technology. Furthermore, Aarseth convincingly argues that we need to move beyond the clichés of linear book and non-linear hypertext. Instead, he proposes a broad media category, "cybertext," as a "perspective on all forms of textuality"[26] that require an interactive, combinative approach to reading, which he describes as "ergodic."

One of the greatest textual precursors of the hypertextual, Jorge-Luis Borges, described Joyce as "the intricate and near-infinite Irishman who wove *Ulysses*."[27] We would do well to remember that this weaving was done in a classical temper and was far from hyper. Joyce's text is what hypertext wants to be, "proteiform yet bounded,"[28] bounded yet proteiform.

[24] Bolter, *Writing Space: The Computer, Hypertext, and the History of Writing* (Hillsdale, New Jersey: Lawrence Erlbaum, 1991) 30.
[25] Kenner, *Ulysses*, 81.
[26] Espen Aarseth, *Cybertext: Perspectives on Ergodic Literature* (Baltimore, Johns Hopkins University Press, 1997) 18.
[27] Borges, "A Defense of Bouvard and Pécuchet," in *The Total Library: Non-Fiction 1922-1986*, ed. Eliot Weinberger, trans. E.Allen. et,al. (London: Penguin, 1999) 393.
[28] Kenner, *Ulysses*, 173.

DONALD F. THEALL
Joyce´s Practice of Intertextuality: The Anticipation of Hypermedia & its Implications for Textual Analysis of *Finnegans Wake*

The history of hypertext usually marks 1945 as the date of an originary moment, for that is when Vannevar Bush first outlined in the *Atlantic Magazine* his ideas about Memex. Bush notes how the conclusion of the war is a moment when there could be a new relationsh p between the thinking person and the sum of their knowledge. The history of grammatology with its perception of virtual hypertext should mark 1939, on the eve of World War II, as the date of an originary moment, for that is when *Finnegans Wake* appeared — a work to which Borges, Derrida, Eco and McLuhan all attribute in one way or another their relative interests in the nature of writing or the relationship between wr ting and other modes of communication. Since the eighties when Derrica, while revealing the importance of Joyce's work to his writings, clearly outlined the affinity of Joyce with computers and digitalization, Joyce's pre-cybernetic intuition has become more and more widely recognized, so that now there even is a journal entitled *Hypermedia Joyce Studies*.

In exploring Joyce's pre-cybernetic intuitions and their relationship to using computers in analysing the *Wake*, I will examine the theoretical implications and the ways in which hypermedia and artificial realities transform processes of reading and understanding. While there will be some discussion of specific examples of text analysis and concor-dancing, the primary consideration will be the implications of a work whose assemblage anticipates cyberculture and whose very existence has implications for all readings of texts subsequent to the digitalization of the docuverse.

At the outset I want to assert a stronger claim that should inform any approach to Joyce's later works. That claim is that living within the same historical frame that produced Vannevar Bush's Memex — a period marked by the rise of contemporary technoculture — Joyce, from the perspective of a cultural producer, intuitively recognized the emergence of digital culture. Joyce's intuition of this cyberculture has been estab-lished in articles by Derrida, Eco and Louis Armand; and in books and articles by Darren Tofts, Lorraine Weir and myself, particularly my *James*

Joyce's Techno-Poetics.[1] Joyce's treatment anticipates such cybernetic concepts as code, surprise or deviation, memory storage, non-linearity, transversality, link, frame and even with a very slight stretch of hermeneutic imagination, bit and bite. Besides, he is most likely the earliest writer to practice so comprehensively, complexly and exhaustively the poetic strategies of intertextuality—or perhaps more properly, of inter-discursivity—in order to create a major anticipation of hypermedia.

The crux of the issue is the peculiar problem that the Joycean text presents because in the *Wake* there is an intrinsic inter-relationship between Joyce as a prophet of cyberculture, self-conscious about its potentialities, and the *Wake* as a uniquely challenging object for processes of interpretation which use computer software and hypermedia as modes to aid understanding. Most of us are familiar with Joyce's remarks about deliberately enticing his readers into interminable interpretation, since his book is directed towards "the ideal reader with ideal insomnia," but the *Wake*'s interdiscursive (or intertextual) aspect as well as its complex intratextuality goes much further—a situation to which the wide variety of nearly a hundred web sites addressing aspects of Joyce's work attest.

First, Joyce's deliberate strategy of introducing the public to his work by gradual stages over the seventeen years he was writing it consciously encouraged his readers to develop an interest in the genesis of the *Wake*. It was initially published in bits and pieces under the working title, *Work in Progress* (first in journals, followed by specific sections in chapbooks). Then he proposed that C.K. Ogden write an introduction to a series of fragments entitled *Tales Told of Shem and Shaun*, encouraging him to include a discussion of the book's mathematics. He also encouraged Beckett to edit and along with others to write a volume of critical essays explicating *Work in Progress* (1929). (Later he would embed the title of the collection of essays into the *Wake* suggesting it to be a partial interpretation by playfully transforming the *Wake*'s title into "Quinnigan's Quake!" and Beckett's collection into "Your exagmination round his factification for incamination of a warping process" [*FW* 497.2-3], just as he would allude to C.K. Ogden in "basically English" and in references to his books). In 1929 he recorded a portion of *Anna Livia Plurabelle* for Ogden, while from the outset of the writing until publication, he continued to provide exegetical guidance to many of his interpreters, such as Mercanton, Giedion-Welcker, Valéry-Larbaud and Frank Budgen, as well as friends such as Harriet Shaw Weaver. This is a program similar to Pope's staged development of *The Dunciad* from *The Scriblerus Papers* through its various versions from 1728 to *The Dunciad Variorum* of 1743.

In addition to his efforts with the staging of *Work in Progress* and critical commentary about it, for some sections of the book he also

[1] Donald F. Theall, *James Joyce's Techno-Poetics* (Toronto: Toronto University Press, 1997).

(whether accidentally or deliberately) left us up to nine various stages of the evolution of the manuscript, including his correction of printed items from *Work in Progress* and the proofs of the *Wake*. These different stages of the manuscript are supplemented by eighteen notebooks that he had used while composing the *Wake* (which now account for 16 volumes of the *James Joyce Archive*). In the digital era the availability of such material for genetic research invites hypertext, just as hypertext invites genetic research. Examples of such a response to Joyce can be found at web sites in Yokohama, Oregon, Zürich, Peterborough, Antwerp, and at Temple University (the latter of which includes the first issue of *Hypermedia Joyce Studies*), for hypertext provides a rich mode for presenting varying layers of composition accompanied by annotations and cross-references to the text of the work when published and links to sites involving places, persons and things interdiscursively involved in the *Wake* (for example, detailed maps, photographs, historical information about Dublin, Ireland, Italy and France). Some of the sites permit interactive suggestions or further suggestions alternative to earlier ones to contribute to the interpretation of the notebooks (whose handwriting is often difficult to interpret), providing for a collaborative act of reading. Jorn Barger maintains a site where all the versions of the segments of the *Wake* from which Joyce began are available to permit an online tracing of the genesis of these key sections.

Joyce's deliberate machination of the genesis of the *Wake* supplemented by the rich fund of genetic material available produces one type of intertextuality. A second type of interdiscursivity involves Joyce's complex and multiple allusiveness, both transversely within the text and externally, to a multitude of persons, places, books and other cultural productions—all sources towards which he deliberately pointed his readers. This latter type of interdiscursivity encourages the early intimations of a primitive online hypertextual variorum edition maintained by Tim Szeliga and me which uses a hypertextual version of my wife, Joan's, and my electronic text of the entire work. *Finnegans Web*[2] at Trent links every reference to the work from most of the major critical books to individual page and line references within the text and also provides a search engine permitting wildcard searches. Frames provide a means for visually presenting Joyce's use of marginalia and foot-notes in the second section of Book II, including graphic material (e.g. scales, doodles, etc.).

What needs to be noted in all of this is the unique importance of Joyce's conception of the reader-writer, producer-consumer relationship, which is referred to immediately following the reference in the *Wake* to "Quinnigan's Quake" cited above: "His producers are they not his consumers?" As early as 1982 in a lecture on *James Joyce: Poetic Engineer*, I related Joycean semiotics with an anticipation of cybernetic

[2] Tim Szeliga, *Finnegans Web* (1999): http://www.trentu.ca/jjoyce/

processes. The Joycean writer comes to be replaced by the reader who re-writes the text—the reader as poet related to processes of coding, to mnemonically pursuing transverse references and to a mimesis of multi-media perception:

> The prouts who will invent a writing there ultimately is the poeta, still more learned, who discovered the raiding there originally. That's the point of eschatology our book of kills reaches for now in soandso many counterpoint words. What can't be coded can be decorded if an ear aye seize what no eye ere grieved for. Now, the doctrine obtains, we have occasioning cause causing effects and affects occasionally recausing altereffects. [*FW* 482.31-483.1]

Jacques Derrida, who described the *Wake* as a "hypermnesiac machine," and noted the potentialities of hypermedia to investigate such a text, suggests that Joyce was:

> there in advance, decades in advance, to compute you, control you, forbid you the slightest inaugural syllable because you can say nothing that is not programmed on this 1000th generation computer—Ulysses, *Finnegans Wake*—beside which the current technology of our computers and micro-computerfied archives and translating machines remains a bricolage of a perhistoric child's toys. And above all its mechanisms are of a slowness, incommensurable with the quasi-infinite speed of the movements on Joyce's cables.[3]

Joyce's "hypermnesiac machine" operates through his readers being "in his memory." By examining his use of pre-digital hyperlinks involving memory and mimesis, this aspect of his creative process provides an interesting way of examining how his virtual or imaginary hypermedia is a pre-digital prophecy of contemporary hypermedia.

One of his prime and complex means of creating networks of inter-linkage within the text (i.e., transversality or intratextuality) is to play on minimal differences within simple syllables by their transformation and/or insertion into a variety of words along with their potential for creating assonance and consonance. The items of minimal difference involved frequently relate to prime clusters of inter-related meanings. Text analysis software with wild card capability, the use of Boolean operators and other such search devices is of considerable value both in ferreting out these groups and in revealing many of the polysemic aspects of their interconnection. To explore memory, mimesis and related concepts take as an example the following chain entered into a search engine of a text analysis and concordancing tool: m preceded by the regular expression "any" (i.e., a single period followed by a wildcard [an asterisk]) then [brackets enclosing aeiou], i.e., indicating any vowel occupying the posi-

3 Jacques Derrida, "Two Words for Joyce: He War," *Poststructuralist Joyce*, eds. Derek Attridge and Daniel Ferrer (Cambridge: Cambridge University Press, 1994) 147.

tion between the two ms the second m being followed by the repetition of the opening sequence, a combination which asks for all words that contain any three letter syllable such as:

m—[aeiou]—m

Applied to the text of the *Wake* this is very productive in generating a multitude of examples illustrative of Joycean excesses of meaning for it selects all the monosyllabic and morphological chains involving mam-mem-mim-mom-mum (interestingly the first two members of which, if the second m is dropped, become ma and me). When the text is searched for occurrences, Joyce's insistence on the relation of the mother to such concepts as mimesis, mimicry, mime, memory, moment, silence (being mum) is established and the chain expands through mul-timimetica (multimedia) to semiotics (the meaning of meaning) and mathematics: "lead us seek, lote us see, light us find, let us missnot Maidadate, Mimosa Multimimetica, the maymeaminning of maimoomein-ing!" (*FW* 267.2-3) to "the deprofundity of multimathematical immaterialities" (*FW* 394.31-2). From the multiple plays on the basic chain of vowel changes, here the reader is led into relating the mimesis and memory to Ogden and Richards, *The Meaning of Meaning* and Ogden's interest in mathematical (Leibnizian) theories of meaning. The strategy being pursued here rises out of Joyce's encyclopaedic design coupled with his practico-theoretic interest in inter-relating such basic textual concepts as imitation, dramatic presentation, memory, meaning and mathematical order. This is similar to that which characterizes hy-permedia links and their rhizomic like organization.

These Joycean links, which pre-date digital culture, are aural-mnemonic; the m-vowel-m sets serving as the anchors for the internal (intratextual) links, as illustrated in how the "maymeaminning of mai-moomeining" cited above evokes *The Meaning of Meaning* because these anchors are supplemented by the visual and auditory structure of words or phrases in the text including puns on the German word for "opinion" and the Irish for "stuttering" to provide the external (interdis-cursive) links. But this interweaving goes further, anticipatorily mimicking some of the more complex aspects of hypertext by inter-relating the maternal, the imitative, the semiotic, the mnemonic and the mathematical (and/or logical) ordering. This is what creates a reciprocity between the Joycean text and the computer programs, which comple-ment (partly, but not solely, by speed) the cerebral processing of the reader reading with eye and ear—the hypertextual path supplementing the path guided by human memory.

As this example attests, text analysis and concordancing software, such as TACT, has become essential in "raiding" Joyce, even more so when, in addition to highly flexible programs for browsing and searching, it also includes programs to produce anagrams, tables of collocations, frequency lists, graphs of distribution and the like.[4] But the Joycean pre-post-modernist (or radical modernist) project makes it even more appropriate since, as established in Thomas Rice's *Joyce, Chaos and Complexity* and my *James Joyce's Techno-Poetics*, Joyce utilized geometrical and arithmetical principles of organization as well as logico-mathematical and structural semiotic ones.[5] This creates a context within which the computer aids and abets the radical type of "raiding" with its "decoding" and "dechording" which the *Wake* envisions in the reader's re-writing. The point is that such an interface does not only assist interpretation or understanding, but it also aids and abets a new mode of advanced modernist (or poststructuralist) reading, radically transverse, as our examples with mam-mem-mim-mom-mum demonstrate. It has been pointed out how the all important "yes" of *Ulysses* becomes associated in the extravagant play of the *Wake* with "eyes." Then the association of the "eye" (e-y-e) with "aye" (a-y-e) and then with capital "I" inter-relate the acts of seeing or vision, of affirmation, and of identity. Computers exponentially increase the capability to investigate the *Wake* not only by their use in concordancing, searching and linking or their statistical power, but also because their hypermediac encyclopaedism is complementary to the *Wake*'s proto-hypermnesiac-encyclopaedism.

Since the Joycean world is consciously a world of permutations, combinations and probabilities, the ability of the computer to provide statistics and distribution graphs contributes further to its reading. I'll take a rather simplistic example. While the *Wake* is often described as a book about death, dream, sleep, trees and rivers, one of the more statistically significant words in it is "old"—there are 463 occurrences of "old" alone (about three times as many as would likely be anticipated). When this is supplemented by the use of "old" as an initial syllable in compounds, the count rises to 539. If a dominant variant of old, "auld" together with its initial appearance in compounds is added, the count increases to 555. One of these compounds combines "auld" with "ancient" in "auldancient," so that if we add "ancient" to the "auld" list another 23 new words are added for 578. (Additionally "auld" provides an interdiscursive node for the entire set of old-ancient-auld.) Distributional graphs further reveal the higher concentration of these occurrences are in the third of the four books dealing with the third and final Viconian era before the conclusion of one cycle and the beginning of another, or in sections dealing with the heroic Finn-HCE figure. The high collocation of the word "old" with "new" indicates the dual role of "old" ("auld") as past and of old as preparing for the new cycle. Al-

[4] Lancashire, Bradley, Stairs, and Wooldridge, eds., *Using TACT with Electronic Texts: Text-Analysis Computing Tools 2.1 for MS-DOS and PC DOS* (New York: Modern Language Association, 1996).
[5] Thomas J. Rice, *Joyce, Chaos, and Complexity* (Urbana and Chicago: University of Illinois Press, 1997).

though with Joyce's incredibly complex word-play statistical results must be tentative—usually erring on the conservative side—such analysis may reveal challenging, counter-intuitive views of the thematics of the *Wake*. Primarily, though, I am using it here to illustrate the potentialities for producing readings of the *Wake*, perhaps even reading the *Wake* in a manner closer to its conception, which can be accelerated and deepened by both a use of the computer and an understanding of the role of digitalisation, memory and hypermedia in the cyberretic.

Finally, by anticipating the emergence of hypermedia and virtual (artificial) realities, Joyce's hypermnesiac differential or calculating engine moved beyond the orality/literacy dichotomy, anticipating digitalization as part of the pre-history of cyberspace, and thus participating in the radical modernist drive to maximize synaesthesia and coenaesthesia (i.e., the integration of the arts). What are the further implications of this overt awareness, over fifty years ago, of the implications of hypermedia? First, concurring with Derrida and Rabaté, Joyce's post-encyclopaedic memory machine—at least for the moment—is beyond the computer in the speed and range of the linkages and the excessive productivity of what Joyce described as his "ambiviolence." His words, phrases, tales and assemblages encompass and yet go beyond the media, yet they simultaneously invite and demand the processes of reading possible in the context of hypertext, hypermedia, telecommunications and artificial reality. His work invites and incites the richest encyclopaedic setting—a setting which will generate readings beyond any specific intention, yet implicit in the global social and cultural context within which it was crafted where the readers (consumers) are perpetual ongoing producers. Second, together with Ulysses, through its very complexity the *Wake* should provide a practico-theoretic ground for the entire humanities computing community, since it attempts to be a summa of all the potentialities of speech and writing.

The current web and other digital projects of the Joycean community are generating a global pan-encyclopaedic hypertextual context for the reading of the *Wake*. This means that an elaborately online networked *Finnegans Wake* consisting of a multitude of international nodes will be generating itself in the next century constituting a practico-theoretic exercise in the limits of reading and understanding with implications for all texts. If one thinks of the complex tools for Joycean interpretation currently available on and off line—gazetteers, maps, collections of music, references to a multitude of books, sets of printed and online annotations, lexicons of classical, Gaelic, Scandinavian, Anglo-Irish and German words and word play, collections of photographs, stages of the manuscript, notebooks used in composition, etc.—the ultimate value of a global interactive cooperation in generating a new context of reading—encyclopaedic, multi-media, yet alphabetic, photograph c, phonographic, filmic, gestural and dramatic—will contribute to our new modes of "raiding" a text in which the computer will be both a tool and an alter-ego to the readers in their act of re-writing—the consumer-producers in their act of reproducing. Joyce's dream, having produced a virtual hypermedia, will generate through its researcher-readers a cyberspatial hypertext.

LOUIS ARMAND
From Symptom to Machine

Writing has no sooner begun than it inseminates itself with another reading. The *Wake*, *fin negans*, begets only beginnings but invalidates all origins, in a system which can be described as a word-machine, or a complex machination of meanings, probing and programming the seedy sides of meaning.*

TEXTUAL MACHINES

In their 1979 book *Autopoiesis and Cognition,* cyberneticists Humberto Maturana and Francesco Varela coin the phrase "autopoietic machines" to describe a process of mechanised autoproduction. In cybernetics the term autopoietic refers to machines organised as a network of processes of production, transformation and destruction. This network gives rise to components which, through their interactions and transformations, re-generate and in turn realise the network or processes that produced them. At the same time these components constitute the network as a concrete unity in the space in which they exist by specifying the "topo-logical domain of its realisation."[1] In other words, the components of autopoietic machines generate recursively, by means of their interaction, the same network of processes by which they themselves are produced.

To a significant extent, the idea of autopoietic machines parallels what Victor Tausk conceived of as "influencing machines," and what Gilles Deleuze and Félix Guattari term "desiring machines." For Deleuze and Guattari, the desiring-production of "desiring machines" coalesces about what Antonin Artaud described as a "the body without organs": a body which "is produced as a whole, but in its own particular place within the process of production, alongside the parts that it neither uni-fies nor totalizes."[2] This sense of a body-machine, produced "alongside" its parts, echoes Tausk's concept of an influencing apparatus as the terminal manifestation in a schizo symptomatology, whose etiology is one of alienation and regressive loss of ego boundaries. Like Artaud's

---

* Jean-Michel Rabaté, "Lapsus ex machina," trans. Elizabeth Guild, *Post-structuralist Joyce: Essays from the French*, eds. Derek Attridge and Daniel Ferrer (London: Cambridge University Press, 1984) 79.
[1] Humberto Maturana and Francisco Varela, *Autopoiesis and Cognition* (Boston: Reidal, 1979).
[2] Gilles Deleuze and Félix Guattari, *Anti-Oedipus: Capitalism and Schizophrenia*, trans. R. Hurley, M. Seem, and H.R. Lane (New York: Viking, 1977) 43.

body without organs, the influencing machine operates as a body prosthesis, whose substitution for the material body initiates a chain of other substitutions, of which it becomes the symptomatic expression, while at the same time nevertheless representing a mechanism of objectification.[3] Hence for Tausk, this machine is above all a symptom, whose relation to the alienating process of its objectification can be described as autopoietic, since it is also a projection and sublimated identification (through which lines of "influence" are preserved and in fact reinforced). Similarly, when the body without organs "turns back upon" its other parts, it brings about what Deleuze and Guattari describe as:

> transverse communications, transfinite summarizations, polyvocal and transcursive inscriptions on its own surface, on which the functional breaks of partial objects are continually intersected by breaks in the signifying chains, and by breaks effected by a subject that uses them as reference points in order to locate itself.[4]

This sense of "transverse communications" emerges in *Finnegans Wake* in terms of an overall apparatus, underwriting a general thematics of identity, autopoiesis, alchemy, duplicity, copyright, historicity and so on. In a key passage towards the end of Book I, Joyce describes Shem-the-Penman, the plagiarist-author figure of the *Wake*, as producing:

> nichthemerically from his unheavenly body a no uncertain quantity of obscene matter not protected by copriright in the United States of Ourania or bedeed and bedood and bedang and bedung to him, with his double dye, brought to blood heat, gallic acid on iron ore, through the bowels of his misery, flashly, nastily, appropriately, this Esuan Menschavik and the first till last alchemist wrote over every square inch of the only foolscap available, his own body, till by its corrosive sublimation one continuous present tense integumented slowly unfolded in all marryvoising mood-moulded cyclewheeling history. [*FW* 185.29-186.02]

Writing with his excrement across the entire surface of his own body, Shem symbolically obscures the divisions between *tropos* and *topos* in a single act of *autopoiesis*. Or rather, this solipsistic reversion crosses between a topological space within language and a tropological space within the *topos* of this relation, whereby we might think of *Finnegans Wake* (whose metonym this excremental writing is) as emerging from a symptomatology of autopoietic involution, or what Joyce calls "morphological circumformation" (*FW* 599.09-17).

Such a mechanism of "circumformation" recalls what Jacques Derrida, in his essay "Two Words for Joyce," terms "a hypermnesiac

3 Victor Tausk, "The Influencing Machine," trans. Dorian Feigenbaum, *Incorporations*, eds. Jonathan Crary and Sanford Kwinter (New York: Zone Books, 1992) 551-2.
4 Deleuze and Guattari, *Anti-Oedipus*, 43.

machine."[5] Following Joyce's writing practice in *Finnegans Wake*, Derrida is interested in how the idea (*eidos*) put to work hypermnemically, as an alternative to the intuition or direct experience of phenomenology, is not the signified concept but the elision of meaning brought about in language by the symptomatic re-alignment of narratives, tropes, themes, genres, but also individual words, letters or phonemes.

In *Dissemination*, Derrida suggests that this elision would give rise to a type of hypertextual apparatus which would operate "in two absolutely different places at once, even if these were only separated by a veil,"[6] an idea he further elaborates upon in "Two Words for Joyce":

> Paradoxical logic of this relationship between two texts, two programmes or two literary "softwares": whatever the difference between them, even if [...] it is immense and incommensurable, the "second" text, the one which, fatally, refers to the other, quotes it, exploits it, parasites it and deciphers it, is no doubt the minute parcel *detached* from the other, the metonymic dwarf, the jester of the great anterior text [...] and yet it is also another set, quite other, bigger, and more powerful than the all-powerful which it drags off and reinscribes elsewhere in order to defy its ascendancy. Each writing is at once the detached fragment of a software more powerful than the other, a part larger than the whole of which it is a part.[7]

The topological structure of the relationship described here, between two textual programmes, recalls what Derrida in *The Truth in Painting* terms *mise en abyme*, wherein a "totality" "is represented on the model of one of its parts which thus becomes greater than the whole of which it forms a part, which it makes into a part."[8] Elsewhere Derrida describes this process in terms of a supplementary "chain of substitutions," or as a "decentring," suggesting analogies to what the mathematician Henri Poincaré termed the "Vicious Circle Principle" and which Bertram Russell in 1908 defined as an *exclusion* of metonymic totality. For Russell,

---

[5] Jacques Derrida, "Two Words for Joyce," *Post-structuralist Joyce: Essays from the French*, eds. Derek Attridge and Daniel Ferrer (Cambridge: Cambridge University Press, 1984) 147.

[6] Jacques Derrida, "The Double Sessions," *Dissemination*, trans. Barbara Johnson (Baltimore: Johns Hopkins University Press, 1981) 221.

[7] Derrida, "Two Words for Joyce," 148.

[8] Jacques Derrida, *The Truth in Painting*, trans. Geoffrey Bennington and Ian McLeod (Chicago: Chicago University Press, 1987) 27. This metaphor describes a two-fold relation that suggests, also, Georg Cantor's set continuum problem, which also came to pre-occupy Gottlob Frege and Bertram Russell. The first is the ambivalent set between two writing/translation softwares, in which one is a "minute" and "metonymic dwarf" which is nonetheless "detached from" and able to "exploit" the other. The second is the equivalent set of relations between two softwares in which both are a "detached fragment of a software" and, simultaneously, a "software more powerful than the other" and a "part larger than the whole of which it is a part."

"whatever involves *all* of a collection must not [itself] be one of the collection."[9]

In the 'Mamafesta' episode of *Finnegans Wake* (I.5), this set theoretical principle of metonymic exclusion is posed against the function of A.L.P.'s letter ("Anna's gramme") as a "metonymic dwarf" of Joyce's "nightbook" as a whole, in which the letters A.L.P. simultaneously describe the recurrent "vicious circle" of a Freudian repetition compulsion in which *Alp* is also the German word for nightmare. As this "epistolear" becomes more and more a part of the textual apparatus that surrounds it, and less distinguishable from its own analysis or exegesis, it begins to take on a mythological aura as the site of endless co-ordinates for an impossible rendez-vous with itself. Like the letters A.L.P. and H.C.E., this "nightletter" serves as a kind of topological, or tropological site of what Jean-Michel Rabaté terms a *lapsus*—a point of "continuity" which at the same time marks out a chain of "dis-continuities," or the symptomatic "disarticulation" of a sequence of encoding and decoding.

As with Derrida, Rabaté envisages a machine in which production is driven by an internal division (memory or desire) which opens a place of potentially limitless substitutions—a movement which finds itself programmed in advance by the irreducibility of the machine's own internal paradox. This paradox is pervasive, but it might be said to be most fully accommodated in the *purpose* of the machine to supersede itself—a form of "built-in obsolescence," which is also a form of projective self-substitution and auto-production. As Rabaté suggests, this paradox functions as a "lapsus" and points to the way in which a programmatic discourse would "attempt to fill the blank space of desire left hollow by—or in—the machine."[10]

This "desiring machine," miming the totalising movement of an exegesis, or exe-genesis, approaches a topological relation to itself similar to that of the Turing machine, or of Cantor's continuum problem (the problem of determining whether there is a set with cardinality greater than that of the natural numbers but less than that of the continuum). In 1901, Russell reformulated this problem as arising from a consideration of the set of all sets which are not members of themselves, since this set must be a member of itself if and only if it is not a member of itself.[11]

Cesare Burali-Forti, an assistant to the mathematician Guiseppi Peano, discovered a similar antinomy in 1897 when he observed that since the set of ordinals is well ordered, it therefore must have an ordinal itself. However, this ordinal must be both an element of the set of ordi-

9   Bertram Russell, "Mathematical Logic as Based on the Theory of Types," *American Journal of Mathematics* 30 (1908): 222-62.
10 Rabaté, "Lapsus ex machina," 79.
11 See Bertram Russell, *The Principles of Mathematics* (Cambridge: Cambridge University Press, 1903). Cf. Bertram Russell and Alfred North Whitehead, *Principia Mathematica*, 3 vols. (Cambridge: Cambridge University Press, 1910).

nals and yet greater than any ordinal in the set. By definition, the paradoxical sets of Forti and Russell deny self-similarity since they must of necessity contain the term that both defines and exceeds them, *ad infinitum*, as a type of interminable destiny. In the absence of any limiting or stabilising "identity," the set paradox tends towards unlimited proliferation—a type of desiring machine caught, like the Lacanian subject, in an inflationary movement of self-projection and re-integration.

This idea can be broadly applied to genetic processes of coding and decoding in which a programmatic identity takes the place of an originary identity, and in which the genetic code can be viewed as structurally antecedent to itself within a sequence of metonymic substitutions. Derrida links this idea to the principle of viral contamination:

> It is precisely a principle of contamination, a law of impurity, a parasitic economy. In the code of set theories, if I may use it at least figuratively, I would speak of a sort of participation without belonging—a taking part in without taking part of, without having membership in a set. The trait that marks membership inevitably divides, the boundary of the set comes to form, by invagination, an internal pocket larger than the whole; and the outcome of this division and of this abandoning remain as it is limitless.[12]

This *destining* (as a form of installation in advance), suggests another way in which programmatic emplacement operates a type of *"paradox lust."* It also suggests a way in which we might consider textual processes as programmed in advance—or as *belonging* to a program which has always already been installed and which cannot be disintricated from the "hardware" with which it will always have been integrated. In "The Question Concerning Technology," Martin Heidegger likewise argues that the essence of technology (as *Ge-stell* or *enframing*) "is an ordering of destining, as is every way of revealing. Bringing-forth *poiēsis*, is also a destining in this sense."[13] Similarly, Maurice Blanchot links discursive emplacement to a certain topology of the "fragment," as an element of metonymic recursion. According to Blanchot:

> the fragment, as fragments, tends to dissolve the totality which it presupposes and which it carries off towards the dissolution from which it does not [...] form, but to which it exposes itself in order, disappearing—and along with it, all identity—to maintain itself as the energy of disappearing: a repetitive energy, the limit that bears upon limitation.[14]

[12] Jacques Derrida, "The Law of Genre," trans. Avital Ronell, *Glyph* 7 (Baltimore: Johns Hopkins University Press, 1980) 207.
[13] Martin Heidegger, "The Question Concerning Technology," *Basic Writings: From* Being and Time *(1927) to* The Task of Thinking *(1964)*, ed. David Farrell Krell, rev. ed. (London: Routledge, 1993) 330.
[14] Maurice Blanchot. *The Writing of the Disaster*, trans. Ann Smock (Lincoln: University of Nebraska Press, 1995) 60-61.

This emplaced-fragmentation, without origin or derivation, would also describe the transversality of the "limit that bears upon limitation" as simultaneously the *aporia* of what Heidegger calls *being placed*. As the mark of discursive emplacement, this *aporia* of limits likewise describes a structural "hesitancy" between the fragmentary resemblance to a system in the process of emerging and to one in the process of dissolution. It suggests a mechanical lability, a technics of the fragmented tending simultaneously towards the infinitesimal and the monstrous through an interminable movement of autopoietic recursion. In place of the incomplete system it will always have seemed to imply, the fragment disseminates itself, engendering each of its elements as the fragmented-whole of which it is not even the whole-fragmented, *mise en abyme*.

HALTING MACHINES

The relation of the fragment to the organisation of semantic structures is also linked, through the material, typographical nature of the "book," to the technological concept of moveable type, echoing to a certain degree Plato's identification of the alphabet itself as a form of *technē* in *Phaedrus*. As Marshal McLuhan and others have pointed out, the invention of moveable type made Gutenberg's press one of the first Western machines of mass production.[15] The limited set of variables required for the press (twenty six Latin characters, plus blank spaces, punctuation marks and diacriticals) provides a basic conception of a typographical grid or matrix, within which a virtually infinite number of permutations and combinations are possible—depending upon assumed conventions of grammar, syntax and orthography used to determine any particular typographical sequence. As Alan Turing has noted, however:

> If we were to allow an infinity of symbols, then there would be symbols differing to an arbitrarily small extent. The effect of this restriction of the number of symbols is not very serious. It is always possible to use sequences of symbols in the place of single symbols. [...] Similarly in any European language words are treated as single symbols.[16]

The Turing "grid" provides a secondary means of organising language as a whole in terms of material combination and recombination, by assigning single values to entire terms, or to any linguistic, rhetorical or schematic unit whatsoever. In this way the cyclical notions of Giambattista Vico or Friedrich Nietzsche, or the structural repetitions of Homer's *Odyssey* and the Bible, can equally be thought of in acrostic terms.

One of the questions raised by Joyce's writing, however, is how to account for the possibility of this acrostic grid exceeding its own rules.

---

[15] Cf. Marshall McLuhan, *The Gutenberg Galaxy: The Making of Typographical Man* (Toronto: The University of Toronto Press, 1962) passim.
[16] Alan Turing, "On Computable Numbers, with an Application to the Entscheidungsproblem," *Proceedings, London Mathematical Society*, 2.42 (1936): 249-50.

In other words, how to account for the assigning of multiple values to individual terms, or to the multiplication of terms within the same grid-space? Moreover, the apparently mechanical nature of the acrostic grid poses questions similar to those raised by Noam Chomsky about the relatedness of such things as grammar and syntax to semantic coherence. This question is partly answered by the contingency of contextuality, or the way in which the acrostic grid motivates a multi-dimensional connectivity between each of its elements. Each connection provides a trajectory of possible interpretation, such that we can say each term is *in place* within its particular context(s).

A simple example of this is the referential function of an index or concordance, in which a basic system of co-ordinates employing two sets of variables (word or phrase and numerical page reference) provides a type of basic hypertextual site map or primitive cybernetic apparatus. In most cases, the first term remains constant for a variable number of second terms. "Plotted" against two-axes on a Cartesian plane, any set of co-ordinates sharing the first term will describe a straight line. The indexical value of the first term thus appears strictly linear

The difficulty arises with a classic Wittgensteinian problem of determining the relative value of the first term, which without appearing to differ, also does not remain constant across all of the contexts in which it appears (which is *not* its indexical value). Plotting the set of co-ordinates as a point-to-point vector across the body of the text, however, will produce a very different diagram—a transversal passing through a topological, "acrostic" space, whose values are not linear in any straightforward sense of that term. Other means of plotting these co-ordinates can also be determined to produce different hypertextual configurations, evolving the acrostic possibilities of the textual co-ordinates in increasingly elaborate ways. As Joyce himself suggests:

> The proteiform graph itself is a polyhedron of scripture. There was a time when naif alphabetters would have written it down the tracing of a purely deliquescent recidivist, possibly ambidextorous, snubnosed probably and presenting a strangely profound rainbow in his (or her) occiput.
> [*FW* 107.08-12]

But while such acrostic possibilities are conceivably infinite, they do pose questions of formal significance which ask whether or not an apparently random constellation of texts whose resemblance is always fractional can exert mutual simultaneous influence at a level which is not merely trivial or at best a fabulation ("a strangely profound rainbow").[17]

---

[17] Cf. *FW* 140-1. The letters A B C and D function here, as elsewhere, as subsectional "indices" of a series of questions, to which it is required "to harmonise your abecedeed responses" (*FW* 140.14).

VICOCICLOMETRY

In *Structure and Motif*, Hart identifies two major patterns of organisation in the structure of *Finnegans Wake*. The first of these is a three-plus-one pattern which Joyce ostensibly borrowed from Vico's *Principi di Scienza Nuova*, of a cyclical model of history comprising three evolutionary stages and a *ricorso*. The second pattern consists of "Lesser Cycles" which "make up a four-plus-one quasi-Indian" pattern.[18] As conceived by Hart, these models sustain the *Wake*'s overall double, cyclic structure: the "Major Viconian Cycle" describing the four books of the *Wake*, while within each of the "three Viconian Ages of Books I, II, and III, Joyce allows four four-chapter cycles to develop," and each of these lesser cycles also sustains an "implicit identification" with one of the four Western "classical elements" of earth, water, fire, and air:

Major Viconian Cycle	Lesser Cycle
Book I (Birth).................................	1. I.1-4: Male H.C.E 2. I.5-8: Female A.L.P.
Book II (Marriage)...........................	3. II—Male and Female battles; fire
Book III (Death).............................	4. III—Male cycle; Shaun as Earwicker's spirit; air

Where Hart's work touches closest on contemporary genetic approaches to Joyce's text is his idea of schemata functioning as prototypical models of different levels of textual production—although where Hart focuses on how these emerge within Joyce's text along more traditional lines of character and narrative, genetics tends to focus on how these schemata emerge from different points in the history of the text's composition. The following analysis of III.1 provides an example of how Hart sees Joyce's text as putting "cyclic ideas to work" in organising individual chapters:

Cycle I

Age i (403.18-405.03): Description of Shaun as a "picture primitive"; he does not speak (first Viconian Age).

Age ii (405.04-407.09): Shaun has become a hero ("Bel of Beaus Walk"); there is an allusion to the heroic slaying of the Jabberwock and an entertaining Rabelaisian description of Shaun's heroic eating habits.

---

[18] Clive Hart, *Structure and Motif in Finnegans Wake* (London: Faber and Faber, 1962) 62.

Age iii (407.10-414.14):   Introduced by "Overture and beginners"
this is the beginning of the Human Age, in
which the gods can appear only in dramatic representation on stage; Shaun has
become a popular representative ("vote of
the Irish"); the word "Amen" brings to an
end the group of three Ages forming the
main part of this first Viconian cycle.

Age iv (414.14-414.18):   A short *ricorso* brings us back to the theo-
cratic Age with the introduction to the
Fable—Thunder (*FW* 414.19).[19]

Hart suggests that the overall structure of the *Wake*—by the three-plus-
one pattern and its four-plus-one schematic complement—can also be
understood in terms of the "cross of the quaternity" or ⊕ symbol. This
cross within a circle corresponds to the siglum in the *Finnegans Wake*
manuscripts used to designate what Hart refers to as the "highly important ninth question in I.6.9":

> if a human being duly fatigued [...] having plenxty off time on his gouty
> hands [...] were [...] accorded [...] with an earsighted view of old hopin-
> haven [...] then *what* would that fargazer seem to seemself to seem
> seeming of, dimm it all?"
> [*FW* 143.4-27][20]

The *Wake*'s answer: "A collideorscope" (*FW* 143.28), can be seen as
one of the many terms with which Joyce's text describes itself, and
Hart contends that Joyce's use of the ⊕ symbol to designate a passage
dealing with the structure of *Finnegans Wake* "suggests that in one
structural sense, the whole book forms a *mandala*," which the ⊕ symbol
represents ("a quadripartite with diametrically inverted ornaments").[21]
This symbol can also be taken as defining a shift across scale, between
trope and schema, describing an implicitly hypertextual relation:

---

[19]   Hart, *Structure and Motif in Finnegans Wake*, 58. Hart then analyses the following sections
of the book along the same lines and demonstrates that Cycle IV brings III.1 "to a conclusion
with a prayer [...] to Shaun the god-figure, who is to be resurrected in the next chapter" (60).

[20]   Cited in Alan Roughley, *James Joyce and Critical Theory: An Introduction* (London: Har-
vester, 1991) 11.

[21]   Cf. Roland McHugh, *The Sigla of Finnegans Wake* (London: Edward Arnold, 1976) 118. For
McHugh the ⊕ symbol "denotes the mental sensation of contemplating the mandala of *Finnegans Wake*, a tranquil equipoise at the hub of time" (ibid., 121). There has been considerable
speculation on the relationship between *Finnegans Wake*'s schematic structures and Jung's
conception of archetypes and collective unconscious (in which Jung employed the mandala
symbol). Although Joyce was acquainted with Jung (who treated his daughter, Lucia, for part
of her illness), and made several references to Jung in the *Wake* ("Jungfraud's" [*FW*
460.20]), he was more clearly drawn to the ideas of Vico and, to a less certain extent, Freud
and the British anthropologist J.G. Frazer.

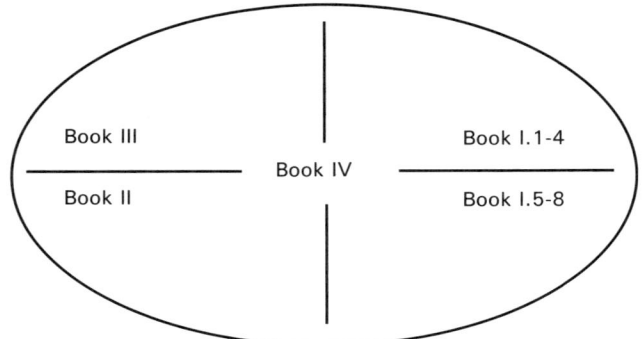

According to Hart, the four quadrants of the circle constitute "the Wheel of Fortune, while Book IV lies at the 'hub.'"[22] One interesting corollary to this analysis arises from a consideration of the apparently "circular" structure of the *Wake* whereby the last line in the book is often considered as turning back upon the first line, so that the book itself becomes literally a circle (a "book of Doublends Jined" [*FW* 20.15-16]), through the "sentence":

> A way a lone a last a loved a long the [| the outside of the book |] riverrun, past Eve and Adam's, from swerve of shore to bend of bay, brings us by a commodius vicus of recirculation back to Howth Castle and Environs. [*FW* 628.15-16, 3.01-13]

But if this sentence belongs to both the first (I.1) and last (IV.1) chapters of the *Wake*, then there can be no simple divide between the first and last chapters. In his seminar "Joyce le symptôme," Lacan suggests:

> déjà son dernier mot ne peut se rejoindre qu'au premier, le *the* sur lequel il se termine se raccolant au *riverrun* dont il se débute, ce qui indique le circulaire?[23]

Lacan goes on to argue that the structure of *Finnegans Wake* should, in fact, *not* be described as circular but rather as knotted, comparing the signifying relation of "the" and "riverrun" to the topological metaphor of Borromean knots. Lacan further relates the idea of the knot back to the "circle and cross" of Hart's mandalic ⊕ schematisation of the *Wake*,[24] arguing that the function of this is not so much to render the *Wake*'s structure as a closed totality, but rather:

22 Hart, *Structure and Motif in Finnegans Wake*, 77.
23 Jacques Lacan, "Joyce le symptôme I," *Joyce avec Lacan*, ed. Jacques Aubert (Paris: Navarin Éditeur, 1987) 29.
24 Lacan, "Joyce le symptôme I," 28.

à savoir l'ambiguïté du 3 et du 4, à savoir ce à quoi il restait collé, attaché, à l'interrogation de Vico.[25]

The exploration of the problem of Borromean knots represented Lacan's attempt at elaborating a topology of the symbolic, imaginary and real,[26] whose ambiguous structure, like *Finnegans Wake*, turns about the seemingly impossible equation $3 = 4$, as a transition from the structure of the "trinity" to that of the "quaternity." Which is also to say that if, according to conventional logics of scale, a sentence cannot be greater than a chapter, then the sentence "A way a lone [...] back to Howth Castle and Environs" belongs to one chapter, and the number of chapters in *Finnegans Wake* is not seventeen but sixteen, and the number of books is three and not four[27] — or rather, there are both possibilities at once. In this way Book IV, the *Wake*an *ricorso*, the "hub" or "doub e axis" of the *Wake*'s mandalic ⊕ structure, initiates this structural turn at the same time as this *turning* effaces it — providing a virtually schematic model of what Blanchot and Derrida describe as a de-centred structure.

Elsewhere in *Finnegans Wake* (293), this topological structuration recurs in the diagrammatical rendering of a doubly articulated "Viconian" mechanism, in which we might detect the solicitation of a particular "technology" of emplacement in the co-ordinates A.L.P.:

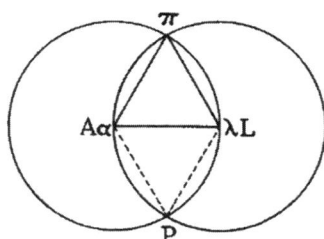

Hart's schematic ⊕ model of the *Wake* in *Structure and Motif in Finnegans Wake* bears particular resemblances to this "vicociclometer." Describing a double chiasmatic movement between the four books of the *Wake* he argues that:

> Around a central section, Book II, Joyce builds two opposing cycles consisting of Books I and III. In these two Books there is established a pattern of correspondences of the major events of each, those in Book III occurring in reverse order and having inverse characteristics. Whereas Book I

[25] Lacan, "Joyce le symptôme I," 28.
[26] See Lacan, "Seminaire," *Scilicet* 6.7 (1976): 40.
[27] Cf. Roughley, *James Joyce and Critical Theory*, 279.

begins with a rather obvious birth (28-9) and ends with a symbolic death (215-6), Book III begins with a death (403) and ends with a birth (590); "roads" and the meeting with the King (I.2) reappear in III.4, the trial of I.3-4 in III.3, the Letter of I.5 in III.1, and the fables of I.6 earlier in III.1. In his correspondence Joyce implicitly referred to this pattern.[28]

Such a Viconian "duplex" (*FW* 292.24) is also suggested in the above diagram (located approximately mid-way through book II) as describing a transversal along the co-ordinates A(α), L(λ), P(π), between a Trinitarian eschatology and an "Hystorical" (*FW* 567.31) cyclic re-birth, in the tri-angulated form of the *vesica piscis*: "between shift and shift ere the death he has lived through and the life he is to die into" (*FW* 293.003-05), becoming:

Uteralterance or
the Interplay of
Bones in the
Womb.
[*FW* 293.L1][29]

In *De monade*, Giordano Bruno describes a similar figure of two inter-secting circles, the *Diadis figura*. The plane of intersection, the *monas*, according to Bruno: "contains its opposite" (*Immo bonum atque malum prima est ab origine fusum*).[30] Leibniz, in the conception of monadology, similarly argued that "in the labyrinth of the continuous the smallest element is not the point but the fold," just as in Joyce's diagram the plane of continuity describes itself through a fold, A(α)–L(λ).[31] Amongst other things, this diagram suggests a mechanism operating on the basis of a type of "paradox lust" whose structural topology (schematic or tropic) is not self-identical but a chiasmatic regeneration—an acrostic convergence of "anaglyptics" (419.10), where: "A is for Anna like L is for Liv. Aha hahah, Ante Ann you're apt to ape aunty annalive! Dawn gives rise. Lo, lo, lives love! Eve takes fall. La, la, laugh leaves alass! Aiaiaiai, Antiann, we're last to the lost, Loulou! Tis perfect" (*FW* 293.18-23).

[28] Hart, *Structure and Motif*, 66-7.
[29] Cf. Donald Theall, *James Joyce's Techno-Poetics* (Toronto: Toronto University Press, 1997) 134f.
[30] *Jordani Bruni Nolani Opera Latine Conscripta*, ed. F. Fiorentino (Neapoli, 1879-91); facsimile reprint by F. Fromman (Stuttgart-Bad Cannstatt: Verlag Gunther Holzboog, 1962); op. cit. is *De Monade Numero et Figura, Secretioris Nempe Physicæ, Mathematicæ et Metaphysicæ Elementa*.
[31] Peter Eisenman, "Unfolding Events," *Incorporations*, 425.

VESICA PISCIS

As Roland McHugh, in *The Sigla of Finnegans Wake*, reminds us, the construction of an equilateral triangle is the first proposition in Euclid's *Elements of Geometry* (*"The aliments of jumeantry"* [*FW* 286.L4]). It is also the mystical figure *par excellence*, derived through esoteric Christian symbolism from the *more geometrico* of the neo-Platonist and Pythagorean cults. The equilateral triangle and its inverted double, moreover, combines the geometry of transcendence and the trinity with the generative principle symbolised by the female. As McHugh further remarks: "the sexual interpretation of this figure has a precedent in the associations of the *Vesica Piscis*, or fish's bladder, which is the central ovoid portion, where the circles overlap."[32]

> It is know to both freemasons and architects that the mystical figure called the Vesica Piscis, so popular in the middle ages, and generally placed as the first proposition of Euclid, was a symbol applied by the masons in planning their temples [...] the Vesica was also regarded as a baneful object under the name of the "Evil Eye," and the charm most employed to avert the dread effects of its fascination was the Phallus [...]. In the East the Vesica was used as a symbol of the womb [...]. To every Christian the Vesica is familiar from its constant use in early art, for not only was it an attribute of the Virgin and the feminine aspect of the Saviour as symbolised by the *wound* in his side, but it commonly surrounds the figure of Christ, as his throne when seated in glory.[33]

Elsewhere in the *Wake* the *vesica* is described as a "kind of a thinglike all traylogged then pubably it resymbles a pelvic or some kvind then props an acutebacked quadrangle" (*FW* 608.22-4).

Joyce's diagrammatic combination of Viconian and Platonic idealities ("Plutonic loveliaks twinnt Platonic yearlings—you must, how, in undivided reawlity draw the line somewhere" [292.30-32]) can be seen as describing a broader schematic function. But this primitive, cyclical apparatus can also be seen as being structured as a *symptom*—a schematic of recursive *aphanisis*. In *The Four Fundamental Concepts of Psychoanalysis*, Lacan adopts a similar diagram in the presentation of his theory of alienation.[34] For Lacan, the *vel*, or space bounded by both circles (the *vesica*), describes the condition *between* Being and Meaning, which is that of non-meaning:

---

[32] McHugh, *The Sigla of Finnegans Wake*, 68.
[33] William Sterling, *The Canon* (1897; London: Garnstone Press, 1974) 11-14; cited in McHugh, *The Sigla of Finnegans Wake*, 68.
[34] Jacques Lacan, *The Four Fundamental Concepts of Psychoanalysis*, ed. Jacques-Alain Miller, trans. Alan Sheridon (London: The Hogarth Press, 1977) 211.

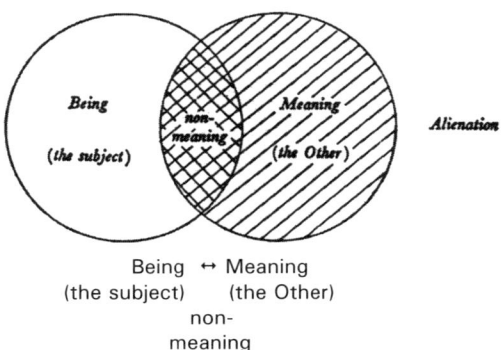

Being ↔ Meaning
(the subject)   (the Other)
non-
meaning

According to Lacan, there is "no subject without, somewhere, *aphanisis* of the subject, and it is in this alienation, in this fundamental division, that the dialectic of the subject is established."[35] Thus the sign of the lack, the "evil eye" (which is, again, the feminine, *castrative* eye of the Freudian Medusa), also becomes the emblem of what *veils* meaning: what elsewhere Lacan calls the *mask* of the Other, the concealment of the gaze, the mirror-illusion of the subject which conceals a "non-meaning." Nevertheless:

> because of the *vel*, the sensitive point of balance, there is an emergence of the subject at the level of meaning [...] from its *aphanisis* in the Other locus, which is that of the unconscious.[36]

Borrowing from Niels Bohr's "complementary sets," Lacan describes the *vel* of alienation as "defined by the choice whose properties depend on this, that there is, in the joining, one element that, whatever the choice operating may be, has as its consequences a *neither one, nor the other*":

> If we choose being, the subject disappears, it eludes us, it falls into non-meaning. If we choose meaning, the meaning survives only deprived of that part of non-meaning that is, strictly speaking, that which constitutes in the realisation of the subject, the unconscious. In other words, it is of the nature of this meaning, as it emerges from the field of the Other, to be in a large part of its field, eclipsed by the disappearance of being, induced by the very function of the signifier.[37]

This state of signification, of *equivocity* ("both and yet neither"), is given a more complex formulation in Lacan's three major seminars on *Finnegans Wake*. In "Joyce le symptôme" I and II, and "Le sinthome, Séminaire du 18 novembre 1975," Lacan suggests that *Finnegans Wake*

[35] Lacan, *The Four Fundamental Concepts of Psychoanalysis*, 221.
[36] Lacan, *The Four Fundamental Concepts of Psychoanalysis*, 221.
[37] Lacan, *The Four Fundamental Concepts of Psychoanalysis*, 211.

can be understood as a type of symptom which it is impossible to analyse. Following from its etymology (Gk. *sumptōma*: occurrence, phenomenon; from *sumpiptein*, to fall together, fall upon, happen), Lacan links the Freudian notion of "symptom" as a condition of the unconscious (of the Oedipal entanglement), to the notion of the unconscious as structured like a language, to the (incestuous) reversion of Joyce's language and ultimately to Joyce himself (as "Shemptôme"), in whom all of these figures intersect as a kind of Borromean knot or "Borumoter" (*FW* 331.27).[38]

BORROMEAN KNOTS
A topological curiosity, the Borromean knot is in fact a set of three rings arranged in a symmetrical pattern, none of which are actually connected but which are intertwined so that they cannot be pulled apart, although with the condition that if any one of them is removed, then all three separate.[39]

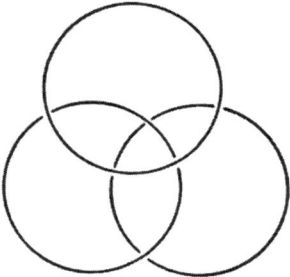

For Lacan, the Borromean knot describes the relationship between *symptom* and a certain *perversion*, which he relates to the Freudian drama of triangulated desire defined in the Oedipus complex. As Lacan argues:

> The Oedipal complex is such a symptom. It is in this sense that the Name-of-the-Father is also the Father of the name.[40]

---

[38] Lacan, "Joyce le symptôme I," 24.
[39] The term "Borromean" comes from the Borromeo family of Renaissance Italy, who used the three interlocking circles on their coat of arms. Cf. *The Mathematical Intelligencer* 17.1 (Winter 1995). There is another interesting historical context in which the image of the rings arises. The diagram was found in picture-stones on Gotland, an island in the Baltic sea off the south-east coast of Sweden. These are dated to some period in the ninth-century and are thought to record tales from the Norse myths. To the Norse people of Scandinavia, a drawing of the Borromean knot using triangles instead of rings is known as "Odin's triangle" or the "Walknot" (or "valknut," the knot of the slain). The symbol was also carved on bedposts used in sea burials.
[40] Lacan, "La Sinthome," *Joyce avec Lacan*, 46.

This chiasmatic turn describes a *perversion* in the relation to the father-scriptor "in as much as *perversion* has the meaning of a translation or transference directed at the Father [*version vers le père*], and that in sum the Father is a symptom, or a sinthome."[41] This relation has to do with the stratification of the individual as *subject* according to the relation of the symbolic, imaginary and real in which the genealogy of the subject describes a topological formulation. What the topological metaphor of the Borromean knot suggests, then, is the *synthetic* nature of the psychoanalytic subject, which, *as subject*, is the unique "solution" to the problem of the incomensurability of what is named by these three terms. Moreover, it is only by virtue of this *synthesis* that the subject can be said to exist *qua* subject. In this way, Lacan argues: "It is not the division of the imaginary, symbolic and real which defines perversion, but rather that they are *already* distinct."[42]

Recalling the Joycean "vicociclometer," Lacan's formulation of the Borromean knot hinges upon the figure described by the *vesica*, or *vel*, although in this case the *vesica* itself is roughly bisected, so that the points at which the three rings initially overlap also describe a triangle, which may tentatively be posed as a figure of the Lacanian symptom (as the "perversion" between *le Nom-du-Père* and *le Père du nom*). As a consequence, it is necessary to posit the Borromean knot in a doubly fourfold manner: as the symptomatic *topos* of the encounter of the imaginary, symbolic and real, and as their *tropological* linkage. It is this tropological counterpart of the symptom that Lacan refers to as *le sinthome*:

> If you find a place [...] which schematises the relationship between the imaginary, symbolic, and the real (as long as they remain separated from one another) you have already—in my preceding drawings, in which this relationship has been clearly set down—the possibility of linking them, but by what? By the *sinthome*. It is necessary for you to see this: it is the re-folding of the capitalised S—that is, of what affirms itself in the consistency of the symbolic.[43]

The *ex-istence* of the symptom is implicated by the position of this "enigmatic link" of the imaginary, symbolic and real, which Lacan describes in the following diagrams:

[41] Lacan, "La Sinthome," 44-5.
[42] Lacan, "La Sinthome," 44.
[43] Lacan, "La Sinthome," 45.

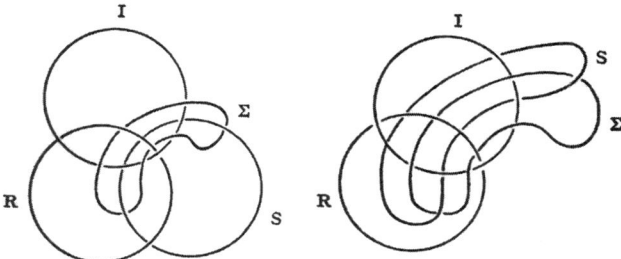

For Lacan, when we attempt to untie the knot of the imaginary (I), the real (R), *le sinthome* (Σ),and the symbolic (S), and thus divide it into four separate parts, the following figure is invariably formed:

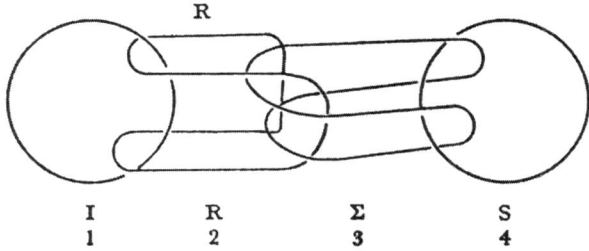

The topological entanglement of these four elements is consequently regarded as describing (by a process of metonymy) the basic condition of Joyce's language in *Finnegans Wake*. In this way, the chiasmatic *perversion* of symptom and *sinthome* also marks a form of transversal, across which each of the relations described above is expressly inter-changeable. Mirroring the subjective determinacy of the "dialectic of identification," the movement from position 1 to position 2 can be re-versed, as 2 to 1, while 3 to 4 can be reversed, as 4 to 3—just as the imaginary identification of the *mirror stage* operates a reversal mecha-nism across the Other-locus in the emergence of the signifier as marking the subject's "entrance" into the symbolic order. In other words, both the symbol and the symptom present themselves in such a fashion that either of the two terms (Σ or S) takes them in their entirety, "so that the other passes over the one which is above and under the one which is below." Following from René Thom's theory of topological folds, Lacan argues that this doubled chiasmus is thus accorded an *immanence* as "the figure we regularly obtain when we attempt to separate the Bor-romean knot into its four parts."[44]

[44] Lacan, "La Sinthome," 46.

In Lacan's view, the "figure" of Joyce is inextricably linked to this topological/tropological antinomy (both as symptom and as sinthome, *synthomme* if not "Saint Homme": "Joyce n'est pas un Saint").[45] Moreover, what Lacan situates as the perversion of Joyce's writing in *A Portrait* and *Ulysses*, with respect to the *Name-of-the-Father* (Dedalus, artificer), serves to aver in the language of *Finnegans Wake* a certain Joyce as *Father of the name*. The translational play between *Joyce* and *Freud* also implies, as a subtext to Lacan's seminar, a further transferential play between the name of *Lacan* and the *lac* against which this "literalising" discourse is projected.

In the chapter of her biography of Lacan entitled 'Mathemes and Borromean Knots,' Elizabeth Roudinesco describes how in his later years Lacan was known to be quite passionately concerned with Borromean knots, and discusses his interest in topological puzzles in collaboration with Pierre Soury, Thom and several other French mathematicians. What she relates bears a peculiar resemblance to certain key aspects of *Finnegans Wake*:

> Soury's teaching, both in private and in public, aimed at constructing a mathematical mould that would facilitate the study of Lacan's logical and topological preoccupations: "What was our point of departure? There was the transition from knot to braid in the special case of the Borromean knot." [...] The solving of the great *casse-tête* took the form of a long correspondence between Lacan and the inhabitants of the planet Borromeo: first with Soury and Thom alone, and then with Christian Léger, who joined them in 1977. There were fifty letters from Lacan, a hundred and fifty from his colleagues: a veritable epic made up of suffering and melancholy, in which everyone involved exhausted themselves in the attempt to solve the riddle of the unconscious by means of telegrams, pneumatiques, and ordinary letters. [...] When they all got together for a discussion, it turned on the possibility of making a knot consisting of four clover leaves, or trefoils, and the transition from the knot to the braid.[46]

In this curious epistolary drama, in which Lacan ties himself in knots attempting to unravel the mysteries of the Borromean puzzle, we can perhaps see a return of the spectre of *Joyce-le-symptôme*: "the Shemptôme and the Shaun," or Shem *the penman* and Shaun ("Joyce Shaunise") *the postman*, inscribing here anew, in the *vel* or *lack* of this "circular" relation, the open mystery of yet another "purloined letter."[47] Joyce's lettristic machine, or synth-tome, described through a metonymic reversion of the name "Joyce," turns back upon its Lacanian symptomatology a figure of "Lacan" as Freudian asymptote. The *joie de livre* in the symptom of the machine.

[45] Lacan, "Joyce le symptôme II," *Joyce avec Lacan*, 33.
[46] Elizabeth Roudinesco, *Jacques Lacan: Esquisse d'une vie, histoire d'un système de pensée* (Paris: Fayard, 1993) 366-67.
[47] Lacan, "Joyce le symptôme I," 24.

DONALD F. THEALL
From the Cyberglobal Chaosmos
to the Gutenberg Galaxy: The Prehistory of
Cyberelectronic Language(s)

In the 1970s a distinguished Québecois author, multimedia artist, broad-caster, and dramatist produced a short book on the cover of which was an illustration of a figure dressed in the jersey of a Montréal Canadien hockey star, the head of which was a famous bust of Pythagoras. The author, Jacques Languirand, entitled his little book *De McLuhan à Py-thagore* — (i.e, From McLuhan to Pythagoras). I begin at this point, for two reasons — both of which will play roles in my remarks: first, Langui-rand had designed one of the multi-media productions within the Man and Community theme pavilions at Expo '67 (Montreal) which has been dubbed "McLuhan's Fair"; second and more significantly he was one of the few Québecois cultural figures of the moment who commented in a playful, offbeat book that emphasized McLuhan's leading us back through the complex traditions of the past in order to understand "the tradition of the new." Probably Jacques did so, because existing in the relatively small cultural complex of Montreal oriented to the past of France and Romance Europe as well as to the future of the United States and North America, he was acutely aware of the coming together of the distant past, the immediate past and the future-oriented transformations of the present at the moment when McLuhan emerged.

My title plays against the same motifs which interested Languirand in McLuhan's work, for it points to the historical connections of the under-standing of modern media with the long march from the birth of civilization in the Near East, Egypt and Greece to the period of McLu-han's *Gutenberg Galaxy* (from the Renaissance until the twentieth century), a work which contemporizes the medley of science, art and the occult in the world of Pythagorean virtuality. By 1950 with the in-ception of electric media the Galaxy signals a present in which the cybernetic global theatre could be partly anticipated. It also weaves together the ways that the arts, philosophy, theology, occult traditions as proto-science and poetry contributed to understandings that were crucial to the early development of humanistically oriented studies of human communication. Two historic intellectual cultures were central as the historical work of Friedrich Kittler and James Peters confirm: first, liberal scholarship with its emphases on the arts, drama, literature, poetry and the historical and archeological study of the past; second, the near immediate history of the arts and literature from the inception of electric media in the nineteenth century to major radical and avant-garde movements of the twentieth. I will examine the second of these clusters, the avant-garde, within the context of the first, the classical and ancient as its ground.

While both of these clusters are intrinsic to those fundamental, yet implicit intuitions of McLuhan, which subsequently became a foundation of media ecology as he understood it, that which relates to the immediate past history is crucial. He never fully articulated his fleeting intuitive sense that the long term drift of electric media, from their inception in the mid-nineteenth century on through to the conclusion of the twentieth century, would be to create a totally new integrated language (oral, visual, verbal, tactile, gestural, digital) which might become more primary than speech and certainly would become more primary than print, since he never felt he could confront all its implications and he also knew that his major audiences in business and conservative academia (as distinct from the avant-garde arts and cultural production) would not understand, even if he provided a comprehensive interpretation and critique. Consequently such paradoxes as his appearing to be concerned about the death of the book, while also appearing to speak of new roles for the printed book, realizing that there would come to be new automated intermedia productions which would constitute a new kind of book. Nevertheless his intuition was possible because he and many others intuited that the thrust of the past century and a half related to connections between electricity, telegraphy and telepathy pointed towards such integration of modes of statement, as had been hinted at late in the nineteenth century by artists such as Wagner in his conception of the "total work of art," which has been seen in retrospect as a kind of proto-virtual reality.

The rise of the so-called avant-garde, directly connected to these theoretical, mathematical, scientific and technological phenomena, is really a coming to terms with the evolutionary (and therefore also devolutionary) aspects of the growth of cities, the taking command of mechanization, the impact of electricity and photography and the "shrinking" of the globe. To understand turbulent transformation it was necessary for those creative minds living through the experience to revisit and re-examine the modes of statement and communication. Walter Benjamin, reviewing the development of the history of modernism from Baudelaire through Dadaism and Surrealism and the emergence of "technological modes of reproducibility," dramatized their intense interest in extending the sense of what language meant, while simultaneously associating it with the esoteric traditions of the occult, particularly the Kaballah. His ability to bridge the work of Baudelaire, of Brecht, of

Kafka, of the surrealists and of new modes of technological production, reproducibility and dissemination arose from his awareness that there existed a spectrum of languages rather than any relatively limited sense of what constituted language.

While Benjamin respected the "language of man" with its propensity towards naming, he still asserted the importance of the language of things which could reach its realization through painting, sculpture, architecture, design or the new modes of production:

> There is a language of sculpture, of painting, of poetry. Just as the language of poetry is partly, if not solely, founded on the name language of man, it is very conceivable that the language of sculpture or painting is founded on certain kinds of thing language, that in them we find a translation of the language of things into an infinitely higher language, which may still be of the same sphere. We are concerned here with nameless, nonacoustic languages, languages issuing from matter; here we should recall the material community of things in their communication. Moreover, the communication of things is certainly communal in a way that grasps the world as such an unidentified whole.[1]

In this essay "On Language as Such and On the Language of Man," Benjamin notes the future importance of the convergence of languages— the blending of modes of discourse—and points out that the artists of the later nineteenth century and of the early twentieth century are the early stages of a dramatic interface with this—an anticipation of the emergence of cyberspace.

This theme of the blending of modes of discourse runs throughout the history of Dadaism and Surrealism and their aftermath, and represents a major unanticipated contribution which Marcel Duchamp and his associates made to the evolution of digital art—a contribution noted early in his career by McLuhan, who entitled his first book, *The Mechanical Bride* after Duchamp's *Large Glass*, or the *Bride Stripped Bare by Her Bachelors, Even*. Duchamp and other avant-garde figures became part of the pantheon of McLuhanesque media ecology, partly because they provided him with such techniques as the collage, the visual punning on cultural icons, the use of headlines and telegraphic comic aphorisms and many of his basic strategies in *The Bride*, and works like *The Medium is the Massage, Counterblast, Culture is Our Business* and *Take Today*. But even more because they were offering comic poetic insights in a variety of modes into the directions in which techo-culture was developing. It is probably through these avant-garde artists and poets that McLuhan was able to first intuit a real role for his classical education in understanding the drift of contemporary culture towards a transformation of the book.

---

[1] Walter Benjamin, *Reflections: Essays, Aphorisms, Autobiographical Writings*, ed. Peter Demetz (New York: Harcourt, 1978) 330.

To digress for a moment, many media ecologists, such as Walter Ong or McLuhan (even Eric Havelock) have obtained initial insights from the work of poets, and artists which fascinated them. Ong's sensitivity to orality and its complex conflicts with literacy were certainly enhanced by his fascination with Gerard Manley Hopkins, just as Shakespeare's *King Lear* and Pope's *Dunciad* provided McLuhan with insights. From *Lear*, as he points out, a sense of "the anguish of the third dimension" as well as "the shift from people being translated from their having roles to having jobs"; from Pope he gleaned how "the mass distributed, printed book [was] leading to a primitivistic and Romantic revival" and how the new emerging collective unconscious was a backwash of private self-statement. From such sources also came insights about the interplay of the visual and the auditory in altering the ratio of the senses.

But the most relevant poetic insights in understanding the processes of change of the actual moment are those of contemporary or near contemporary artists, since their impact extended beyond Ong and McLuhan to other critics and historians of media. The Dadaists and other avant-gardists, including Mallarmé mentioned earlier, became involved with the fluidity of language as manifested in its polsemy. A little known figure in this history of the pun, Jean-Pierre Brisset, who until recent years was a barely remembered figure of French intellectual life, was adopted by Jarry, Duchamp, Apollinaire and others.

Duchamp included Brisset in his "ideal library" with authors such as Mallarmé. As Hans Richter, one of the early Dadaists, points out, Brisset "attributed to language a sort of divine consciousness... From the sound of speech and from affinities of sound he deduced a deeper divine meaning and on it based his 'Great Law, Key to Words.'" In Brisset's vision and its echoes in Apollinaire, Breton, Duchamp and other Dadaists and Surrealists resides one aspect of the roots of Joyce's *Finnegans Wake*, which became not only a text-book for McLuhan, but for writers on hypertext and VR such as J. David Bolter, Michael Joyce and Darren Tofts as well as my essays on hypermedia especially "Beyond the Orality/Literacy Dichotomy: James Joyce and the Pre-history of Cyberspace." The entire movement of the avant-garde during this period is directed towards the creation of "new languages" which could be various blends of multiplicity of different modes—gestures, sounds, images, words and their movement.

This is certainly part of what was implicit in the *symboliste* and *avant-garde* interest in Rimbaud's "alchemy of the word"—an alchemy which about five decades later has been partly co-opted by the post World War II advertising industry. This motif of "alchemy" is specifically linked by Antonin Artaud to his conceptions about the theatre, for in 1938 he links the theatre to multi-modal language and the creation of virtual realities. "The theater, which is in no thing, [Artaud says], but makes use of everything—gestures, sounds, words, screams, light, darkness rediscovers itself at precisely the point where the mind requires a language to express its manifestations."[2] Later he points out that the theatre is "a mirage" just as the alchemical symbol is and he continues noting the perpetual allusion to the materials and principle of the theater found in alchemical books, concluding that this express2s an identity between "the purely fictitious and illusory world in which the symbols of alchemy are evolved" and "the world in which the characters, objects, images, and in a general way all that constitutes the virtual reality of the theater develops."[3] With the coming of age of VR in the digital world during the closing decades of the second millennium, it is intriguing to note such an anticipation of the affiliation of the "theater" as an inclusive form—a convergence of modes of communication and statement. Furthermore, Artaud concludes his essay by putting the "essential drama" at the "root of all Great Mysteries."[4]

Artaud's corroborating the twentieth century thrust towards the goal of an all encompassing language integrating a wide spectrum of modes of statement, also stresses the poetic as intrinsic to the complexities of cognition and neurology that constitute the realities of mind and the external world. In the first half of the twentieth century avant-garde movements in all of the arts were moving in the same direction—a direction which not too surprisingly anticipated the evolution of a digital world and of cognitive science that would re-establish some new links between the arts, science and technology: Artaud's 'Theatre of Alchemy"; Duchamp's envisioning the "alchemy" of Rutherford's theories on radiation and later the splitting of the atom; and Joyce's making Shem the poet in and of *Finnegans Wake*, an "alshemist," whose dream vision plays with complex paranomasia and with scientific and mathematical theories from Helmholtz, Rutherford and Poincaré to Heisenberg, Planck and Gödel.

The simultaneous inter-relationship of all these writers with such motifs as linguistic ambivalence, engineering, science, the occult (such as alchemy) and the intuitive modes of daydream and vis on are in many ways rooted in the histories of science itself and its connections with the histories of memory, statement and the occult. If Duchamp regarded his activity as a mode of engineering, as many other avant-garde artists did, Joyce spoke of himself as "the greatest engineer"—something he found easy to put into juxtaposition with being a musicmaker and a philosopher. Joyce, like Duchamp, regarded himself as enmeshed in the alchemy of the word, which leads to the splitting of the atom and the "etym." Linking language through etymology with atomic science, Joyce predicts the explosions and detonations of the coming world war, simultaneously noting the transformation of language itself in this new world of Rutherford's alchemy.

---

[2] Antonin Artaud, *The Theater and its Double*, trans. Mary Caroline Richards (New York: Grove Press, 1958) 12. Originally published in France in 1938.
[3] Artaud, *The Theater and its Double*, 49.
[4] Artaud, *The Theater and its Double*, 51.

This linguistic alchemy—a language-oriented modality of chaos—simultaneously lays the groundwork for the ongoing transformations of media, since it underlines the fluidity of modes of communication, linking them with transitions in science and technology. It leads to Joyce's speaking in the *Wake* of "chaomos"—the world as cosmos transformed in a multi-dimensional earth—which became a key word in later discussions in Eco, Deleuze, Guattari, Baudrillard and many others since complexity and chaos emerged as ruling theoretical principles—a phenomenon reflected throughout popular culture. Simultaneously it lays the groundwork for a growing acceptance of the quest for hypermedia, since it presents the probes which provide the linguistic fluidity and the synaesthetic consciousness that are requisite to understand the accelerating convergence of modes of statement that had earlier been intuited by film makers, photographers, typographers and many others. All of this is grounded within the satiric exposure of the ecological problems of media that permeated the work of avant-gardistes, especially Marcel Duchamp, Wyndham Lewis and James Joyce.

I am primarily using the insight gained from such associations as an exemplum of how all the arts—the traditional fine arts; what were then in the 1930s called by Gilbert Seldes the newer "lively arts"; and subsequent pop arts and media—were with varying degrees of consciousness developing a vision of newly transformed *paraoral* and *paraverbal* languages. (I am coining these terms to indicate that the new, potentially primary language would exist beyond, beside and above existing oral languages.)

A key document in this pre-history is Laszlo Moholy-Nagy's *Vision in Motion*. Along with Wyndham Lewis he was a strong influence on the early McLuhan. Moholy-Nagy, invited to the U.S. to become director of the New Bauhaus, ultimately became director of the Chicago Institute of Art. Within his own creative work he had explored a variety of approaches and media: photograms, painting, sculpture, design, industrial design, experimental film and writing. He also articulated the importance of the growing inter-relation of art, technology and science in developing contemporary solutions to living in a global society.

Moholy-Nagy's basis for this project is his assertion that the primary discovery contemporary artists and poets had made is the significance of "vision in motion." In his writings he demonstrated repeatedly that painting, sculpture, architecture, music, film and contemporary poetry and creative writing along with many other artistic developments were all becoming more conscious of the ancient awareness of the arts as aspiring to reproduce "vision in motion." He also stressed that "vision in motion" had a particular relationship with the new space-time world in which everyone in the twentieth century had become immersed, and consequently with the increasing importance of electricity and electronics, all of which he specifically mentions. In this respect, Moholy-Nagy is building on the work of the Dadaists and the Cubists, but particularly

Duchamp, whose *Large Glass* was so intrinsically involved with electricity, with new technologies, with the new space-time continuum and the fourth dimension. *Vision in Motion* is, therefore, an exploration of the possibilities of an assemblage of new languages, which partly reflect his own lifelong practice as an artist, designer and teacher.

Moholy-Nagy in many ways is the pioneering founder of what led through his successors, particularly his student Gyorgy Kepes, to the MIT visual arts program and then to the MIT media lab with its exploration of cyberspace and the World Wide Web. He stressed the importance of linking Joyce's work to the new directions of vision in motion as well as indicating the intimate association of advertising, comics and industrial art with the avant-garde critique of media. As McLuhan realized through his study of and association with Wyndham Lewis, the early avant-garde were involved in an ecologically oriented satiric critique of the rise of new electric modes of communication. Such a critique is not intended to be purely negative, since there is always within it a positive element of what might come to be along with a powerful comic critique. It is from this critique by the early avant-garde as well as from the perceptions of modernist poets and artists that there arose the intellectual satire of media ecology which vitiated the work of McLuhan, and then moved in differing ways into that of such successors Ong, Kroker, Baudrillard, Neil Postman, Bob Dobbs and John Cage.

Beyond McLuhan and in his *Wake* there came the pragmatic practices and critical discussions of the exploration of hypertextuatlity and cyberspace. These practices and discussions are beginning to provide a new ecological perspective to what Ong called "secondary orality" and what McLuhan, and later Baudrillard, could see as the next transformation of the idea of the libris, which has moved through history from stone and papyrus to manuscripts, printed words, illustrated words and the like. As Baudrillard pointed out, tactility (and the ratio of all the senses) was always more crucial in the Mcluhanesque understanding of media than specific biases toward the acoustic sphere or the visual range. Implicit in that transformation was an acceptance of the "chaosmic" nature of our complex cosmos, which is the context in which the new cyber-electronic language(s) is taking form. Understanding the cyberglobal chaosmos takes us back to the *Gutenberg Galaxy* (just as McLuhan's work naturally led back to Pythagoras). This enables us to appreciate the complexities involved in exploring the transformations of the modes of statement and their dissemination, while also demonstrating that we have always already been moving towards our parahuman—not posthuman—vision of virtuality.

The reason it is important to appreciate the roots of this in the avant-garde movements and the roots of such artistic movements in the poetics and rhetoric of the ancient world is both to return to them for a deeper understanding of the problems of media ecology (or in a play on McLuhan's ratio of the senses—an ecology of sense) and to appreciate the need to attend to and study the mature contemporary artists and poets (particularly playing with the new hypermedia) as a guide to understanding the ecological implications of the future of the twenty-first century. The examples of anticipation and illumination are legion, arising in visions such as Jorge Luis Borges's parabolic stories on "The Library of Babel" and "The Garden of the Forking Paths" or in the cultural productions of Rauschenberg, Cunningham and Cage—but that is a tale for another time and place. What we have looked at here is the importance of realizing that there is a musical, choregraphic, visual art and poetic presence side by side with the techno-scientific in the emergence of our new cyber-electronic languages (our contemporary thrust for the para-oral and para-verbal) and that the history and current immediacy of that presence is an important aid to media ecologists.

DARREN TOFTS
"Where are we at all? & whenabouts in the name of space?"*

I

When Dante entered the abject world of hell, it was Virgil, a classical poet who accompanied him and explained its mysteries. In a similar retro gesture, it is James Joyce, as opposed to William Gibson or R.U. Sirius, whom I adopt as my guide to cyberspace. Part of Virgil's appeal for Dante was ancestral, for he had previously taken a journey into the underworld in *The Aeneid.* As we continue to forge a brave new electronic frontier that goes by the name of cyberspace, Joyce seems a most appropriate guide. He too has been there before, and *Finnegans Wake* is my *Aeneid,* since it embodies the convergence of paperspace and cyberspace.

Marshall McLuhan was one of the first to recognize Joyce's importance in the age of media, describing him as a clairvoyant.[1] The radio, telephone and cinema feature prominently in *Finnegans Wake,* as does the emergent apparatus of television ("the bairdboard bombardment screen," [*FW* 349.8]). On the basis of the way television is represented in the *Wake,* predominantly in Book two, chapter three, Joyce's interest in its historical formation as a mode of communication is bound up with his familiarity with contemporary understandings on the nature of time and space. We should, of course, expect nothing less. One of the first discussions of television occurs in the context of references to Einsteinian physics (*FW* 149) and Planck's quantum mechanics (*FW* 149-50). Joyce was quick to recognize that television warps perceptions of space (his "faroscope" [*FW* 150] is not so far removed from our "telepresence"). He was even quicker to recognize that new technologies also warp language, and provide the opportunity for invention. To someone who felt that he could do anything with words, the emergent invention of television must have excited Joyce's verbal membranes, an excitement detected in formations such as "teleframe" (*FW* 349.9) and

---

* Author's note: This paper was originally published in the inaugural issue of *Hypermedia Joyce Studies.* It should be noted that the ethos from which it was written seems very dated now: such is the speed of techno-change. In other words, it should be noted that it is very much of its time.

[1] Marshall McLuhan, *The Gutenberg Galaxy* (Toronto: University of Toronto Press, 1968) 74.

"teilweisioned" (*FW* 345.35). His conceits seem to also indicate a fascination with the luminous nature of the new "medium" (new in the sense that through language and imagination he was contributing to its invention). The charge of light down this "nightlife instrument" (*FW* 150.32) stimulated ideas of representability, producing very early in the piece some of the grammar of the medium (the "fade" [*FW* 349.6], the "double focus" [*FW* 349.13]). Contemporary screen theorists don't seem, though, to have mastered Joyce's language. The term "verbivocovisual" (*FW* 341.18) doesn't have any currency in contemporary discourse. This is a great pity, for no other term in use suggests as efficiently the interdiscursive nature of television as a medium.

The television program also makes its first appearance in the *Wake*, well before it was a cultural fact. In typically Joycean presentiment, the two staple television genres, domestic drama and comedy, are broadcast in the *Wake* with an air of routine network programming: and tonight on BBC1, the "Taff and Butt Show" and "The Charge of the Light Brigade." The episode in Earwicker's bar in Book two has all the trademarks of late night channel surfing (the pun in this context has not been lost on me) between "swapstick quackchancers" (*FW* 342.31) and "the scanning firespot of the sgunners" (*FW* 349.15), complete with commercials "from our sponsor" ("The Irish Race and World" [*FW* 341.21]), and, of course, a favourite "compeer" ("Tancred Artaxerxes Flavin" and "Barnabas Ulick Dunne" [*FW* 337.35]). Dream logic proved for Joyce to be a useful, and indeed accurate model for imagining the shifting, collage-like qualities of television; a feature of the medium that has been increasingly discussed in recent years by communications theorists and the like.

Apart from the uncanny sense of commonplaceness about the television show, there is also in this chapter an undeniable wonder generated by the novelty of moving pictures. Earwicker's customers bawl for the show to begin ("We want Bud. We want Bud Budderly. We want Bud Budderly boddily" [*FW* 337.31]). Joyce seemed to be in no doubt that television would become the dominant form of popular culture in this century. The social context of the medium as spectacle, which creates its own audience and sustains the desire for continuous theatricality, is indicated in the setting of this chapter in a "public plouse" (*FW* 338.4). Joyce's timing here is superb in the way that television program and pub rattle and hum blend into a soundscape in which there is no identifiable foreground and background. As a cultural apparatus, the television is very much *mise en scène*.

The *Wake* has also proven to be something of an index of telecommunicative change, anticipating the cultural impact of the succession of different media forms ("Television kills telephony... Our eyes demand their turn" [*FW* 52.18]), as well as the advent of hypermedia, such as virtual reality ("a dreariodreama setting, glowing and very vidual") and hypertext ("The proteiform graph itself is a polyhedron of scripture" [*FW*

107.8]). In their predictable search for ancestry, commentators from William Gibson to Michael Heim frequently describe *Finnegans Wake* as an exemplar of hypertext. Ted Nelson, too, has drawn attention to the literary characteristics of the medium; indeed, his most famous axiom, "everything is deeply intertwingled," is distinctly *Wake*an. Joyce's exploitation of equivocation is well recognised as a method of dreamwork. But it is less well known as a form of electronic thought, of hyperlogic. Joyce extended verbal freeplay to such a degree that his language space becomes a manifestation of the marvelous, the phantasmagoric, where diversity and convergence know no bounds. The inclusiveness made possible by the *Wake* in this respect makes Lautréamort's chance encounter of a sewing machine and an umbrella on an operating table seem positively banal. We can learn also learn a lot about the concept of extension from the *Wake*, for its systematic patterns of self-reference create the dense, web-like organization of information ("messes of mottage" [*FW* 183.22-3]) that we associate with the term "network." All this was not lost on Jacques Derrida who, in the burgeoring days of the personal computer, recognised such parallels, describing the *Wake* as a "hypermnesiac machine" that links information about different cultures, religions, philosophies and mythologies at incalculable speed.[2] As a dream of human history, it is a collective unconscious. where all language, all identity fuses into the public domain of universal memory. Nelson's dream of Xanadu still awaits fruition (it is, as the *Wake* was called before publication, a *Work in Progress*). Joyce has already created Babel.

The parallels between Joyce's "nightmaze" (*FW* 411.8) and the Internet are, of course, irresistible. The common response of newcomers to both is of unmanageable excess; in their own ways they are both unreadable. The lack of co-ordinates entails untintelligibility in Joyce, disorientation on the Net (they are "too dimensional" [*FW* 154.26]). The defining metaphors of both suggest liquidity, formlessness; Joyce's "riverrun" is cyclical, without beginning or end, and the Net is a bit-stream, a data-sphere. It's worth remembering that cyber is Greek for navigate; a fitting prefix for an environment that, by its very nature, lacks pre-determined grids. The type of involved textual analysis that has persistently been applied to the *Wake*, exegesis (from the Greek, *egeo-mai*, to lead) is also aptly named. In both cases the need for guidance contributed to the rapid formation of communal identity. On-line help, bulletin boards, chat groups and the overall ambience of a shareware culture are the Net's equivalent to the reading groups and collective study seminars that enabled a generation of Joyceans to negotiate the matrix of *Finnegans Wake.*

[2] Jacques Derrida, "Two Words for Joyce," *Post-Structuralist Joyce: Essays from the French*, ed. Derek Attridge and Daniel Ferrer (Cambridge: Cambridge University Press, 1984) 148.

Cyberspace, in Michael Benedikt's words, is "a territory swarming with data and lies, with mind stuff and memories of nature, with a million voices and two million eyes in a silent, invisible concert of enquiry, dealmaking, dream sharing, and simple beholding."[3] Joyce's "babbelers" (*FW* 15.12) are no less garrulous than today's virtual community, and just as various. The *Wake*'s central character, H. C. Earwicker, is impossible to "idendifine" (*FW* 51.6), and the abundant permutations of his name (Here Comes Everybody, Haroun Childeric Eggeberth, Heinz Cans Everywhere) parallel the diverse interest groups populating today's Huge Cyber Ecology, as well as the role-playing and shifting subjectivities that takes place in IRCs and MOOs.

Both cyberspace and the *Wake* are parallel realities, consensual hallucinations that allow for infinite variety and difference. But a crucial question, equally applicable to both, is asked in the *Wake* of itself: "Where are we at all? and whenabouts in the name of space?" (*FW* 558.33). Joyce, as we know, was besotted with the written word. The *Wake*, a space literally made of words, is an "allaphbed" (*FW* 18.18), a verbal terrain where the same letters are combined and recombined in ways that hypertext culture struggles to compete with (perhaps there's something of a Joycean reference in the initials HTML). *Finnegans Wake* is as much concerned with *Finnegans Wake* as with anything else in its orbit. Whoever it is that speaks to us in the name of the narrator is hyper-conscious of the formidable challenge of entering this language space, especially when armed with literary assumptions formed by *critique vraisemblable;* assumptions that involve passing beyond writing to a represented world: "[Stoop] if you are abcedminded, to this claybook, what curios of signs [please stoop], in this allaphbed! Can you rede [since We and Thou had it out already] its world?" (*FW* 18.17-9). You've got to hand it to the guy. It wasn't just any group of professors he sought to keep busy. Anyone who would play around with the word "Peirce" clearly had a certain audience in mind.

Book one, chapter five is Joyce's most sustained exposition of the grammatological nature of the *Wake*'s "spatiality" (*FW* 172.9). In a fit of diacritical pique, writing in this chapter almost collapses to its barest scriptural essentials. Morphology, signification, clear the decks of this claybook. Like that postcard (so beloved of Derrida) of Socrates writing and erasing at the same time, Joyce reminds us here that literature (understood as an imaginary world created by writing) begins its life as so many marks, or "paper wounds" (*FW* 124.3):

These paper wounds, four in type, were gradually and correctly understood to mean stop, please stop, do please stop, and O do please stop respectively, and following up their one true clue, the circumflexous wall of a singleminded men's asylum, accentuated by bi tso fb rok engl a ssan dspl itch ina,—Yard inquiries pointed out→that they ad bîn "provoked" ay

[3] Michael Benedikt, ed., *Cyberspace: First Steps* (Boston: MIT Press, 1993) 2.

Λ fork, of à grave Brofèsor; àth é's Brèak—fast—table; ;acùtely
profèššionally *piquéd*, to = introdùce a notion of time [ùpon à plane (?) sù '
' fàçe'e'] by pùnct! ingh oles (sic) in iSpace?! [*FW* 124.3-12]

Remarkably (thanks to plenty of Heavy Critical Exegesis), out of the "riot
of blots and blurs" (*FW* 118) that is the punctured space of the *Wake*,
we manage to form something beyond the page; it's "the same told of
all... They lived und laughed ant loved end left" (*FW* 18), "... as human a
little story as paper could well carry" (*FW* 115). Some kind of imaginary
space comes into being when the *scriptible* insomniac reader begins
"again to make soundsense and sensesound kin again" (*FW* 121.15-6).
I've always been struck by the astonishing sleight of hand in this chapter, which deconstructs the very language of the *Wake* itself, through
the very language of the *Wake* itself. Here, as in many passages
throughout the text, Joyce anticipates the Janus-faced textuality so
characteristic of postmodern fiction (think of Borges and Calvino). If you
want to create a world, an imaginary space, dear Reader, you had better
like words, and be prepared to play with a them "a full trillion times for
ever and a night" (*FW* 120.12-3).

Imaginary space, in Joyce's verbal universe, comes into being
through the reader's negotiation of textuality, which is in itself the acti-
vation of certain learned habits about the nature of language as
representation. But where are we, exactly, in cyberspace? The cyberpunk vision of being jacked into the machine imagines an alternative
sensory condition beyond language altogether, a downloading of the
mind into the matrix of pure information. While virtual reality environments offer convincing experiences of immersion in artificial worlds,
other media such as the Internet are inevitably rehearsing familiar terrain.
The predominantly text-based character of Internet clearly means that if
we are somewhere else, we are there notionally (to use William Gibson's
term). The people we communicate with, perhaps fall in love with, swap
ideas with, or simply chat with, are imagined in much the same way that
we have traditionally come to know fictional characters, or the person
whose letter we are reading. Writing entails a virtual reality through acts
of faith and consent, the conceptual location of its participants in an
"elsewhere," be it novel, office memo or MUD. Cyberspace, itself, is
something many Netcruisers would have initially "entered" in just this
manner, through reading cyberpunk novels such as *Neuromancer*. The
Wake clearly occupies "paperspace" (*FW* 115.7), but t doesn't behave
according to the predictable logic of typography and its associated reading practices. Its hyperlogic necessitates the use of an augmented form
of artificial memory only conceivable in the computer age (which was
not that far away, for in 1939 Vannevar Bush postulated the idea of the
Memex, or memory extender, the theoretical system recognized as the
foundation of hypertext). The best Joyce could hope for in 1939 was
"an ideal reader suffering from an ideal insomnia" (*FW* 120.13-4).

The place of the *Wake* within the lineage of hypermedia clearly evidences the ongoing evolution of writing as a technology, which needs to continually extend itself to accommodate cultural change: Thoth begat Joyce begat Xanadu. McLuhan asks the question at the end of *The Gutenberg Galaxy:* "What will be the new configurations of mechanisms and of literacy as... older forms of perception and judgement are interpenetrated by the new electric age?"[4] With Joyce the writing was on the wall, "telesphorously" speaking (*FW* 154.7). He was, as the vanguard saying goes, ahead of his time in making the jump from paperspace to cyberspace. However it is a mistake to think that with the *Wake* he simply wrote a book that *looks like* hypertext. In fact he didn't write a book at all. He provided a complex system of prompting, the primary node in an interface to be activated by the reader. Interface design is in the process of reflecting this generative principle, for as Brenda Laurel has noted, computer scientists have only just begun to incorporate into software development an awareness of the collaborative nature of the human/computer relationship.[5] Before software there was "joyceware."[6]

The *Wake* embodies the fundamental desire implicit in the history of writing: the artificial extension of memory, and the displacement of the self through technology. Hypertext and the Internet respectively have become Western culture's most advanced response to this grammatological desire. In this new media formations are not merely catching up with Joyce. They are, as Derrida has noted, "*in memory of him.*"[7]

II

> In the heliotropical noughttime following a fade of transformed Tuff and, pending its viseversion, a metenergic reglow of beaming Batt, the bairdboard bombardment screen, if tastefully taut guranium satin, tends to teleframe and step up to the charge of a light barricade. **Down the photoslope in syncopanc pulses**, with the bitts bugtwug their teffs, the missledhropes, glitteraglatteraglutt, borne by their carnier walve. [*FW* 349.6-12; JJ's italics; my emphasis]

Joyce created a language of "syncopanc pulses" (*FW* 349.10-1), of "doublin existents" (*FW* 578.14), of synchronicity. Always on the move, always displacing, splicing into something else in the same word, and at the same time elsewhere in the matrix of the dream of Finnegan. The whole of history, the babble of all languages compressed into a "hypermnesiac machine."[8] "In the buginning is the woid" (*FW* 378.29).

4 McLuhan, *The Gutenberg Galaxy*, 278.
5 Brenda Laurel, *Computers As Theatre* (London: Addison-Wesley, 1993).
6 Derrida, "Two Words for Joyce," 147
7 Derrida, "Two Words for Joyce," 147
8 Derrida, "Two Words for Joyce," 146

Joyce's words come at you with the force of association, the riotous logic of the unconscious, the "law of the jungerl" (*FW* 268.F3). An inexhaustible language, a language, after Duchamp, definitively unfinished.

The fourth dimension was more than a poetics; it was a prototype of electronic thought. How else do we account for *The Large Glass*; it is not an object; it's a node in a network of ideas of "indefin te" possibility. Consult *The Green Box*. Start a chain reaction. Duchamp's "catalogue of ideas" never takes form; it keeps you guessing, invites you to think about it from any possible angle. You can't do it all in one moment of viewing. Dip in today, dip in tomorrow— anything may happen.[9]

In exploiting randomness Cage went beyond the concept of the line. The line imposes limits, it enforces an obliged movement in one direction. Indeterminacy is the promise of extension, of going beyond the predictable next step. Use a star chart to create a score, imperfections on a sheet of paper, throw dice. Overlap, collision, resonance. "Our ears are now in excellent condition."[10] What you thought you were listening to turns into something else. You need to be "omni-attentive" when "everything happens at once." Don't close the window. Leave it open. All sounds are welcome here. With indeterminacy you no longer take steps. You meander, like a river.

"riverrun"—where does it run? "from swerve of shore to of Bay, brings us by a commodius vicus of recirculation back to Howth Castle and Environs" (*FW* 3.3). Go with the flow. The energet c charge of the incipit, of first words. "Once upon a time...," "riverrun..." With first words you haven't gone anywhere, but can still go anywhere. Stories don't have to be the same every time you read them. Don't be fooled. The river isn't the same in any two spots. Make your own rivulet. Don't finish a train of thought. Jump trains. We've gone beyond finished books. It's not the time to finish anything.[11]

Duchamp never finished anything. He created "delays." You never completely look at *The Glass*. In fact you don't even look at it, since you are already in it. How do you know your not in it when your not looking at it? Fragments from *The Green Box* can spark a myriad of associations, and these change over time through the very fact of their ambiguity. You never come back to the *same Glass*. You return in "indecisive reunion." You continue to think about *The Large Glass* over time. Who knows when you will think about it. But you think about it nonetheless. It exists not as an object but as a series of anachronous moments. *The Large Glass* is concerned with ideas in time. The fourth dimension is unpredictability in action. Bring things together. See what happens.

The prepared piano creates unexpected sounds that the instrument was not designed to make. What do *you* hear when you listen to four minutes and thirty-three seconds of silence? Like Duchamp's fragments,

[9]   John Cage, *Silence: Lectures and Writings* (London: Marion Boyars, 1937) 59.
[10] Cage, *Silence*, xii.
[11] Pontus Hulten, ed. *Marcel Duchamp* (London: Thames & Hudson, 1993) npag.

sounds are as "free as air," liberated for "an infinite play of interpreta-tion."[12] Cage envisaged that no two experiences of any of his works would be the same. Active listening is not removed from the environment. The active listener is already in the environment, is already "inter." In between, amongst other things. Inter: prefix used in English as a formative element. *Inter*active, *inter*action, *inter*activity. In Joyce there is no beginning, no middle, no end, there is only the state of being inter. "A way a lone a last a loved a long the riverrun." In the midst of things. Look at *The Large Glass* "from all associative angles"[13]: you are always in it. *Inter alia*.

III

Once upon a time there was a lifeform called typographic man. He told stories, stories that had a beginning, middle and end. His kind listened to these stories, but had no part to play in their performance. He evolved into meanderthal man, the nomad, the wanderer. He lives in the waterless ocean of information society. He no longer tells stories that have begin-nings, middles and ends, for he works with a different form of narrative— the theorists call it indirect freestyle. His narrative is interactive. He in-volves others in the development of interfaces, networks. Instead of sitting and listening to a pre-determined sequence of events, meanderthal man creates his own terrain, establishes his own connections. Meander-thal man comes into being with the birth of the personal computer, which provides him with a powerful new form of reasoning, a hyperlogic.

This is an interesting story, isn't it? My interest in it is twofold. First, like most historical narratives it is very linear; passive typography yields to dynamic electronic text and with a point and a click we've revolutionized all previous concepts of narrative, writing and reading. Secondly, what, or more specifically when is an interface? This story assumes that it only exists in the cybernetic domain, when someone sits in front of a pc and clicks a mouse. An interface, on the contrary, is any act of conjunction which results in a new or unexpected event. A door-handle is an inter-face. So too is the "chance encounter, on an operating table, of a sewing machine and an umbrella." Joyce didn't write books. Duchamp didn't create works of art. Cage didn't compose music. They created interfaces, instances into which someone intervened to make choices and judgements that they were not willing to make. All three actively promoted chance discovery over any notion of authorial pre-determination; Duchamp's celebrated indifference is their signature. To be indifferent is to encourage indiscrimination; come into this work and feel free to go anywhere you like, do anything you like, and whenever

[12]   Hulten, *Marcel Duchamp*, npag.
[13]   Hulten, *Marcel Duchamp*, npag.

you like. You are empowered, you are in control; cough during a John Cage recital and you are part of the performance. That's an interface.

Given that these features, interface and indeterminacy are a characteristic of interactive media, a question arises about contexts of use. Joyce, Duchamp and Cage had all been called unintelligible during their careers. However such accusations are firmly premised on the understanding that unintelligibility is to be expected in the experimental arts. It is where transgression and idiosyncracy are played out. Indeed, the links between certain tendencies in modernist art and hypermedia are striking. Surrealist cinema, for instance, was, in Adrian Martin's terms, the search for a hyperlogic, a "dizzying, revelatory version of psychoanalytic free association."[14] There's that word again, hyperlogic, that distinctive marker of electronic difference. Similar charges of unintelligibility have also been laid against new media. First time cruisers of Internet frequently complain about its vastness, its lack of pre-determined grids and the ease with which one can get lost, or spend a lot of time wandering aimlessly with little to show for all that URL jumping. Interactive adventures such as *Myst* or detective comedies such as *Sam 'n Max Hit the Road* are equally criticised for being frustrating, since so much is left up to the player. You have to navigate an unfamiliar terrain with little internal assistance, find things and learn how to use them, all the time assembling a narrative sense of where it is all ultimately heading. But there is more. You are also required to uncover secret functions, weapons or sources of information so cunningly hidden that an entire culture of cheat codes has developed to aid the hapless gameplayer, who by this stage may be on the verge of flinging his rom into the rubbish bin. Try playing *Doom* without the aid of IDDQD or IDKFA and see how you like it—and I'm not talking about Hurt Me Plenty; check out Ultra Violence! Perhaps every interactive gameplayer secretly yearns for our old friend, the pastoral narrator, who does all the work and spares us from such anxiety. Just sit back and enjoy the ride. Of course such interactive features have also been highly praised, for all the the opposing reasons; so much *is* left up to the player, etc. And as far as vicarious experience is concerned, *Doom* can't be beaten. It gives a whole new dimension of meaning to the concept of catharsis. Indeed, if Aristotle were living in the late twentieth century, I'm sure he would have developed his theory of pity and terror while playing *Doom.*

Similar feelings of abandonment and disorientation have been raised concerning hypertext. When I first used a multi-media encyclopaedia I was struck by the speed and facility with which I moved from a high resolution image of an African village to plate-tectonics to Geosyncline theory to the Devonian period. It was impressive in that I had pursued a series of unexpected links that opened up an ever-expanding web of

[14] Adrian Martin, "The Artificial Night: Surrealism and the Cinema," *Surrealism: Revolution by Night* exhibition catalogue (Canberra: National Gallery of Australia, 1993) 194

information that was not linear and was not restricted to following a single topic. You can hardly call it a narrative, in any conventional sense of the term, though it observes the important narrative principle of contiguity; the proximity of any given piece of information to something with which it has affinities (the prehistorical evolution of the African continent). And all this, of course, was merely one of many possible paths I could have strolled down. On the other hand, I was troubled by the fact that I had lost interest in returning to my African village. This is the nature of a virtual document, such as a hypertext; you are somewhere doing something (reading screen-text about an African village), and all the time you are being prompted to go somewhere else, to a parallel, linked document. This can have its drawbacks, and feeling lost in the woods is certainly one of them. Disorientation and information overload are the price to be paid for such a powerful medium. But within archival and recreational contexts this is to be expected, and people will be happy to pay such a price in return for the rewards, or simply concede it as an occupational hazard. After all, it is just a matter of degree. You can just as easy feel dazed and confused watching *Last Year At Marienbad* or cross-referencing a topic in the *Anglo-American Cyclopaedia*.

Hyperlogic, or thinking electronically, is not actually confined to hypermedia. It is a form of thinking based on association, on accident, on suggestion. It is exactly the kind of logic usually implied by the term brainstorming. In other words, the kind of electronic thinking made available by interactive media, rapid linking and lateral jumps, unexpected fusions of ideas, indeed, the invention of ideas, is something we are all familiar with in pre-electronic forms. Just think of Surrealism. Or think of how much accident plays a part in writing an essay or a TV script. In terms of the question, "What has interactive media given us that we didn't have before?," I suppose it is a heightened, very powerful extension of this mode of thought. My observations have largely been confined to ready-made multi-media. Authoring software, on the other hand, is what interactivity is really all about. Instead of a mental image of *The Large Glass* when I read Joyce on the screen, I can import one, and if a piece of John Cage comes to mind, I can blend it into the entire ensemble. My matrix of ideas has become a multi-media "docuverse."

The term "enabling technology" is used a lot these days. I think it is fairly accurate. Interactive media don't necessarily offer us anything new, but rather enable us to improve the creative potential of things we are already doing. Multi-media brings together or converges different, previously discrete media forms; for instance, video, or quick-time movies can accompany text, a picture of a Fender Strat can be enhanced by sampled sound.

But does hyperlogic have a function beyond the archival and recreational contexts I have referred to? What happens when you shift context? Claims have been made that the non-linearity of interactive media offers us a new form of communication. But is anything communicated in the interactive environment? Given that so much emphasis is placed on navigation and discovery, or role play and problem-solving, it seems to me that nothing is actually being communicated. Communication assumes an end point, something being transported, re-located from one context to another. In this sense, it is a transitive form of language use; an activity that takes an object, which gives meaning to the activity. The activity, the process of communication (be it a news broadcast or a recipe in a cookbook) completes itself by delivering its message. The academic lecture is typical in this respect. My own experiments with introducing interactivity into the lecture format reveal that students have very deep expectations about the verbal presentation of information: the lecture is linear and has an endpoint outside itself. It is ultimately going somewhere. Multi-media lecture presentations, according y, run the risk of being unreceivable; there is too much information, not all of it verbal, and it has no clear endpoint. Such presentations demand reciprocal activity in a context in which students expect narrative guidance. Rather than being told a story, they have to negotiate various informational sources, determine in what ways such information is to be linked, and then work out how it relates to the topic at hand, whatever that may be. As with the example of my African village, purposive action (the exchange of knowledge) is frustrated by purposeless distraction. Some lectures have been more succesful than others, and as a style it can be very useful in drawing students into the productive nature of the learning process. But when they don't work, you'll be told in no uncertain terms that the lecturer has lost the plot. This situation reveals both the trouble with, and the attraction of interactivity: it is intransitive. It is activity that does not lead to a point, or give up an object. And being intransitive it is all-consuming and self-absorbing. Think of the San Fransisco lawyer who stayed back all night playing *Myst* after a hard day at the office: "The only problem was when I began clicking on things in real life. I'd see a manhole cover and think, 'Hmmm, that looks pretty interesting', and my forefinger would start to twitch. And then I'd realize, 'No, it's real life. Real life is the thing that happens in between *Myst*'" (Carroll 1984: 70).[15] Cage talked of a purposeful purposelessness, Joyce demanded an ideal, insomniac reader doing nothing but read *Finnegans Wake*, Duchamp wanted the experience of his work to be "indefinite." Communication or absorption, that is the question.

This is for me the most fascinating aspect of interactive media. They share with the experimental arts the desire to sustain the creative act, the act of engagement, and the pleasure of feeling that you don't have to go somewhere, but are simply going. You are as much interested in what you are doing as any reason you might be doing it for. I am listening to John Cage, I am playing *Doom*. Please don't ask me why. The

[15]   John Carroll, "Guerrillas in the *Myst*," *Wired* (August, 1994) 70.

concept of communication as a transitive act holds no truck here. I've got another inter word to add to the list: *"inter*plication." Unlike explication, which opens outward to arrive at a meaning, interplication, to quote Stephen Heath, is a "folding and unfolding in which every element becomes always the fold of another in a series that knows no point of rest."[16] Although he was referring to *Finnegans Wake*, Heath's term is a nice description of electronic thinking, and it neatly focuses the emphasis on doing, on process, on making and discovering that interactive media offer us. No one I know has found the out door of **the** Internet, because they are not interested in trying, and there isn't one anyway. I gave up trying to *get through Sam 'n Max* a long time ago. The longer I can keep putting off completing it, all the better.

[16] Stephen Heath, "Ambiviolences," *Post-Structuralist Joyce: Essays from the French*, ed. Derek Attridge and Daniel Ferrer (Cambridge: Cambridge University Press, 1984) 39.

DONALD F. THEALL
Transformations of the Book
in Joyce's Dream Vision of of Digiculture

The digital, pre-cyberfied Joyce, precursor of hypermedia, first emerged at the conclusion of the First World War during his exile to Zürich (1915-20). The first major shift in Joyce's stylistic and structural directions in his writing of *Ulysses* occurred while he was composing the "Cyclops" episode in 1919 and continued through the composition of "Circe" and "Ithaca" in Spring and Summer of 1920.[1] Stylistically and structurally, these episodes, together with those of "Aeolus," "Sirens" and "Oxen of the Sun" are the sections of *Ulysses* which are the ones that most clearly approximate the style, structures and techniques of *Finnegans Wake*. The unremitting "interetexuality" of the redrafting of "Cyclops," followed later by the complex multiphonic allusiveness of "Oxen of the Sun" began Joyce's sophisticated experimental transformations of the mechanics of the text.

This transition fully launched his role of becoming the prime explorer of the place of the book in the post-electric world—a road which was to permit him to explore poetically the accelerating modes of synaesthesia, the orchestration of the arts and contextual fluidity which would provide a new language, a new sense of structure and a probing of the depths of the social as well as the individual unconscious in dreams that had always already provided the sense of art as virtuality.

Zürich at the end of the second decade of the twentieth century provided Joyce with encouragement and influence from Dadaism—particularly through Tristan Tzara, Hugo Ball and Hans Arp—as well as a medley of trans-European artistic and poetic influences wielded by others sheltering there. Further Euro-American currents reinforced and expanded that impact temporally, spatially and intellectually. He did not achieve this ex nihilo, for that historic Dadaist moment in Zürich during World War I was coupled shortly after with Dadaistic movements in New York, Berlin and Paris, later supplemented by Surrealism. These were further complemented and supplemented by the major impact of French symbolisme, late Nineteenth Century art, and the Americo-British-Gallic

---

[1] Michael Groden, *Ulysses in Progress* (Princeton, NJ: Princeton University Press, 1977) 115-18.

poetic movement marked by Imagism (particularly Pound, Eliot and Yeats) and Vorticism. Continental European art, literature and theory of the first three decades of the twentieth century provided Joyce with key debates about the impact of science, mathematics and technology on cultural production, particularly with regard to their importance in the post-electric age which became a focal point for the poetic prophecy of *Finnegans Wake*.

Joyce's connection with these continental artistic currents is further confirmed by his close friendship with Carola Giedion-Welcker and her husband, the historian-theorist of architecture and art, Sigfried Giedion; by the combination of his fascinating admiration for, and his sharp artistic, intellectual and satiric criticism of, Wyndham Lewis; and by his close friendship with Frank Budgen. Rather than operating as specific influences on Joyce, this historic complex—a multi-logical, polysemic "context of situation"—opened up new ways of perceiving and thinking about events and phenomena that Joyce jointly shared with a contemporary community of artists and intellectuals. Historical awareness of these influences provide an important prolegomena for exploring Joyce's vision of the digital world. They demonstrate a significant presence of a variety of influences from the contemporary intellectual, scientific, artistic and literary world, and indicate the influence from the cities where he lived as he was in the final stages of the writing of *Ulysses* and beginning the composition of the *Wake* (Zürich 1915-20 and Paris after June 1920). This is of considerable assistance in elucidating some of the reasons for his quest for new stylistic and structural directions. But, as we shall see, they also simultaneously provide some understanding of how Joyce came to occupy a unique role in what has recently been called the "prehistory of cyberculture."[2]

Whether or not the *Wake*'s speaking of the "twattering of bards" (*FW* 37.17) is a reference to Paul Klee's famous Twittering Bird completed in 1922,[3] or Joyce's speaking of his book as a "claybook," or Glasheen's suggesting that he is alluding to Klee's relation with Marcel Duchamp (*Moy jay trouvay la clee dang les champs* [*FW* 478.21]) by playing on the French phrase for "freedom of the fields" and on the German word for clover (i.e., Klee)) is consciously intended, the affinity of Joycean interests with the techno-scientific and electromagnetic in-

[2] See Darren Tofts & Murray McKeich, *Memory Trade: A Prehistory of Cyberculture* (North Ryde, NSW: A 21*C Book published by Interface, 1997); and Donald F. Theall, "Beyond the Orality/Literacy Dichotomy: James Joyce and the Prehistory of Cyberspace."

[3] Cf. "And so they went on, the fourbottle men, the analists, unguam and nunguam and lunguam again, their anschluss about her whosebefore and his whereafters and how she was lost away away in the fern and how he was founded deap on deep in anear, and the rustlings and the twitterings and the raspings and the snappings and the sighings and the paintings and the ukukuings and the (hist!) the springapartings and the (hast!) the bybyscuttlings and all the scandalmunkers and the pure craigs that used to be (up) that time living and lying and rating and riding round Nunsbelly Square. And all the buds in the bush. And the laughing jackass. Harik! Harik! Harik! The rose is white in the darik! And Sunfella's nose has got rhinoceritis from haunting the roes in the parik! So all rogues lean to rhyme" (*FW* 95.27).

terests of Klee, Duchamp, Picabia, Ernst, the Dadaists, Surrealists and Expressionists is noteworthy. If Duchamp, Picabia, Klee and a number of other contemporary artists explored the impact of techno-scientific phenomena such as X-Rays, atomic structure, electricity and magnetism, radiation, radium and aspects of chemistry on the visual and optical arts, Joyce extended this exploration into their impact on language, gesture, speech and print/writing.

If Duchamp's *The Large Glass* (1914) marks a turning-point in the marriage of art, science and technology, Joyce's beginning major new directions in and revisions of the style of *Ulysses* (1919) marks the moment of his moving toward his complex merger of narrative, science, mathematics, technology and poetics in *Finnegans Wake*. While Apollinaire, Tzara, Duchamp, and Picabia had noted the value of the transgressive potency of the "pun" in their new "playful science" of the new post-electric arts, Joyce consciously set out to develop the polyvalent, polysemic "pun" using it along with grammar (traditional grammatica, early linguistics and semiotics), mathematics and mnemonic theory to achieve the "abnihilisation of the etym."[4] While the efforts of these artists and of Joyce may initially seem far removed from questions of digitalisation, virtuality or hypertextuality today, they actually contribute to an understanding of the social, artistic, intellectual and practical (i.e., applied) contexts leading to their development. In discussions of art and technology in the 1960s and after, Duchamp, Max Ernst and others stand as figures on the road to the MIT Media Lab, for at the root of the evolution of digital, artificial or virtual reality (i.e., cyberspace) are the early post-electric visions of synaesthesia, of the "orchestration [or integration] of the arts" and of the networks of connections and allusions to other arts, science and technology.[5]

That Joyce appropriately occupies a unique place in that pre-history is attested first by the fact that he established these motifs at the very outset of the *Wake* when he began drafting the work starting with the earliest fragments: the satirico-comic debate between St. Patrick and Berkeley about the nature of light and its relations to the physics of light and quanta; the scene of his anti-hero as an inebriated King Roderick O'Connor, whom Joyce dubs the last "pre-electric king of Ireland"; and the "Mamalujo" fragment introducing the four senile psychoanalysts-historians (also playing on the four evangelists) — who later become the "four claymen" (clay + Klee + 'klee', Ger. key) electronically probing and cross-examining Yawn. These fragments together with: the portrait

---

[4] See Derek Attridge, "Unpacking the Portmanteau, or Who's Afraid of *Finnegans Wake?*" *On Puns: The Foundation of Letters*, ed. Jonathan Culler (Oxford: Basil Blackwell, 1988) 140-55. It is also useful to note that Duchamp, Apollinaire and others promoted Jacques Brisset's near deification of the pun in the second decade of the twentieth century.

[5] See Douglas Davis, *Art and The Future: A History/Prophecy of the Collaboration Between Science, Technology and Art* (1973; rpt. New York: Praeger Publishers, 1975); and Stewart Brand, *The Media Lab: Inventing the Future at MIT* (New York/Toronto: Viking Penguin, 1987).

of HCE; with the semi-incestuous seduction of Isolde ("Izzy"); and with the description of St. Kevin at Glendalough, are the first moments of Joyce's unique modernist carnivalesque Rabelaisian (or Menippean) satire of the post-Dadaist world—and like the Dadaists and their progeny produce a playful techno-scientific poetic. The first three vignettes— Patrick and the Archdruid, Roderick O'Connor and "Mamalujo"—play with the techno-scientific and with the emergence of the cyborgian but always respecting the human person in the context of a quest for a "parahumanism."

Joyce's final commitment to the importance of his book as a literary machine is underlined by the fact that in 1938 during the last stages of writing the *Wake* he produced a newly composed paragraph to introduce the final version of Anna Livia's concluding letter which provides a bridge between Anna's letter and Patrick and Berkeley's debate, that immediately precedes it. This new passage (about one page in length) overtly reasserts the machinic, synaesthetic, coenaesthetic and hypertextual aspects of the *Wake* for his book becomes for Joyce, "Our wholemole millwheeling vicociclometer, a tetradomational gazebocroticon, the 'Mamma Lujah" (*FW* 614.27-8). The description of this machinic assemblage, which is identified with "Mamalujo," the "Four" an[n]ali[y]sts-historians-evangelists-gossips as the consumer-producers of Joyce's book, is introduced by references to memory processes which constituted part of the earliest drafts of *Work in Progress*:

> What has gone? How it ends? Begin to forget it. It will remember itself from every sides, with all gestures, in each our word. Forget, remember![6]

The process of remembering is the book, the dream, the vision itself as Joyce had asserted at the outset.

In the subsequent paragraphs Joyce's playful exploration of the mnemonic process involved in remembering is linked to codes in which there is not only a complex blending and interplay of icon, image, writing, sound, movement, and structure, but of past and present, of multidimensionality, of chance and of the metamorphic potentialities of matter, as exemplified in phrases such as:

> a tetradomational gazebocroticon [*FW* 614.27-8];

> autokinatonetically preprovided [*FW* 614.30];

> their homely codes, [*FW* 614.32];

[6] David Hayman, ed., *A First Draft Verson of Finnegans Wake* (Austin: University of Texas Press, 1963) 281. Original version of *FW* 614.19-22.

the heroticisms, catastrophes and eccentricities transmitted by the ancient legacy of the past type by tope, letter from litter, word at ward, with sendence of sundance... all, anastomosically assimilated and preteridentified paraidiotically, in fact, the sameold gamebold adomic structure... as highly charged with electrons as hophazards can effective it [*FW* 614.35-615.7].

What Joyce is able to dramatically demonstrate at the conclusion of the seventeen year process of writing the *Wake* is that through his transformations of poetic language he has moved writing and speech into that new post-electric world which was rapidly moving beyond media to a hypermedia and virtual reality. As Sergei Eisenstein, film director and theorist, and Laszlo Moholy-Nagy, design theorist and visual artist, intuited, *Wake*se—which can easily be described as a hyperlanguage or paralanguage—positions language for an era in which new modes of communication and expression would permit an integration of media in which the goals of synaesthesia, the orchestration of the arts and syncretism would be achieved, thus producing a new language.

Motifs suggesting that Joyce consciously developed this integrated, metamorphic character of *Wake*se occur in other passages in which crucial elements were added toward the end of the 1920s. In one of these the interplay of eye and ear in the poet's invention of his language simultaneously refers to the merging of the verbal and visual just as it refers to the interplay of writing and speech in which, incidentally, there is clearly a musical element of "dec[h]ording":

The prouts who will invent a writing there ultimately is the poeta, still more learned, who discovered the raiding there originally. That's the point of eschatology our book of kills reaches for now in soandso many counterpoint words. What can't be coded can be decorded if an ear aye sieze what no eye ere grieved for. Now, the doctrine obtains, we have occasioning cause causing effects and affects occasionally recausing altereffects.
[*FW* 482.31-483.1]

That Joyce had both the merging and the interplay in mind is confirmed by observations such as "Television kills telephony in brothers' broil. Our eyes demand their turn. Let them be seen!" (*FW* 52.18), or in the repetitive playful interlinking of the beginnings of modern art and of modernist writing such as juxtaposing the American author, John DosPassos, and the founder of French impressionism, Edouard Manet: "Willed without witting, whorled without aimed. Pappapassos, Mammamanet, warwhetswut and whowitswhy" (*FW* 272.5).

What needs to be noted when interpreting such passages is Joyce's unique conception of the reader-writer, producer-consumer relationship, which is articulated much later than the passage on "decording" cited above that speaks about eye-ear, code-cord. In a reference to the book itself as "Quinnigans' Quake," he asserts, "His producers are they not his consumers?" (497.1). The Joycean writer comes to be replaced by the reader who re-writes the text—the reader as poet related to processes of coding, to mnemonically pursuing transverse references and to a mimesis of multi-media perception. Jacques Derrida, who described the *Wake* as a "hypermachinic engine" and noted the potentialities of hypermedia to investigate such a text, suggests that Joyce was:

> in advance, decades in advance, to compute you, control you, forbid you the slightest inaugural syllable because you can say nothing that is not programmed on this 1000th generation computer—*Ulysses, Finnegans Wake*—beside which the current technology of our computers and microcomputerfied archives and translating machines remain a bricolage of a prehistoric child's toys. And above all its mechanisms are of a slowness incommensurable with the the quasi-infinite speed of the movements on Joyce's cables.[7]

Joyce's "hypermnesiac machine" operates through his readers being "in his memory." By examining his use of pre-digital hyperlinks involving memory and mimesis, this aspect of his creative process provides an interesting way of examining how his virtual or imaginary hypermedia is a pre-digital prophecy of contemporary virtuality and hypermedia.

While the machinic had been one of the central motifs in the unfolding explorations by Dadaists, Surrealists, Futurists and other avant-garde movements, what Derrida describes as the "hypermnesiac machine" is a distinctly Joycean invention. Joyce intersects with the Dadaists and their successors with respect to the recognition of: the need for a new language subsequent to the rise of the new science and of post-electric technologies; a new emphasis on chance and, as in the work of such Dadaists as Arp and Richter, ordered chance; convergence of media involving synaesthesia, the orchestration of the arts, and the merging of media; incorporating in their work an interest in the new mathematics, including geometries and science. But Joyce added to this a specific interest in the mnemonic and his perceived post-Viconian recognition of the inter-relatedness of imagination, creative intellect and memory. In these latter concerns he was perhaps closer to Richter's so-called "fathers of Dada"—Klee and Kandinsky—than to Duchamp, who like Wyndham Lewis , critiqued Henri Bergson. Early in writing the *Wake* Joyce suggested the rhizomic nature of memory rooted in "increasing, livivorous, feelful thinkamalinks; luxuriotiating everywhencewithersoever among skullhullows and charnelcysts of a weedwastewoldwevild" (*FW* 613.19-21). Along with Vico Joyce viewed memory as the foundation of all invention, imagination and intellectual activity.

Joyce's hypermnesia complements and supplements the range of the Dadaists, the Surrealists and other avant-garde figures. He is closer to

---

[7] Jacques Derrida, "Two Words for Joyce," *Poststructuralist Joyce: Essays from the French*, ed. Derek Attridge and Daniel Ferrer (Cambridge: Cambridge University Press, 1984) 147.

Kandinsky and Klee because their theories stressing the interaction of the material and the immaterial recognise the fundamental presence of the "mnesiac" in the growth of form as an inner landscape. Yet even more particularly in the case of Klee, whose Bauhaus lectures provided the only "Principia Aesthetica" of modernism in the visual arts and whose theory arises from the rhizomic existence of the tree in nature and from such motifs of motion as the natural flows of water in a river.[8] Joyce, Klee, and Kandinsky like the Dadaists, Surrealists and other avant-garde artists were involved with the concept of the artist as an engineer designing and building ideographic constructs. These new art movements had been recognised in the avant-garde modernist movements in the visual arts by the development of modes such as collage, ready-mades, techno-constructs (e.g. Duchamp's *Large Glass*), optical art, mobiles and the like.

While the *Wake* contains key references to collage, to ready-mades, to mobiles and to optical experimentation along with other terms associated with the avant-garde artistic movements, Joyce's poetic engineering by having to utilise the semiotic, dialectical and rhetorical could also encompass the playfulness of Apollinaire and Jarry supplemented by the entire symboliste tradition from Baudelaire through Mallarmé to Valéry in order to achieve the complex virtuality of the dream. One reference to collage: "and flaunt on the flimsyfilmsies for to grig my collage juniorees who, though they flush fuchsia, are they octette and virginity in my shade but always my figurants" (*FW* 279F1) is embedded with references to music, to film, to attending college, to erotic play and to fucking thus creating a verbal collage; another appears in the Schoolroom, "Triv and Quad," episode in a playful note which continues with references to comic strips such as Popeye and other forms of popular culture (*FW* 279.n1). A reference to a mobile is included in a painterly and optical introduction to the episode concentrating on Shaun the Post (III.1) where it is included within a vision of the spectrum occurring in a "fogbow" (a phenomenon similar to rainbows but generated by a fog):

White fogbow spans. The arch embattled. Mark as capsules. The nose of the man who was nought like the nasoes. It is self tinted wrinkling, ruddled. His kep is a gorsecone. He am Gascon Titubante of Tegmine sub Fagi whose fixtures are mobiling so wobiling befear my remembrandts. She, exhibit next, his Anastashie. She has prayings in lowdelph. Zeehere green eggbrooms. What named blautoothdmand is ycn who stares? Gugurtha! Gugurtha! He has becco of wild hindigan. Ho, he hath hornhide! And hvis now is for you. Pensée! The most beautiful of woman of the veilch veilchen veilde. [*FW* 403.6-15]

8 Herbert Read, *A Concise History of Modern Painting* (New York: Praeger, 1959).

As the "White fogbow spans. The arch embattled." (*FW* 403.6) the colors of the spectrum appear—"ruddled" (red), "gorse" (orange), "green eggbrooms," (green and yellow—"broom" = yellow), "blautoothdmand" (blue), "wild hindigan" (indigo), "veilde" (violet—German, veilchen, violets). Embedded in that vision is an image of King Mark described as one "whose fixtures are mobiling so wobiling befear my remembrandts" (*FW* 403.9-10). Here Joyce's play with Rembrandt's name is in counterpoint with modern mobiles, while simultaneously playing on the presence of memory within the virtuality of the contemporary visual object of art, whether optical or painterly.

The word "mobile" also appears later in the pre-cyborgian, para-human image of HCE as innkeeper with which the barroom scene opens (II.3). Here it appears in the acoustic equivalent of a collage—a sound collage—and takes on a sexual, conjugal spin, for this "tolvtubular high fidelity daildialler" (*FW* 309.14) is:

> equipped with supershielded umbrella antennas and connected by the magnetic links of a Bellini_Tosti coupling system with a vitaltone speaker, capable of capturing skybuddies, harbour craft emittences, key clickings, vaticum cleaners, due to woman formed mobile or man made static and bawling the whowle hamshack and wobble down in an eliminium sounds pound so as to serve him up a melegoturny marygoraumd, eclectrically filtered for allirish earths and ohmes.
> [*FW* 309.17-310.1]

Here the convergence of the arts and of the new media of technological reproducibility within a world that is moving beyond media (or at least within Joyce's prophetic dreamworld where that convergence is a dream that is always already beyond specific technical artifacts) is explored in relation to sound and acoustic modes of technology.

Their interplay is even more striking in Joyce's numerous forays into the evolving avant-garde interest in optical aspects of art marked in the *Wake*, for example, by such playful compounds as the following which include the morpheme "-scope": " after those few prelimbs made out through his eroscope the apparition of his fond sister Izzy" (*FW* 431.14-5); looking through at these accidents with the "faroscope of television" (*FW* 150.32-3); "Hippohopparray helioscope flashed winsor places as the gates might see. (*FW* 341.23-4); "Amid a fluorescence of spectracular mephiticism there caoculates through the inconoscope stealdily a still, the figure of a fellow" (*FW* 349.16-8); "Two makes a wing at the macroscope telluspeep" (*FW* 275.L3-6); "When I'm dreaming back like that I begins to see we're only all telescopes. Or the comeallyoum saunds" (*FW* 295.10-2); "myrioscope" (*FW* 127.35); "neviewscope" (*FW*

449.34); "pudendascope" (*FW* 115.30); "spectrescope" (*FW* 230.1); "big Willingdone mormorial tallowscoop " (*FW* 8.35, cf. *FW* 9.34).[9] A passage playing on the kaleidoscopic which concludes a riddle (I.vi #9) indicates how central this cluster is to the book, its dream structure and its synesthetic modes of virtuality. In that riddle which includes references to a "panaroma of all the flores of speech" (*FW* 143.4) and "an earsighted view of old hopeinhaven," (*FW* 143.9) Joyce links this merging of traditional stylistics and electrified matter with the spectral nature of light:

> what roserude and oragious grows gelb and greem, blue out the ind of it! Violet's dyed! then what would that fargazer seem to seemself to seem seeming of, dimm it all?
>   Answer: A collideorscape! [*FW* 143.25-8]

One aspect of this "collideorscape" is that it brings together the sound, motion, movement and sights of the city through time as well as space as a series of chaotic (hence, colliding and escaping) bits of the city. Danis Rose's way of paraphrasing the passage is helpful in underlining this:

> ... Shem asks could a human being, fatigued after a day n the city and given in sleep a view of Copenhagen whereby he could behold the vast, infolding panorama of its history, the countless events, vicissitudes that were enacted there in the course of its history, could such one, as the vision continued on throughout the night, integrate or differentiate alll the millions of particulars, make sense out of the whole or even a part, discern what is static and what kinetic? In short, what would such a dreamer seem to himself seemingly to be seeing?
>   Shaun is not to be foxed and answers succinctly: a kaleidoscope![10]

What "that fargazer seem to seemself to seem seeming of," is clearly virtual, for this is a "collideorscape" produced by the "dreams of accuracy" of a "camelot prince of dinmurk" (*FW* 143.6-7). The *Wake* is thus not only a verbal recreation of a film ("the reel world' [*FW* 64.25]), but its dreamworld can also become a virtual reality. With respect to filmmaking, Duchamp's colleague, Hans Richter, noted that there is a merging of the dreamworld and reality which permeates the various films that constitute his film Dreams That Money Can Buy. Eisenstein's remarks on Joyce implicitly and prophetically suggests that the tendency of film is

---

[9] By 1931 Walter Benjamin was using the phrase "optical unconscious" in his "Small History of Photography." A more recent use of "optical unconscious," which takes exception with Benjamin, is Rosalind E. Kraus, *The Optical Unconscious* (Cambridge. MIT Press, 1949) 178-9 is using a Lacanian-Freudian sense of unconscious, while Benajmin is closer to Gregory Bateson and ultimately to Joyce, since the optical unconscious is the virtual making visible of the social unconscious.

[10] Danis Rose and John O'Hanlon, *Understanding "Finnegans Wake": A Guide to the Narrative of James Joyce's Masterpiece* (New York: Garland Publishing, 1982) 92.

toward creating just this type of convergence of media—a moving beyond media and beyond language as we know it.

Joyce's "collideorscape" provides an escape for "making sense" out of this world which he underlines through an interplay of the phonetic sound spectrum of the vowels and the visual spectrum of light producing colours—a blending of visual and verbal and ambivalence. For in recounting history or recounting the story of "his tory," conservative innkeeper "will [have] been having recourse" to the reverberration of knotcracking awes, the reconjungation of node binding ayes, the redissolusingness of mindmouldered ease and the thereby hang of the Hoel of it" (FW 143.12-5). And if the sounds blend creating ambiguous signs, the light creates spectral colors: "what roserude and oragious grows gelb and greem, blue out the ind of it! Violet's dyed! then what would that fargazer seem to seemself to seem seeming of, dimm it all?" (FW 143.24-7). These phenomena are the stuff of hypermedia, creating the resonance ("reverberration"), the node-binding ("reconjugation"), and the fluidity ("redissolusingness") that shape the virtual city ("Copenhagen") .

The optical spectrum permeates the Wake in conjunction with the image of the rainbow, as we see in an example such as the description of the "fogbow" noted above. The final appearance of the spectrum in the climactic debate between the Saint and the Sage is immediately followed by an explanation of the nature of Joyce's "vicociclometer," the "tetradomational gazebocroticon" (FW 614.27-8). At the heart of Joyce's projects in the composition of the later stages of Ulysses and the Wake was a recognition of a series of transformations which would have to occur in the "book" of the future as the Dadaists had perceived in their merging of the modes of expression by their inclusion of music and poetry in a visual and performance-oriented art movement. So Joyce within the "unique" language of Finnegans Wake provides a constant "fluxion" (FW 297.29) between vision, gesture, movement, sound, speech, printed word and light itself. Like the Dadaists, their immediate progenitors and their successors, Joyce commingled in print what they had commingled in their performances and presentations. In the process the groundwork was being laid for the hypermnesiac machine and the production of hypermedia and digitalised virtual reality, Prior to a development of hypermedia integrating fully text and originary writing with motion, vision, sound, gesture and speech is the creation of a yearning for hypertext in the complex intra- and inter-textuality of "ambiviolent" Wakese which gives shape to its rhizomic "chaosmos."

One of Joyce's prime and complex means for creating networks of interlinkage within the text (i.e., transversality or intratextuality) is to play on linguistic minimal differences. He transforms and/or inserts minimal phonetic or orthographic changes in words, combining these transformations with possibilities for creating assonance and consonance. The items of minimal difference involved frequently relate to prime clusters of words with inter-related meanings, frequently involving an interplay of different national languages, all of which provides further means for achieving their polysemic interconnection.[11] Interconnections between memory, mimesis and related concepts both exemplify this phenomenon while they simultaneously shed light on this subject of the "hypermnesiac machine." The sequence "m" plus any vowel plus another "m" either with the "m"'s in inital or final position or preceded or followed by other letters [i.e., m — [aeiou] — m] generates a multitude of relevant examples illustrative of Joycean excesses of meaning, for it selects all the monosyllabic and morphological chains involving mam-mem-mim-mom-mum (interestingly the first two members of which if the second m is dropped become ma and me).

When the text is searched for occurrences, Joyce's insistence on the relation of the mother to such concepts as mimesis, mimicry, mime, memory, moment, silence (being mum) is established and the chain expands through multimimetica (multimedia) to semiotics (the meaning of meaning) and mathematics: "lead us seek, lote us see, light us find, let us missnot Maidadate, Mimosa Multimimetica, the maymeaminning of maimoomeining!" (*FW* 267.2-3) to "the deprofundity of multimathematical immaterialities" (*FW* 394.31-2). From the multiple plays on the basic chain of vowel changes, the reader is led into relating mimesis and memory to Ogden and Richards, *The Meaning of Meaning* and Ogden's interest in mathematical (Leibnizian) theories of meaning. The strategy being pursued here rises out of Joyce's encyclopedic design coupled with his practico-theoretic interest in inter-relating such basic textual concepts as imitation, dramatic presentation, memory, meaning and mathematical order. This is similar to that which characterises hypermedia links and their rhizomic like organisation.

Joycean aural-mnemonic links, which pre-date contemporary digital culture, serve as nodal points for the rhizomic organisation that generates the intratextual and the intertextual. A phrase such as the "maymeaminning of maimoomeining" (*FW* 267.3) evokes an allusion to *The Meaning of Meaning* because these nodal-points are complemented and reinforced by the visual and auditory structure of the words or phrases, including verbal play on the German word for "opinion" (meinung) and the Irish for "stuttering" (meanne, minne) to provide the interdiscursive connections. This interweaving situated in a slightly larger context ("lead us seek, lote us see, light us find, let us missnot Maidadate, Mimosa Multimimetica, the maymeaminning of maimoomeining!" (*FW* 267.1-3)) goes further anticipatorily mimicking some of the more complex aspects of hypertext by inter-relating the maternal, the imitative, the dramatistic, the semiotic, the mnemonic and the mathematical (and/or logical) ordering. This chaotic, yet ordered, complexity is what creates a reciprocity between the Joycean text and the computer pro-

---

[11] Text analysis software such as TACT with its wild card capability, its use of Booleans operators and other such search devices is of considerable value both in ferreting out these groups and in revealing many of the polysemic aspects of their interconnection.

grams which complement (partly, but not solely, by speed) the cerebral processing of the reader reading with eye and ear—the hypertextual path supplementing the path guided by human memory.

There is an extremely strong affinity between those features which text analysis and concordancing software dramatically illustrate and Joyce's concept of the "raiding" (FW 482.32) of the Wake. But the Joycean pre-post-modernist (or radical modernist) project makes it even more appropriate since, as established in Thomas Rice's Joyce, Chaos and Complexity and my James Joyce's Techno-Poetics, Joyce utilised geometrical and arithmetical principles of organisation as well as logico-mathematical and structural semiotic ones. This creates a context within which the computer aids and abets the radical type of "raiding" with its "decoding" and "dechording" which the Wake envisions in the reader's re-writing. The point is that such an interface does not only assist inter-pretation or understanding, but it also aids and abets a new mode of advanced modernist (or poststructuralist) reading, radically transverse, as our examples with mam-mem-mim-mom-mum demonstrate. Parallel-ling this there is a strong affinity between what digitalisation of texts has made possible, since this not only increases our ability to investigate the Wake in ways in which the Joycean conception of the text itself invites, but also because its hypermediac encyclopedism is complemen-tary to the Wake's proto-hypermnesiac-encyclopedism.[12]

While returning in such a specific way to the verbal textuality of the Wake, it is important to consider how the influence of radical modernist artists interested in sound, the visual, the sculptural and the typographic interplays with the intra- and inter-textuality which is essential to the virtuality of Joyce's hypermnesiac dream machine. The fluidity of Joyce's "new" language more readily encompasses the revolution of artistic expression and communication which began in the first decades of the twentieth century. If we have associated Joyce's development in the last stages of Ulysses and in beginning the Wake with avant-garde movements during the period he lived in Zürich, and then the early pe-riod in Paris, one major aspect of aesthetics associated with the Dadaist revolution from the Zürich years, represented primarily by Apollinaire, went back to the relative beginnings of the printed book and the early moments of Alexandria. This was "pattern poetry" or "figured" poetry which took advantage of the spatial arrangement of the words and lines in the poem to make a variety of shapes which complemented the verbal text. Apollinaire's "calligrammes" as he entitled his collection of such

[12] The preceding four paragraphs have been adapted from a paper presented to a joint meeting of the Association of Canadian University Teachers of English and the Canadian Association for Computing in the Humanities. In the paper, which has been published by CACH, there are specific examples applying statistical programs from the Text Analysis and Concordancing Tool (TACT) to the interpretation of Finnegans Wake as well as a fuller amplification of the arguments surrounding the preceding four paragraphs. A complete text of the article may be found at their web site: http://www.chass.utoronto.ca/epc/chwp/theall/

poems possibly reinforced Joyce's interest in Mallarmé's *Un Coup de Dès*. It is further apparent that in *Ulysses*, in the composition of which he coupled these interests with experiments such as Wyndham Lewis's vorticist magazine, *Blast*, Joyce had become acutely aware of the potentials of typographical form in shaping his book, as evidenced in many of the later revisions of *Ulysses*.

While it is impossible in a short essay to encompass the relations of Joyce with the history and theory of the printed book as an entirety (not just its contents, but particularly its status as an artifact through a multitude of transformations), yet to understand the relationship of the *Wake* to the emerging digiculture of hypertext and hypermedia it is essential to look at some aspects of this problem—contemporary and historical. The transformations of the book (originally an inscribed medium) clearly indicates that contemporary digital culture has produced completely new potentialities for electronic inscription, providing new possibilities for what the book has been at various moments from its early history through Gutenberg into the electro-mechnical era. The importance of Joyce's description of the *Wake* as a "vicociclometer" has already been noted, but it is equally as important to note that the description of this "tetradomational gazebocroticon" (*FW* 614.27-8) immediately follows the debate about the nature of light between the Saint and Sage with its emphasis on the spectrum. In fact, the variety of references to books repeatedly emphasise the fluidity of the radical modernist post-electric vision of the book—"Jungfraud's Messongebook," "claybook," "tellafun book," "new book of Morses," "lingerous longersous book of the dark," "our book of kills," "his book of craven images," "comicsongbook," "a most moraculous jeerymhead sindbook," "his morse-erse wordybook."

From the modern vision to the classical roots of the book, Joyce touches on important moments in its nature as an artefact. His renewed interest in the typographical and other material aspects of the book further appears to have added to the role that the key eighteenth century satirists- Pope, Sterne and Swift—played in the *Wake*. Their own interest in the book as a production (*The Dunciad*, *Tristram Shandy*, and *A Tale of the Tub*) and the processes of promotion, publication and production (e.g. *Of The Art of Sinking in Poetry* and the various versions of *The Dunciad* and *The Dunciad Variorum* had been replayed in the processes of promotion, publication and production of the *Wake* (e.g. the role of *Our Exagmination* and Joyce's manipulation of commentary about various episodes). At the most obvious level this is reflected in the use of marginalia and foot-notes in the Schoolroom episode of the *Wake* (II.2), but it is also reflected in the poetic treatment of such issues within his verbal poetry. Simultaneously Joyce associates the very nature of the manuscript and book with a fluidity. At various moments in the *Wake* he affiliates it: with illustration and ornamentation (e.g., the *Book of Kells*); with electrification and codification ("morse-erse wordybook"); with popular visual and auditory presentation ("comicsongbook"); and finally as a "gazebocroticon." His fascination with the mechanics of the book is complemented by his awareness of its potentiality for metamorphoses. The ultimate comedy of such metamorphoses is Belinda the Hen, pecking up the letter (i.e., manuscript) from a dung heap (*FW* 111.5ff), which is later simultaneously transformed into a multiplicty of media—newsreels, nursery rhymes, dreams, a diary, a wireless transmission of music ("bostoons"):

> —This nonday diary, this allnights newseryreel.
> —My dear sir! In this wireless age any owl rooster can peck up bostoons.
> [*FW* 489.35-490.1]

What must be noted here is that Joyce's vision of the book is one that recognises its past historic transformations and its potentialities for a near infinite set of possibilities for future transformations. But all of this contributes to the prophetic, poetic vision of the metamorphoses of the postelectric book. If various moments in history could play with the shape and mechanics of the book, then the book could undergo further transformations as it does in the language and dream of the *Wake*, but also in the way the *Wake* provides the prime exemplar for Derrida's hypermnesiac machine. The potentialities for that conception of the book came to Joyce from symbolism, from the Dadaists and Surrealists and the avant-garde in general who were acutely sensitive to the exponential increase to the transforming power of modes of production, reproduction and dissemination in the post-electric era. Yet from whatever Joyce learned, particularly in Zürich and Paris, it was his unique contribution to craft "a vicociclometer, a tetradomational gazebocroticon," which would anticipate the impacts on communication and expression of digitalisation and the convergence of media that would accompany it.

LAURENT MILESI
Joycean Choreo-Graphies in
Stephen Hero & *A Portrait of the Artist as a Young Man*

One of the best known landmarks of early Joycean aesthetics is the writer's theory of the epiphany as the essence of (involuntary) artistic manifestation, inseparable from the juvenile figure of the alter ego Stephen Dedalus. Less well documented, however, is how the successive stages in the theory's presentation and implementation, from *Stephen Hero* to *A Portrait of the Artist as a Young Man*,[1] turn around a formal orchestration of correlated concepts, usually with an awareness of their etymology or even their Indo-European roots, involving gesture, rhythm but also emotion and energy. What follows is an attempt to chart the gradual development of this aesthetics of the epiphany in the light of these cognate "root words" and themes, and show how they paved the way for a more full-blown "choreography of writing," to be further refined in *Ulysses* and *Finnegans Wake* (outside the scope of the present essay), whereby the figure of the artist as dancer emerges from a kinetic conception of art and of writing as a dance.

More broadly, this essay arises out of the following question: how does Joyce the *poète manqué* who, via several evolving artistic personae (Stephen Dedalus(es), Shem the Penman), never abandoned his interest in theories of language and the place these allocate to the poetic, feature among a range of practitioners who foregrounded the mechanics of writing, using as an analogical touchstone similes with rhythm, dance, gesture, e-motion, etc, in order (ultimately) to work out alternative genealogies for the practice of writing? I shall review some of these "figures of the dance(r)" or key moments in an ongoing choreography: writing the dance or writing-as-dance, the variously inflected, ceaselessly renegotiated and increasingly self-ironic "movements" and tempi of Joyce's oeuvre, by focusing on its incipient stages in *Stephen Hero* and *A Portrait of the Artist as a Young Man*.

---

[1] Editions cited: James Joyce, *Stephen Hero*, ed. and intro. Theodore Spencer, rev. ed. with additional material and a Foreword by John J. Slocum and Herbert Cahoon (London: Granada, 1977), also identified as *SH* after quotations; *A Portrait of the Artist as a Young Man*, with six drawings by Robin Jacques (London: Granada, 1977).

1. THE RHYTHMIC E-MOTION OF EPIPHANY IN *STEPHEN HERO*: ART AS GESTURE

The "early Joyce" — both as writer and delimited literary corpus — is generally associated with the juvenile artistic figure of Stephen Dedalus and his theory of the epiphany as the essence of (involuntary) artistic embodiment. Within the broader context of remarks on (poetic) language, the word, gesture and rhythm, it is arguably the undramatic nature of the theory's early exposition towards the end of what was preserved of *Stephen Hero* — and prepared by notetaking on rhythm, dance (consonantia, harmony) in the 1903 Paris Notebook[2] — that will lead Joyce to want to recast the verbose "classical" end-of-19th-centuryish novel into the more economical modernist *Portrait*. A close-up on the moment of the theory's presentation in relation to earlier remarks on cognate terms is therefore necessary.

The theory is first glimpsed at through the first evocation of rhythm in supple terms that conjure up its Indo-European root, from **rei-*: to flow, the "beauty of verse" being described as a pulsating movement of "concealment and revelation" (not unlike the ancient Greeks' conception of Truth as *aletheia*) after the short following passage (which occurs after two missing pages):

> of verse are the first conditions which the words must submit to, the rhythm is the esthetic result of the senses, values and relations of the words thus conditioned. [*SH*, XV.29]

I have deliberately underscored the tacit etymology since, as the text says — and that was also one of Joyce's best-known interests — Stephen's budding aesthetics of poetry-as-rhythm was informed from its inception by an acquaintance with the historical palette of words: "He read Skeat's Etymological Dictionary by the hour. [...] People seemed to him strangely ignorant of the value of the words they used so glibly" (*SH*, p. 29). Indeed the etym — or atom; both will be fused later in several portmanteau words of *Finnegans Wake* (e.g. p. 353) — provides the artist with a kernel of aesthetic energy, and modern poetic creation is interestingly conceived as a retrogressive dismantling of words back into their letter constituents (note "doubling backwards into the past" in the following excerpt, to which I will return):

> He sought in his verses to fix the most elusive of his moods and he put his lines together not word by word but letter by letter. He read Blake and Rimbaud on the values of letters and even permuted and combined the five vowels to construct cries for primitive emotions. [...] Stephen did not attach himself to art in any spirit of youthful dilettantism but strove to

---

[2] See *The Workshop of Dedalus: James Joyce and the Raw Materials for "A Portrait of the Artist as a Young Man,"* ed. Robert Scholes and Richard M. Kain (Evanston, IL: Northwestern University Press, 1965).

pierce to the significant heart of everything. He doubled backwards into the past of humanity and caught glimpses of emergent art as one might have a vision of the plesiosaurus emerging from his ocean of slime. He seemed almost to hear the simple cries of fear and joy and wonder which are antecedent to all song, the savage rhythms of men pulling at the oar, to see the rude scrawls and the portable gods of men whose legacy Leonardo and Michelangelo inherit. [*SH*, XVI.34]

Further on, two distant textual fragments can be counterpointed as they both strengthen the connection between rhythm and emotion in Stephen's art:

For him [the critic] a song by Shakespeare which seems so free and living, as remote from any conscious purpose as rain that falls in a garden or as the lights of evening, discovers itself as the rhythmic speech of an emotion otherwise incommunicable, or at least not so fitly. [*SH*, XIX.74]

—I know a few elementary things and I express them in words. I feel emotions and I express them in rhyming lines. Song is the simple rhythmic liberation of an emotion. Love can express itself in part through song. [*SH*, XXIII.158]

These constitute the prelude to the full-blown articulation of a theory of an art to come ("should"), as rhythm gives way to the more quintessential gesture—cf. earlier: "the savage rhythms of men pulling at the oar" —, as all the above is subsumed, integrated and transformed into Stephen's "theoretical" disquisition on that experience that crystallizes aesthetic energy: the epiphany:

[from a longer conversation with Cranly on rhythm and gesture]
—There should be an art of gesture, said Stephen one night to Cranly.
—Yes?
—Of course I don't mean art of gesture in the sense that the elocution professor understands the word. For him a gesture is an emphasis. I mean a rhythm. You know the song 'Come unto these yellow sands'?
—No.
—This is it, said the youth making a graceful anapaestic gesture with each arm. That's the rhythm, do you see?"
[*SH*.XXIV.165]

Just after the thoughts "dancing the dance of unrest" in Stephen's brain before his composition of the "Villanelle of the Temptress," comes the famous definition—the passage is soon followed by a full exposition of the three qualities of beauty, the third of which, the Aquinean *claritas* (radiance), which Stephen equals with *quidditas*, constitutes the epiphanic moment proper:

This triviality [an overheard snippet of "the most commonplace conversation," whose hypnotic spell on his mind was recalled also on p. 29] made
him think of collecting such moments together in a book of epiphanies. By
an epiphany he meant a sudden spiritual manifestation, whether in the
vulgarity of speech or of gesture or in a memorable phase of the mind itself. He believed that it was for the man of letters to record these
epiphanies with extreme care, seeing that they themselves are the most
delicate and evanescent of moments. [*SH*, XXV.188]

The epiphany can thus itself be a gesture recording kinetically—or, precisely, as etymology tells us, e-motively (from e*[x]*-movere: to move out,
set in motion, stir up)—the intrusion of the vivid external reality of lived
experience into the realm of artistic expression, the successful embodiment of something real and objective into something linguistic and
subjective (to adapt Pound's terms for the "image," with which it has
technical affinities).[3] Its choreo-graphic nature can be apprehended in
ironic contrast to the seemingly more casual, implicitly more negative
references to the pantomime but especially dance in its socially domesti-
cated form, the more overtly classical ballet:

She [...] asked Stephen what he liked best in pantomime. Stephen said he
liked a good clown but she said she preferred ballets. Then she wanted to
know did he go out much to dance and pressed him to join an Irish danc-
ing-class of which she was a member. [*SH*, XVII.64]

What is striking about the above excerpts is how key concepts, components like "emotion," "rhythm," "gesture," "dance," "energy" also, and
finally "epiphany," are made to interact two by two (or three by three) in
such arresting moments of aesthetic observation or theorization, per-
forming at intervals, as it were, a rhythmic two/three-step dance, a
lexical choreography—Joyce's own logopoeia, which Pound again described as "the dance of the intellect among words"[4]—whose aesthetic
function would be to gradually shape and forward the theory to its full-
blown, rhythmic disclosure. It is this kinetic build-up to the epiphany of
the theory of the epiphany, as much as its conception, which, together
with a modicum of the yet insufficiently dramatized third-person narrative, at once redeems the juvenile novel from failure by the terms of

---

[3] See Ezra Pound, "Vorticism," *Gaudier-Brzeska. A Memoir* (New York: New Directions, 1970)
89. Note also the following passages, still in "Vorticism," which hover around the same
cluster of concepts Joyce had played with via Stephen Dedalus: "*Every [...] emotion presents
itself to the vivid consciousness in some primary form. [...] If [...] movement, to the dance or
to the rhythm of music or verses.*" (81); "I said [...] that I believed in an absolute rhythm. I
believe that every emotion and every phase of emotion has [...] some rhythm-phrase to
express it." (84); "[...] I realized quite vividly that if I were a painter, or if I had, often, that
kind of emotion, or even if I had the energy to get paints and brushes and keep at it [...]"
(87).
[4] Ezra Pound, "How To Read," *Literary Essays of Ezra Pound*, ed. and intr. T.S. Eliot (London:
Faber, 1954) 25.

Joyce's own aesthetic theory as it is filtered through his fictional alter ego, and yet removes the possibility for the epiphany to inform the presentation of the novel's action outside such crucial theoretical, metanarrative moments. Such an inchoate artistic treatment of the epiphany—both the theory's content as much as its practical manifestations or illustrations—had thus to be radically revised and its raw material, too ostentatiously foregrounded in *Stephen Hero*, subjected to modernist economy for the rewriting as *A Portrait of the Artist as a Young Man*. In this novelistic transformation, the more straightforwardly kinetic dimension of the epiphanic experience will modulate into the stasis of dramatic equipoise at the heart of the "rhythm of beauty."

2. EPIPHANIC PRESENTATION IN *A PORTRAIT*

The admixture of first- and third-person narrative agencies and the more prevalent, defter use of irony—which we can test in Lynch's boisterous remarks during Stephen's aesthetic peroration, instead of his predecessor's more patient listening—helped focus the overhaul of the earlier novel in order to bridge the gap between the "rhythmic-abstract" theorizing and the modernist aesthetics of dramatic distancing. Hence also the more deliberate alignment, in the crucial disquisitions in chapter five, of the threefold qualities of beauty with the three forms into which art divides itself: lyrical, epical, dramatic, so as to equip the reader with the critical vocabulary with which to judge how Stephen's subsequent sketch of a villanelle—the "rhythmic movement of a villanelle" (A Portrait, p. 197) which his mind conjures up after seeing his beloved—belies a lyrical immature artistic self whose practice falls short of the grand theorizing (the theory's wording percolates into the description of the protagonist's sexually charged emotions during the literary elaboration). Let us compare the passage, cited earlier, about the laden value of language in Stephen's juvenile poetics with the artist's definition of the lyrical form and tacitly note the quickened recirculation of the cluster of key words seen before as well as of one significant image:

> He sought in his verses to fix the most elusive of his moods [...]. He [...] even permuted and combined the five vowels to construct cries for primitive emotions. [...] He doubled backwards into the past of humanity and [...] seemed almost to hear the simple cries of fear and joy and wonder which are antecedent to all song, the savage rhythms of men pulling at the oar. [*SH*, 34]

> The lyrical form is in fact the simplest verbal gesture of an instant of emotion, a rhythmical cry such as ages ago cheered on the man who pulled at the oar or dragged stones up a slope. [...] The personality of the artist, at first a cry or a cadence or a mood and then a fluid and lambent narrative, finally refines itself out of existence, impersonalizes itself, so to speak. [*P* 5.194]

In the light of Stephen's advocacy of an artistic maturation process, from the lyrical to the dramatic, Joyce's decision to turn the end of *A Portrait* into a series of shorthand (lyrical) entries from a first-person diary further underscored the accrued ironic distancing between writer and fictional alter ego in terms of artistic creed and execution, and can be interpreted as a retrograde "doubling backwards into the past" for strategic compositional purposes, an overall choreography of writing of which there will be many numerous examples in *Ulysses* and *Finnegans Wake* (which *inter alia* will rehabilitate the pantomime as a salvational, yet ironic mode for art). The writing becomes Janus-faced, both turned towards the artist's lyrical self in a language that betokens aesthetic immaturity, and informing the ironic portraiture and (self-) revelation through concise narrative presentation.

Such a shift is best registered towards the climax of the fourth chapter, when the artistic calling takes off from a drawn-out epiphanic scene which recasts the earlier tones of sacerdotal vocation. The radiance evoked earlier in religious contexts and absent as such in what has survived from *Stephen Hero* is redeployed into the highest form of beauty and epiphanic manifestation. Let us compare for instance the following passages, the first one from the most sacerdotal vein of Stephen's search for a vocation, the second from the turning point in chapter four (the revelation of the artist's calling, amid recurrent rhytmic "hither and thither"'s), but also a third one, from the framing of the composition of the Villanelle:

Every part of his day [...] circled about its own centre of spiritual energy. [...] every thought, word and deed, every instant of consciousness could be made to revibrate radiantly in heaven [*P*, ch. 4]

His heart trembled; his breath came faster and a wild spirit passed over his limbs as though he were soaring sunwards. His heart trembled in an ecstasy of fear [...] and the body he knew was purified in a breath [...] and made radiant and commingled with the element of the spirit. An ecstasy of flight made radiant his eyes and wild his breath and tremulous and wild and radiant his windswept limbs. [*P* 4.154]

To him she would unveil her soul's shy nakedness, to one who was but schooled in the discharging of a formal rite rather than to him, a priest of eternal imagination, transmuting the daily bread of experience into the radiant body of everliving life.
The radiant image of the eucharist united again in an instant his bitter and despairing thoughts, their cries arising unbroken in a hymn of thanksgiving.
[six lines from the Villanelle, featuring the word "ardent"]
He spoke the verses aloud from the first lines till the music and rhythm suffused his mind. [*P* 5.200]

In order to reach a better understanding of what is at stake in this passage from religion to art, let us turn back to two excerpts from *Stephen Hero*—and tacitly note in the second quotation the Yeatsian-cum-Nietzschean echoes: Aherne and Robartes, related to the all-integrating figure of the dancer who realizes the artist's personality and his opposite (the all-powerful figure of the dancer in *Thus Spoke Zarathustra*, with Nietzsche's advocacy of writing as dancing)[5]:

> [just before the fragment featuring Rimbaud's vowels, quoted before:] He wrote a great deal of verse and, in default of any better contrivance, his verse allowed him to combine the offices of penitent and confessor. [*SH* 4]

> He repeated often the story of The Tables of the Law and the story of the Adoration of the Magi. The atmosphere of these stories was heavy with incense and omens and the figures of the monk-errants, Ahern and Michael Robartes strode through it with great strides. Their speeches were like the enigmas of a disdainful Jesus; their morality was infrahuman or superhuman. [*SH* 160]

What Stephen had looked and hoped for in religion, and could only find in art, is the harmonious integration of opposites—of the kind praised by Nietzsche in equally mythical evocations: the artist's inhumanity as *Übermensch*, hence the famous passage in *A Portrait* about the artist being like the god of creation, everywhere but invisible (*A Portrait*, ch. 5, pp. 194-5). The quintessential, quasi-alchemical sifting of epiphanic ingredients and the conditions of epiphanic revelation, paradoxically through a dissolution of its centrality in *A Portrait*, had thus to retain and transform in the crucible of art this crucial difference between religion and aesthetics in order to recast more effectively the still predominantly rhythmical-gestural, quasi-mythical foundation of art. In that respect, the next stages of "evolution" in Joyce's choreographic aesthetics (*Ulysses*—especially the revisiting of rhythm, gesture and dance in the sexual phantasmagoria of "Circe"—and *Finnegans Wake*) will mark a fuller coming to terms with the necessity of compromising with polar opposites (for e.g. in the overall "redemption" of Stephen the effete artist by Bloom the *homme moyen sensuel*) and with what the younger fictional artist had despised about the President in *Stephen Hero*: the "hermaphroditic gesture" (*SH* 90).

---

[5] Cf. the notebook entry on VI.B.17.71: "Dance — / extensions / personality" (used for Issy in *Finnegans Wake* 144.22-23).

ANDREW NORRIS
Joyce & the Post-Epiphanic

MEANING AND REVELATION

Joyce's epiphanies and the accounts of the epiphany he stages in his
work, lack claritas. They leave us wondering what exactly an epiphany
is. While we may be able to separate the epiphany off from the conceptual void or plenitude, and appreciate it as a conceptual complex in
itself, its final harmony or whatness eludes us. The set- piece presentations of the theory, in *Stephen Hero* and *Portrait*, signally fail to work as
epiphanies of the epiphany, while taking their place no doubt in the relation of part to part, in reading as an exercise in consonantia. The
collected epiphanies, numbered and presented sequentially as discrete
texts,[1] resist this potential affiliation between consonantia and narrative.
When inserted into longer texts, however, they lose their capacity to be
what they are as they take on other functions; subjected to the relational
science of part to whole, they achieve functionality as compositional
units. The instantaneity of the imagistic prose poem is co-opted to the
episodic temporality of the novel, and such a transposition threatens the
integritas, even perhaps the claritas, of the epiphany as unit. The beginning and end of the classical Thomistic epiphany as glossed by Stephen
Dedalus, is swamped by the intermediate stage, all is consonantia, an
ongoing differentiation and adjustment, a revelation in the making. Gone
is the notion of an image as sufficient unto itself, a form of truth which
owes its force precisely to its rejection or transcendence of sequence. If
differentiation fails, and logically this possibility must be included, what
was once a resonant whole incorporating itself as aesthetic object into
the revelation it projects, will collapse back into a state of formlessness,
which may be figured as a plenitude of brute matter without name, an
anti-claritas.[2]

---

[1] Most readily available in James Joyce, *Poems and Shorter Writings*, eds. Ellmann et al.
(London: Faber, 1991).
[2] This collapse of the first and third terms of the Thomistic epiphany into the second term
implicates both the syllogism and the Hegelian dialectic as forms of differentiating thought
served by and serving the distinction between an object or subject and all that it isn't. Consonantia, in this sense, might be figured as a syllogism blocked at its second term, a subject
or object as a postulate stuck with a predicate which has the potential to define it but which
can never disclose the necessity of their relation. The subject or object co-exists absurdly
with this hypothetical predicate. In *Peculiar Language* (Ithaca, New York: Cornell University

Narrative, then, stalls the epiphany at an intermediate stage, and is thus one of the problematic contexts raised by the Joycean epiphany, one of its inevitable ironies. The peripatetic Dedalus, instructing Cranly and Lynch in the ways of beauty, hesitates between theory and practice, or attempts perhaps to reconcile them in a critical discourse which will ideally achieve the claritas of which it speaks. While exposition would seem on the face of it to participate in this consonantia of the ongoing Joycean epiphany, adjusting part to whole in a progressive refinement of comprehension, Stephen's bid to epiphanise his critical thought, if that is indeed what he is up to, would put an end to the verbal round. At one moment in the *Portrait* monologue the transcendence of criticism in an epiphany of thought seems actually to have been achieved: "Stephen paused, and though his companion did not speak, felt that his words had called up around them a thoughtenchanted silence" (218). The "though" here is odd, since it is precisely the muteness of Stephen and Lynch which reveals and sets the seal on the "thoughtenchanted silence." Is Stephen so obsessed with logomachy that he is incapable of recognising an epiphany when he is having one? Does he privately doubt that verbal structures can ever be brought to a form of non-verbal perfection? "What I have said...," he continues, in full academic mode, breaking the silence to continue the adjustment of his critical instrument, "refers to beauty in the wider sense of the word, in the sense which the word has in the literary tradition. In the marketplace it has another sense." Differentiation, adjustment of part to part, criticism as composition, consonantia in perpetuity. In *Stephen Hero*, Stephen breaks the silence with awkward humour:

> Having finished his argument, Stephen walked on in silence. He felt Cranly's hostility and he accused himself of having cheapened the eternal images of beauty. For the first time too, he felt slightly awkward in his friend's company and to restore a mood of flippant familiarity he glanced up at the clock of the ballast Office and smiled:
> — It has not epiphanized yet, he said. [*SH* 190]

Here there is no "thoughtenchanted silence" to be dissipated by further speech, merely a sense of intellectual betrayal and social failure. The theory, in being related to the real world of objects, is gently ridiculed and condemned to repeat itself as theory. And if the presentation of epiphany was intended to work as an epiphany, it has turned out instead to be an episode in the ongoing narrative of Stephen's development, a part to be related to another part in the hope of eventually revealing the

Press, 1988) Derek Attridge refers to the *Wake*'s "denial of the logic of opposites" (202), and in arresting the Thomistic epiphany at its second term, the episodic epiphany might be said to present a "logic of opposites" minus the logic, or a confrontation of statement and anti-statement without the synthesis, an unviable yet persistent state which hesitates between self-assertion and self-cancellation as possible solutions to its inconclusive engagement with dialectic as a principle of active understanding.

Portrait of the artist as aesthetic object, epiphanised by his work. As such, the episode and the work of which it is a part, cries out for criticism.

Stephen's mockery of the clock (which is also mockery of himself as a theory-addicted subject who hesitates to epiphanise) retracts the moves which have been made towards claritas, opening a space for criticism to fill. A similarly inviting space is opened by the break in the text in *Portrait*, which turns Stephen's talk with Lynch into an episode by dividing it from the following section in which Stephen composes his villanelle.[3] Just before the divide we have the description of the girls on the steps of the colonnade seeing out the "the few last raindrops." This paragraph was drawn from the epiphany collected as number twenty-five, but in the *Portrait* its self-revealing sufficiency (or perhaps the moment which it reveals) is not enough to satisfy the needs of narrative, and it is immediately followed by a contextualising passage of criticism provided by Stephen: "And what if had judged her harshly? If her life were a simple rosary of hours..." (221). And then we have the break in the text which reinforces its episodic nature and obliges the reader to step into the breach and play the critic. If Dedalus hesitates between consonantia and claritas, between letting the revelation stand and refining it further, so does the Joycean text. Narrative and the criticism it sponsors here suggest a certain diffidence before the epiphany as revelation. Perhaps, after all, we are more interested in meaning than revelation, in signifying rather than signification, and this may have been Jacques Lacan's point when he responded to Joyce's famous professor-baiting remark about the puzzles he was putting into *Ulysses*.[4] "Ces gens," wrote Lacan, meaning the professors, "sont uniquement occupés à résoudre les enigmes, au minimum à savoir pourquoi Joyce a mis ça là. Ils trouvent toujours une raison—il a mis ça là, parce qu'il y a juste après un autre mot." This "autre mot" points to the consonantia in criticism, the balancing of part to part, the procession from word to word.

---

[3] Interestingly, in *Stephen Hero* the "Villanelle of the Temptress" is mentioned before Stephen's exposition of his epiphany theory (see page 188). If in *Portrait*, the composition of the villanelle is inspired by Stephen's epiphanic waking, in Stephen Hero it is inspired by an actual epiphany—the Eccles' Street flirtation between the drawling Young Lady and the all but inaudible Young Man. While in the later version the object of inspiration is extra-textual, in the earlier work it is present as text, the epiphany, as it were, refuses to be displaced by the poem which it inspires. The two versions taken together, then, give us the object of inspiration and the composition of the finished poem; the narrative of this poem's creation, its consonantia, is spread across the two books, while its claritas, its presence, is squeezed into textual absence.

[4] It is interesting that Joyce should have made such remarks in relation to *Ulysses* and not *Finnegans Wake* which would seem, at first sight at least, to be by far the more baffling book. We might speculate that Joyce considered academia to have been completely overtaken and routed in the shift of writing practice between the two books. It will be one of my contentions that the structures which make such riddling possible in *Ulysses* are no longer present in the *Wake*.

There will always be in criticism another word which justifies the last, and Stephen's "though," which reveals his expectation that Lynch will consecrate with speech the epiphanic "thoughtenchanted silence," betrays his own uneasiness before the moment as instant rather than episode. Stephen represses his symptom by displacing it onto Lynch, and his malaise might be compared with Sartre's account of Roquentin's need to master the indescribable: "Ca ne pouvait pas se décrire, il aurait fallu pronocer très vite: 'C'est un jardin public, l'hiver, un matin de dimanche'" (64). The claritas of epiphany, in transcending narrative, annihilates the sequentiality of description and cuts directly, as it were, to the final scene: all parts must work together as the whole, the linear axis which makes the other word possible is exchanged for a supercharged present which, according to Roquentin at least, is a source of joy:

> Tout s'est arrêté; ma vie s'est arrêtée: cette grande vitre, cet air lourd, bleu comme de l'eau, cette plante grasse at blanche au fond de l'eau, et moi-même, nous formons un tout immobile et plein: je suis heureux.[5]

Roquentin's joy is founded on a double suspension—of linear time and of the distinction between subject and object—a double victory over the kind of hesitation Stephen and the tripartite Thomistic epiphany is subject to in Joyce's texts. Roquentin's withdrawal from the episodic nature of experience represents a decisive move beyond consonantia, a move which seems to be beyond the powers of Stephen, and the "full, static whole" he declares himself to form with the rest of his visible universe serves to evoke a second problematic of the Joycean epiphany.

AGENCY IN BETWEEN

Alongside the hesitation in the Joycean epiphany between consonantia and claritas, meaning and revelation, there is a confusion of agency: we are not sure who or what does what to what or whom. In the act or process of epiphany, it is difficult to be clear about the positions and roles of subject and object, which is active and which is passive in the transaction. This uncertainty about the relative positions of subject and object will, as we shall see, loom large in the evolution of Joyce's work towards a mode of writing pitched beyond the epiphanic, where we will be faced with the possibility that subject and object no longer have any fixed positions of their own.[6] Let us for the moment address it as the

[5] Jean-Paul Sartre, *La nausée* (Paris: Le livre de poche, 1965) 84.

[6] In "Mind your Genderous: Toward a *Wake* Grammar" (*New Light on Joyce from the Dublin Symposium*, ed. Fritz Senn, Bloomington: Indiana University Press, 1972) Strother B. Purdy refocuses attention on the sentence as a unit of meaning in *Finnegans Wake*. His provisional grammar of the *Wake* is derived from a set of "selection restrictions" which exert downward pressure on the number of readings possible for each morpheme within a sentence. These restrictions are themselves based on context, which is a spatio-temporal model reliant on a logic of proximity: that which has the greatest influence on the meaning of any unit is that

second of our three problematics, and attempt to isolate the most interesting questions it raises about the hypothesis of the post-epiphanic in Joyce. We might begin by asking why, if in *Stephen Hero* Stephen defines the epiphany as a "sudden spiritual manifestation" (*SH* 188), do the two set-piece discussions of the concept staged in that book and its successor revolve around a clock and a butcher's basket?

In scholastic epistemology, confusions or doubts concerning the question of what is in us and what is beyond us, the nature of the relation between subject and object, invariably served as proofs of the existence of God, an all-knower beyond the scene, an exemplary epistemological plenitude to stand against the relative emptiness of the conclusions which secular philosophy was capable of reaching. The concept of epiphany stands at the centre of such issues, and we would do well perhaps in discussing Joyce to imagine the possibility of a secular epiphany which, like its theological counterpart, intervenes at the point of intersection between epistemology and aesthetics, subject and object, but which does not entail a proof for the existence of God. In the secular epiphany, revelation is philosophical or psychological rather than divine, a function of the subject's relationship to its objects. God as all-knower is beyond causality, but the subject and object groping towards the revelation of epiphany are lost in epistemological doubt and confusion. Causality, as a line of force transmitting itself from agent to reagent warps into a multi-directional and perhaps even circular play of tensions. Is it the subject who epiphanises the object through an adjustment of spiritual focus precisely calibrated to the unique qualities of the object? Or does the object reveal itself ontologically to the subject under certain specific conditions of attention and desire? Do subject and object work together? Do they compete? Or is epiphany an accident or

which is closest in space and time to the unit in question, hence Purdy's emphasis on the sentence. The assumption is that we understand language and the world sequentially; when the sequence is broken we are required to make a leap of understanding if we are to keep hold of meaning. The sentence provides a mediate check on this expanding sequence, permitting us to grasp its developing structure in convenient bits. Epiphany, however, offers a challenge to this episodic epistemology, raising meaning to revelation through the suspension of sequence and context. Within *claritas* it is not possible to think in terms of sequence and units. Revelation, indeed, might be defined as meaning without context, a form of knowledge that is unlimited by further proximate forms. While we do indeed employ contextuality as a tool in our attempts to read *Finnegans Wake*, its utility (or even validity), I would suggest, is severely compromised by the posthumous nature of the text's epiphanic project. The contextlessness projected by epiphany overbalances into a form of total contextuality, where the arbitrariness of any attempt to elect one thing as the context of another is so apparent that selection takes on an ironic, or even sardonic, inflection. While the text is divided into sentences articulated by conventional punctuation, the link between the unit and the sequence it serves is wholly conjectural; in spite of the sequential structure we don't know where to start. Purdy himself admits that he is intimidated by infinity (see page 60) and that his desire to limit each morpheme to one meaning is motivated by resistance to the almost infinitesimal number of possible combinations (see page 63). His grammar, we might say, is inspired by anxiety, which is itself triggered by the persistence of meaning in the *Wake* of revelation.

cognitive quirk along the lines of the common yet unnerving experience of déjà vu?

Stephen seems to imagine a collaborative effort, as if subject and object achieve epiphany together by pooling their resources, each complimenting the other as active and passive partner in a pragmatic exchange designed to provoke a manifestation of transcendent beauty. Working from the butcher's basket, he tells Lynch that "your mind first of all separates the basket from the rest of the visible universe which is not the basket. The first phase of apprehension is a bounding line drawn around the object to be apprehended." (*SH* 333-4). This is clear enough, the subject acts on the object. But then the object seems to respond in kind: "you pass from point, to point, led by its formal lines" (*SH* 334) Stephen tells Lynch, and agency is reversed as the object takes the subject on a tour of its formal contours. The subject here, it would seem, is acted on. In the final phase of apprehension the status of active partner again seems to be divided between the two. The moment of claritas is qualified as the "instant wherein that supreme quality of beauty, the clear radiance of the aesthetic image, is apprehended luminously by the mind which has been arrested by its wholeness and fascinated by its harmony" (*SH* 334). The subject as mind apprehends the object which has arrested and fascinated it. Whose, then, is the epiphany, since both seem to have caused it? Morris Beja employs an open construction to cover this mystery when he gives a "general working definition" of the epiphany as:

> a sudden spiritual manifestation, whether from some object, scene, event, or memorable phase of the mind—the manifestation being out of proportion to the significance or strictly logical relevance of whatever produces it.[7]

The "from" here leaves us wondering whether the object in the light of the subject is capable of such a manifestation, just as the subject may manifest its spirituality suddenly in the light of God. This recessive structure, whereby God may apprehend the epiphany of the subject who may apprehend the epiphany of the object would simplify if not annihilate our problematic (though we would be left to discover what it is that may manifest its spirituality in the light of a butcher's basket), but it hardly helps with the divided agency we have noticed in Stephen's account. The word "whatever" in the second part of Beja's definition serves only to confirm its openness. Close attention to the verbs used by Stephen in his account of epiphany would lead us to dispute Beja's claim that Joyce's treatment of the epiphany effects a transition from "revelation by the object to insight on the part of the subject."[8] The object's power to arrest the subject and declare itself a formal whole seems already to

[7] Morris Beja, *Epiphany in the Modern Novel* (London: Peter Owen, 1971) 18.
[8] Beja, *Epiphany*, 77.

spoil the neatness of this formulation. To go along with Beja's partition-
ing of subject and object one would have to read Stephen's attribution
of agency to his objects purely as a figure of speech, an instance of
pathetic fallacy. But can we ever be sure that Stephen is being purely
rhetorical in his accounts of epiphanising objects? Trace pathetic fallacy
as rhetorical gesture back to its origins in animist belief, and the metaphysical problems which Beja would seem to leave out leap back into
Joyce's language. The text, any text, like the object in Stephen's account, has the power to arrest the subject which apprehends it, just as it
has the power to hesitate between the rhetorical and the metaphysical.
In the prehistory of its career as a figure of speech, the pathetic fallacy,
we might say, was an instance of pure textuality.

The pathetic fallacy, I would suggest, is actually a very appropriate
choice of rhetorical figure for any discussion of the epiphany since it
takes us to the heart of that mysterious manifestation of the object in
the light of the subject, which may equally be the reverse. The fact that
it is a verbal form should also serve to remind us that the problematics
of the Joycean epiphany are essentially linguistic. The butcher's basket,
like the Ballast Office clock, is a linguistic textual object. Stephen does
not know how to formulate his description of the epiphany, he hedges
his bets, hiding behind the rhetoric of exposition; he lets himself go, as
he does again in "Scylla and Charybdis."[9] His account plays on its own
textuality and this inevitability of speech again serves to bring us closer
to the problematic of the epiphany—its inter-involvement of subject and
object.

If the secular epiphany is to remain so, it must struggle against a
metaphysics of the textual object, and in the way Stephen's epiphany
speeches acknowledge and play off their social context we can detect
the tension inherent in a theory of transcendent beauty which must not
however be allowed to transcend. The fraught encounter of subject and
object in Stephen's exposition and in the Joycean epiphany itself is a
struggle for an aesthetics of grace stripped of God. It involves, as William T. Noon notes, a subjective extension to the objective parameters
of Thomist aesthetics:

[9] Where we have the feeling that Stephen's text is running away with him and that he is
caught between the generation of material as meaning and its mastery as revelation. His
inward comment expresses his fear of never -ending consonantia, of being permanently
arrested on the cusp of claritas: "What the hell are you driving at? / I know. Shut up. Blast
you. I have reasons" (170). Stephen asks himself if he has been "condemned to do this"
(170), and his question takes us back to Father Arnall's sermon in *Portrait*. By rejecting the
biblical hell with his satanic non serviam, Stephen confirms his submissiveness to the scrip-
tures as text. One may separate oneself from faith as a conscious state of mind, but the
textuality of one's former belief lives on in language and iconography. The subtext of non
serviam, then, might be "I will serve (the signifiers of the church)." The biblical hell which
Stephen has rejected has been replaced, perhaps, by a discursive hell where the pain of loss
as evoked by father Arnall becomes the subtler torment of consonantia, an eternity of studying the formal qualities of the object, of being led on from part to part, without ever pushing
through to a realisation of its whatness.

The Scholastics for their part have almost always spoken, as Aquinas does, of integrity, proportion (consonantia), and clarity as objective qualities, or existential properties, in things, and though they may not always have been very clear as to whether these existential qualities belong to the things represented by the work of art or inhere in the representation, they have not treated these qualities as though they belong to the act of apprehension, as Stephen does.[10]

Stephen describes the "luminous silent stasis of aesthetic pleasure," or claritas, as a "spiritual state" (SH 334), and in this we can hear how difficult it is for him to pursue his quest for ideal beauty without falling into emotional states or stances characteristic of religious belief. The problematic of the subject and the object in the epiphany is grafted onto Stephen's bid to secularise his vision of divine beauty. The admixture of fin de siècle aestheticism in his "applied Aquinas," however, leads him paradoxically to spiritualise his secular account of beauty (notwithstanding his rejection of "symbolism" as a possible analogue for claritas), and a confusion of categories ensues in which the apostate Stephen encounters spirituality where the Christian philosophers found only beautiful objects. These spiritual habits or needs are ingrained enough to animate him even when reality makes its strongest bid to convince him of its brute objectivity. I am thinking of the moment in "Proteus" where he attempts to penetrate beyond the "ineluctable modality of the visible" only to discover a "world without end" (U 3.28-9) which is independent of his subjective perspective and which insists ineluctably on the material dimension of its existence. Throughout Ulysses Stephen seems to be in urgent need of a new conceptual context in which he may thrill to the luminosity of the revealed object, and gloomily realistic about the remote chance of ever finding one.

AFTER CLARITAS?

A third problematic raised by the Joycean epiphany is simply the question "What succeeds it?" or, more precisely, "What can succeed it?" If this mysterious relationship of subject to object in language can be brought to this mysterious but revelatory point of climax called claritas, what happens afterwards, given that language itself is bound to continue? While the epiphany in its various forms has been used extensively as a formal and conceptual model in Joyce criticism,[11] have we suffi-

[10] William T. Noon, Joyce and Aquinas, (North Haven: Archon Books, 1970) 45.
[11] From William T. Noon's Joyce and Aquinas, through Hugh Kenner's Dublin's Joyce (New York: Columbia University Press, 1987) to Jacques Aubert's The Aesthetics of James Joyce (Baltimore: Johns Hopkins University Press, 1992). More recently, we can find Laurent Milesi arguing in his introduction to James Joyce and the Difference of Language that the epiphany as a form of linguistic expression survives as a trace element in Joyce's ultimate work: "One may even still register something of the former epiphany in the multi-layered portmanteau word or syntactico-rhythmic modulations of the Wake's nonce-idiom." Laurent Milesi, ed. James Joyce and the Difference of Language (Cambridge: Cambridge University Press, 2003) 2.

ciently considered the possibility that certain later phases of Joyce's writing are specifically post-epiphanic? The transitions between Joyce's major works (most crucially between *Ulysses* and *Finnegans Wake*) pose interesting problems of discontinuity, which may be governed at least in part by the changing nature of the subject-object relationship within the rise and fall of the epiphanic epistemology and its inscription.

If there is an afterwards to the epiphany, chrono-logic dictates that it will be a consequence of claritas. The post-epiphanic, if indeed it exists, occurs when the "luminous silent stasis" of claritas fades, is reconfig-ured or succeeded. When meaning passes into the revelation of the subject or the object, or of each in the light of the other, something happens perhaps which makes it possible to imagine an afterwards. This something is more inevitable, it would appear, and therefore more con-ceivable within the limited context of the linguistic epiphany. In the light of post-Saussurean linguistics it is easier to imagine language carrying on beyond a point of maximal lucidity. The signifier, we are told by Derrida and Lacanian psychoanalysis, will carry on regardless; while writing, in spite of a mounting scepticism or indifference to its own functionality, persists in its bid to place subjects in relation with objects and thus cre-ate meaning. Epiphanic writing strives to bring this relation to a state of perfection, convinced that the nearer it attains to this goal the more definitive will be the meaning it produces. If the linguistic epiphany, brings subject and object into some kind of revelatory focus, perfects their relation in some way, we might well wonder where writing can go afterwards, given that in the *Wake* of this perfection it is obliged by the signifier to go somewhere.

This becomes clear if we return to the pathetic fallacy and recover it from its prehistoric origins in animist belief, reinstating it in the present as a rhetorical figure. Claritas, we have seen, sets a limit to the rhetori-cal mode of presenting one thing in terms of something else; whatever happens to the subject and object in epiphany, it is beyond the scope of the pathetic fallacy. The transposition of qualities from object to subject or vice versa is superseded by the manifestation of the subject's or ob-ject's whatness. While we can trace the pathetic fallacy back to its origins in magical belief, it remains to be seen whether we can project it beyond the epiphany, where its survival depends on the new configura-tions of subject-to-object relations in post-epiphanic language. One of the characteristics of such a language may well, then, be its post-rhetoricity, its shift into a mode beyond figuration in which writing must carry on without the facility to speak of one thing in terms of another. In *Finnegans Wake*, for example, it is impossible to identify metaphors with any certainty, while metonymy is dispersed into a general fragmentation of the substantive—the object which names the subject by association is also, more often than not, a new subject. The space in which figuration normally operates has been crowded out with indeterminate forms. Tak-ing its cue, perhaps, from the "Aeolus" chapter of *Ulysses*, *Finnegans*

Wake seems to glory in the condition of rhetoric as a repertoire of exhausted forms.

Another indication of this crisis of rhetoricity, perhaps, is the chiasmus, a figure which jumbles its terms and says again in reverse what has already been said, seeking to squeeze a supplement of meaning out of the gesture of repetition. In Joyce, the chiasmus signals the imminent collapse of signification into epiphanic revelation, the moment where consonantia brings its tour of the object's formal features back to the point of departure. Part IV of *Portrait* ends with Stephen's epiphanic ramble on the beach at Dollymount, where he encounters the girl who is like a bird. As he analyses the contours of her beauty in an erotic consonantia, Stephen falls into the chiasmus: "Her bosom was a bird's soft and slight, slight and soft as the breast of some darkplumaged dove" (175). Apart from the refinement of the bird into the 'darkplumaged dove," the second half of the sentence repeats the first. Language is wheeling around its object, its forward movement has been arrested, and the suspension announces the silent stasis of claritas. Which we never see, of course, since this last rhetorical gasp leaves the girl fluttering metaphorically in the shallows.

Having had his vision, Stephen retires to the dunes and falls asleep in ecstasy. His passage out of consciousness is described in hallucinatory terms and includes an exploding chiasmus: "A world, a glimmer or a flower? Glimmering and trembling, trembling and unfolding, a breaking light, an opening flower, it spread in endless succession to itself, breaking in full crimson and unfolding and fading to palest rose, leaf by leaf and wave of light by wave of light, flooding all the heavens with its soft flashes every flush deeper than the other" (177). This is rhetoric without an object and is one stage closer to claritas than the description of the wading girl; it is epiphanic writing pregnant with the post-epiphanic. The chiasmus, as variation on a strictly limited theme, is coming apart here ; in its ecstatic and despairing attempt to bind the signifier to the signified it hints, perhaps, at what writing might be like, how it might perform, on the far side of claritas.

The epiphanic writing we have seen so far suggests a post-epiphanic mode without actually writing it. While claritas itself seems to be unwritable, we might at least ask how it functions as a point of transition or transitional blank between what comes before and after. The epiphany of the clock or the basket (or of any object in fact) projects a radical equivalence of things (a term which here includes both subjects and objects) where everything is as real as everything else since everything may become the subject of its own epiphany. Claritas, as the moment of the revelation of the whatness of a subject or object is naturally, filled with this object or subject ; coterminous with this whatness, it is an autonomous and exclusive state in which the object or subject, in signifying itself, excludes everything else, including the signifier. According to Stephen's account, the subject is, up to a point, responsible for the epiphany of an object which it perceives. Beyond this point the object shows itself as radiant to the scrutinizing subject who experiences knowledge of its whatness as absolute beauty. But the object at this point has moved a crucial step beyond signification ; it may be what it is, but it cannot be represented as such, least of all by the scrutinising subject, whose minute study of its form is only a prelude to claritas. In moving beyond signification, the object has also, in a sense, moved beyond form, which cannot survive its own epiphany. Is it, perhaps, resistance to this terrifying potential of the epiphanised object (which, like the wading girl in *Portrait*, threatens to explode signification by over-signifying itself) which guides Joyce's writing toward the post-epiphanic, which might then be conceived as an experimental mode for testing the hypothesis that form and signification do survive claritas, albeit in altered states? Or is this resistance really the signifier's, which is condemned to perpetuate itself in the eternal experiment of signification to which claritas stands in the relation of a limit which must be loquaciously repressed?

ARRESTING THE NAME AND BEING OTHER
The object is subjectless in its whatness: Stephen can admire the radiance of the epiphanised object, but the object itself is monopolised by its own whatness ; signification continues at the margins of revelation, before and possibly afterwards. In the objectless epiphany, the subject similarly monopolises the ontological field, becoming all that is, subject and object plural, and acceding to that undifferentiated totality of presence from which writing seeks to abstract particular cases of subjectivity. We can glean a hint of this from epiphany number four, which moves towards a revelation of the subject as the incomparable object to which everything must nevertheless be compared:

> [Dublin: on Mountjoy Square] Joyce — (concludes)... That'll be forty thousand pounds. Aunt Lillie — (titters) — O, laus!... I was like that too......... When I was a girl I was sure I'd marry a lord... or something... Joyce — (thinks) — Is it possible she's comparing herself with me?[12]

As one of the 1902-1904 epiphanies, this dialogue predates the formulation of the theory of the epiphany as we find it in Stephen's fictional account in *Portrait*,[13] it may also, in that case, predate the theory. Instead of a subject and an object as in the fictional scenarios imagined by Joyce and theorised by Stephen, what we have here are subjects and language. If, at this early stage in Joyce's career, something is to progress towards epiphany, it can only be one or perhaps both of the subjects. It is too soon to speak of an object achieving claritas or the

---

[12] Joyce, *Poems and Shorter Writings*, 164.
[13] Though it might coincide with the drafting of *Stephen Hero*, which, according to Theodore Spencer's introduction, took place between 1901-1906 (12).

epiphany of language itself. The final line takes us into the mind of "Joyce," which immediately envelops Aunt Lillie and readies itself to become the subject of the epiphany-in-the-making: "Is it possible she's comparing herself to me?" The Joyce who writes has sought to reveal the Joyce who is written and the "me" at the end of the piece marks the moment at which the two Joyces come together to be jointly absorbed into a subject which strains the limits of the signifier "Joyce." The "me" here, in its scale and appetite, is gargantuan, capable of absorbing Aunt Lillie, the "lord or something," the forty thousand pounds, the social jest and the sociological truths it vectors, Mountjoy Square and the whole of Dublin. All the subject and object matter of the sketch is absorbed by the "me" and integrated as an approximation of its whatness. As it passes beyond signification this approximation is in turn absorbed by its object, as the whatness of "me" marks an end to writing as a process of differentiation. The epiphanic trajectory here reverses the dynamic of the legend which Stephen writes on the flyleaf of his geography book in *Portrait*, where the subject undergoes atomic dispersal into the maximum of matter:

Stephen Dedalus
Class of Elements
Clongowes Wood College
Sallins
County Kildare
Ireland
Europe
The World
The Universe

[*P* 15-16]

The young Stephen experiments chiastically with this text, first reading it backwards, as if to try out the epiphanic potential of his own name encountered at the top of a list beginning with the Universe, and then forwards again, passing beyond the limits of matter into the presence of God: "It was very big to think about everything and everywhere. Only God could do that" (*P* 183). For the jejune schoolboy under the tutelage of the jesuits, nothing could be bigger than God, as every whatness, whether of subject or object, is subsumed by His singularity expressed by the sublime tautology "and God's real name was God" (*P* 184). The apostate post-adolescent who speaks through the epiphanies names himself as God ; the "me" of epiphany number four is subject to nothing beyond itself, which is to say that it is subject and object, sufficient unto itself. But God and ego as they appear in these early works gradually give way to something else (which I hesitate to name) as the epiphanic mode of revelation is itself subjected to a range of linguistic experiments which project the subject-object duality into a subject-object identity, where no single thing, subject or object, is coincident with itself. Post-epiphany, it is no longer possible to establish these hierarchical trajectories of revelation leading to God or to "me"; there is no longer a single biggest thought or a single biggest thing which may be expected to manifest itself at the end of writing.

In contrast to the epiphany of Joyce as "me" and the anti-epiphany of Stephen as atom in the Universe as thought by God, we might turn to Bloom's play on his own name as revealed through the cosmic neutrality of "Ithaca." Here there is no question of the hyperbolic ego or of God as all-subject absorbing the world as object ; revelation as reduction to one whatness is replaced by a playful inquiry by the subject into the possibilities of being other. Derek Attridge registers throughout *Ulysses* "a questioning of the straightforward blending of a mind and a body in a unity that can be called by a single proper name or pronoun,"[14] and it is a certain ontological restlessness in the face of this singular unity consecrated by the name which inspires Bloom's experiment in self-extension. Post-epiphanic style (I have named it) enters the field as the principle of plurality in language which allows writing to continue in the face of an epiphanic revelation of singularity:

What anagrams had he made on his name in youth ?

Leopold Bloom
Ellpodbomool
Molldopelboob
Bollopedoom
Old Ollebo, M.P. [*U* 11.404-09]

In order to live the epiphany of himself as artist according to his tripartite Thomistic scheme, Stephen must first of all distinguish himself as a separate thing in the world, and while the name would seem essential to this process, it is also the point at which he is most vulnerable to the interventions of the signifier as abstract combinatory potential. While Stephen's swoon towards the end of Chapter IV of *Portrait* is brought on by the ecstatic revelation of the bird girl, it might also be seen as a narcoleptic episode triggered by permutations on his name shouted out by Shuley, Ennis and Connolly: "Stephanos," "The Dedalus," "Bous Stephanoumenos," "Bous Stephaneforos," "Stephanos Dedalos" (*P* 300-1). While Stephen's subjective experience focuses to a point of unparalleled clarity, provoking a union with the object pitched beyond the range of language, he must grapple with a renewed sense of himself as a subject in language, the bearer of a name as primary signifier which may be arrested in its progress through the linear logic of the epiphany by the manipulations, multiplications and substitutions of an Other whose otherness is irremediable. Bloom by contrast seems happy to exploit the transitional space between himself and his image as represented by his

[14]   Attridge, *Peculiar Language*, 187.

name; the game is to multiply the transformative potentia of the name as signifier, the objective perhaps being to render his self-image as protean as style. To exploit the structural and associative resources of "Bloom" rather than propel it towards a revelation of its essence. With the exception of the first and possibly the last names in the list, his anagrams might equally be the names of objects and this might be taken as an indication of how writing on the far side of epiphany harbours an indifference to the distinction between subject and object which aligns it in a curious sense with the moment of claritas which it succeeds. If the revelation of whatness collapses the distinction between subject and object, post-epiphanic style seems grudgingly to acknowledges this distinction as a trace element in a writing practice it has inherited and must adapt to a new set of conditions.

POLYKINESIS

Let us return, in the light of this projected realm of the post-epiphanic, to the second of our key problematics, which revolves around the relative positions and valencies of subject and object in the epiphany. Morris Beja writes that in his epiphanic writing:

> Joyce's emphasis is generally on the perceiving consciousness, the subject who actively adjusts his "spiritual" vision to focus on the object, which in turn is "epiphanised." Realizing this point helps us to understand Joyce's attitude toward epiphany, which is related to his whole view of the act of perception and consequently to his aesthetic theory. His stress on the perceiver is in line... with the general development in epistemology from an emphasis on the object that reveals itself, fundamentally through God's grace, to an emphasis on the role of man's mind and imagination: from revelation by the object to insight on the part of the subject.[15]

Hugh Kenner, in *Dublin's Joyce*, disagrees: "it is radically impossible to understand what Joyce is talking about from the standpoint of the post-Kantian conviction that the mind imposes intelligibility upon things."[16] The question "whose epiphany is it?," which is one way of summarising the apparent disagreement between Beja and Kenner, only makes sense before claritas, when the subject and object retain the capacity to signify each other and remain distinct, either ontologically in the world or linguistically as grammatical elements in a sentence. It is, in this sense, a proleptic question, and should be written "whose claritas will it be?"; but attribution is no longer conceivable in a realm where possession of and possession by complete each other and cancel each other out in the same movement. Post-epiphanic language, which is predicated on the unaskability of the question, voices from the far side of nonsense the perpetuity of the signifier and the persistence of subject and object in

15 Beja, *Epiphany in the Modern Novel*, 77.
16 Kenner, *Dublin's Joyce*, 138.

new inter-involved configurations. In Epiphany number four the creative Joycean ego gives a clamorous reply to the above question: "me" it says, "this claritas will be mine!" Bloom's new names speak back to the Joycean "me" from the other side of claritas, bearing witness to the nonsensicality of ego assertion in a realm where language either plays on the distinction between subject and object, or bypasses it completely. Bloom's onomastic burst of post-epiphanic style says "Ours!" to all of those questions which will no longer be askable. In *Finnegans Wake*, rather surprisingly, the name of the subject is once again at issue: the trajectory I have sketched above and which is characterised by the un-asking of the question "who is who?" is, against all expectations of continuity, reversed. The compulsive and apparently aberrant re-asking of a question whose philosophical grounding seemed to have been finally swept away in the dispersal of Stephen and the ludicrous multiplication of Bloom is perhaps the key discontinuity in the transition from *Ulysses* to the *Wake*.[17] We have seen that this transition which, to reiterate my basic position, I am theorising as a shift from the epiphanic to the post-epiphanic mode, entails the displacement of the singularity of revelation by a principle of plurality in style. The question of the subject, like all other elements carried over from the history of writing into the *Wake*, is subject to this principle. While the *Wake*, then, re-asks the question of the subject's name, it does this within a post-epiphanic framework; and rather than re-launch an epiphanic progression towards the revelation of a subject's perfection, in the manner of Stephen Dedalus, it theorises and thematises its own capacity to name the subject without inaugurating a categorical exclusion of all that the subject isn't. It stages a self-defeating bid to save naming as a grammatical and psychological function, opening and occupying an anxious space of pseudo-identity where the disintegrating neurotic ego constantly falls short of what Lacan identifies as the "delusional metaphor" of psychosis.[18] Suspended between neurosis and psychosis in a realm of indeterminate figuration, the *Wake* names without principle. Just as it is imposible to say according to what the *Wake*an subject is named, so we have the impresion that almost any name will do. The notion of a proper name (a name proper to the subject) is no longer tenable in this realm where the naming of the subject can only be accomplished in conjunction with the naming of everything

---

[17] Jacques Aubert traces Joyce's compulsive interest in "Names, those asemantic vocables, signifiers par excellence," to an anxiety he shared with James Clarence Mangan: "Joyce betrayed the same anguish when he decided to sign his private correspondence, not merely his public literary production, 'Stephen Dedalus'" (73).

[18] For Lacan it is the absence of the Name-of-the-Father which triggers the collapse of neurosis into psychosis: "It is the lack of the name-of-the-Father in that place which, by the hole that it opens up in the signified, sets off the cascade of reshapings of the signifier from which the increasing disaster of the imaginary proceeds, to the point at which the level is reached at which signifier and signified are stabilized in the delusional metaphor." *Ecrits, A Selection* (New York: Norton, 1977) 217.

else. This impossibility naturally imposes itself as one of the most urgent aporias of any reading of the *Wake*.

The assertion of the plurality of post-epiphanic style contains a fading echo, perhaps, of what happens during claritas. It allows us to revisit the first two of the three key problematics I have identified in relation to the Joycean epiphany (the hesitation between consonantia and claritas, meaning and revelation; and the confusion of agency between subject and object), with the hope of drawing them together for futher more consolidated consideration. Narrative, consonantia and Lacan's "other word" of criticism all involve a deferral of the ideal presence of the object or subject in claritas. These forms of deferral might remind us of the "improper" arts, the "pornographical or didactic" which Stephen cites in the philosophical preamble to his theory of epiphany in *Portrait*. These arts are inferior according to Stephen because they insp re movement, and this kinesis is opposed to the aesthetic stasis of claritas. Now stasis is also presence, the self-coincidence of the object beyond the minute oscillations pertaining between the sign and the thing, which constitute the kinesis of representation. Claritas, at least in the visua realm, implies a seeing without representation; while in the conceptual realm of language, the object exceeds its name and passes beyond the scope of denotation. Words gravitate around the thing which has "epiphanised" (as Stephen would have it), they can no longer stand in for it; any evocation is fleeting and partial and the subject can no longer entertain the illusion that he or she may lay hold of the world and pass it on through language. A discrepancy opens up between the movement which is inherent to the signifier and the fixity of the thing in its non-episodic existence beyond language: while the signifier moves on, the object or subject is obliged to stay put.[19]

As the thing enters the presence of its whatness, the sequential thought which characterises the kinesis of consciousness is arrested. Beauty is neither in the eye of the beholder nor in the thing beheld, but in the perceptual moment of stasis in which both are clearly involved. Perceiver and perceived, subject and object, are united in an ultimate form of thinghood predicated on the suppression of two forms of absence—narrative and name. As the object's structural relations "coincide with the stages of aesthetic apprehension" (*P* 213), epiphany is simultaneously experienced by the mind as a new way of relating to itself, almost as if the object in namelessness is part of the mind itself. The mind is "raised above desire and loathing" (*P* 209), as Stephen puts it. In this stasis of common presence questions of aetiology become historical (dependent on narrative and its consonantia of meaning); it is no longer possible to ask whether the leap into whatness is dependent on the mind's capacity for suspending the kinesis of sequential consciousness,

---

[19] Freed from the dialectical movement of narrative, "L'objet reste là," wr tes Roland Barthes in relation to the descriptive practice of Alain Robbe-Grillet in "Littérature Objective" in *Essais critiques* (Paris: Editions du Seuil, 1964) 29-30.

whether the object has been perceived into whatness by the mind, or whether the object itself provokes such a reaction in the perceiver.

Stephen says that the true "produces a stasis of the mind," but we might prefer to suppress the kinesis of the verb and say simply that stasis is truth. The epiphany, whatever else it is, is certainly a form of truth; and the post-epiphanic, whatever else it is, is a problematisation of this singular form of truth. Whatness cannot accommodate several truths, and the common presence of subject and object in epiphany cannot be split into two separate but equally valid essences; there is no longer any room for complimentarity or opposition. Style, as I have argued above, is inherently plural and partial and cannot therefore accommodate the True.[20] This plurality does not however imply a return to the kinesis of narrative. Within style, narrative is also plural and partial, and the kinetic which is resolved into stasis by epiphany here becomes polykinesis. If the whatness of epiphany coincides with the true, then in the polykinesis of style this whatness takes on an interrogative rather than a revelatory sense. As we enter an environment in which theory again becomes conceivable, the question "what is that?" or "what could the whatness of that be?" re-occurs with a frequency which rapidly renders theory impracticable. Theory must cope with a constant tension between the need to ask and the need to answer, two needs which epiphany had resolved into one form of rapturous satisfaction. Or rather it must strive to keep this tension constant in the face of an accelerating sense of ignorance, a burgeoning epistemological deficiency which threatens to become overwhelming.

If kinesis is a form of absence susceptible to epiphany, polykinesis is a form of hyperpresence which we may postulate as post-epiphanic. Style plays on the structures which render kinesis susceptible to epiphany, as we have seen with Bloom's variations on his name. It is this playing on (and on) which characterises polykinesis. In the sense that it reveals the whatness of thought in the whatness of the object and wraps up the problematic separation of subject and object in an instance of the true, epiphany stands as some kind of solution or culmination to

---

[20] This association of truth with stasis takes us back to the problem of eternal return and the Viconian structure of the *Wake*. If history is circular and the cycles will repeat themselves to infinity it is difficult to see how it can contain truth, if truth is stasis. In "Ecclesiastes" we can read: "the eye is not satisfied with seeing nor the ear filled with hearing. What has been done is what will be done, and there is nothing new under the sun" (1.8-9). This "nothing new under the sun" might be compared to the Joyce's Viconian notion of the "seim anew" (*FW* 215.23). In the biblical context, eternal return works as a proof of God's monopoly on truth since he is the stasis beyond the revolving system, a singulartity beyond duplication. Without God, eternal return functions as a negative representation of truth as repetition, the return of the same is all the truth there is. Eternal return precludes stasis and the truth of epiphany: the same, or that which is, is constantly renewed (or "anewed"), it is cyclical, but, more importantly, the cycle implies motion. To return to "Ecclesiastes" in the light of the *Wake*'s godlessness, we might say that the senses are not satisfied because they have never perceived whatness, instead they are confronted through post-epiphanic style with an infinite sequence of whats.

the kinesis of consciousness. Style, then, might be seen as an expanding relativisation of this "solution," which multiplies kinesis through play and re-provisionalises the relationship of consciousness to its objects, casting both into a realm of unknowableness which is radical enough to be distinct from mere absence.[21]

As many critics have noticed, while the opening chapters of *Ulysses* might be seen to move towards a manifestation of presence in the classic epiphanic pattern, the stylistic "thickening" which gradually takes over complicates this intial narrative absence with a playful polykinesis.[22] Further attempts at epiphanic transcendence (for example Bloom's orgasm in "Nausicaa" and Stephen's "Nothung" crisis in "Circe") which occur during the burgeoning of style in the latter part of the book, mark points of tension between the epiphanic and the post-epiphanic, and might suggest ways of defining the special kind of difficulty *Ulysses* generates in relation to its readers.

While epiphany transposes the subject and object into a realm of truth which is inaccessible to theory, style plunges this truth into a linguistic environment which is over-productive of alternative forms of unknowableness.[23] The polykinesis of style, one might even say, is dedicated to this overproduction; it takes the subject-object synthesis which I have asociated with claritas and opens it up to hesitation and confusion. In the *Wake* we are not even sure what it is we don't know, and *Ulysses*, through the incursions of style, prepares the ground for this inflationary doubt by teaching us how little we knew about the limitations of our knowledge, how beguiled we had been by the epiphany as a model of literary meaning and satisfaction. Until, as a parodic post-epiphanic echo of the revelation of epiphany, we might imagine theory, or indeed any non-specialised act of reading, etertaining the question: "what is the whatness of what?"

In *A Portrait* Stephen evokes Aristotle's statement that "the same attribute cannot at the same time and in the same connection belong to and not belong to the same subject" (212), and this law of non-

---

21 In distinguishing the effects of the pun from those of the portmanteau word, Derek Attridge notes that in the *Wake* "the context itself is made up of puns and portmanteau words" (*Peculiar Language*, 202). This loss of the bounding line of integritas, which is supposed to separate the thing from everything that it is not, may be taken as a symptom of the polykinesis of style.

22 The classical critical developments of this idea are Karen Lawrence's *The Odyssey of Style in Ulysses* (Princeton: Princeton University Press, 1987), James Maddox's *The Assault on Character in Joyce's Ulysses* (New Brunswick: Rutgers University Press, 1986), both of which draw on Hugh Kenner's notions of the narrative norm in *Dublin's Joyce*. See also Kenner's meditations on objectivity and incursions of subjective style in *Joyce's Voices* (London: Faber and Faber, 1978).

23 While Joyce's earlier writing might be said to move towards "one great [epiphanic] goal," the *Wake* moves in every direction at once, making it impossible, as Attridge states, "to draw out any single thread as central—whether it be plot, time sequence, character, symbolic structure, mythic framework, voice, attitude, dogma, or any of the other threads that run through conventional novels" (*Peculiar Language*, 217).

contradiciton is just one of the totality of philosophical statutes which epiphanic presence renders inadmissible. In passing from consonantia, with its analysis of part to whole relationships, to claritas, epiphany exceeds the recognition of attributes. And while in the epiphanic mode Aristotle's principle is a cornerstone of rationality on which theoretical edifices can be constructed, in the post-epiphanic realm theory becomes something which can only be attempted, something which is purely theoretical. Obliged by language to exist beyond the revelation of its whatness, the subject or object enters a realm of indeterminate irrationality where it is plagued by attributes. In Book Four, for example, as waking is underway, we encounter "A kind of a thinglike," a thing which is one of a kind in its approximation to a thing. A description of sorts is attempted:

> all traylogged then pubably it resymbles a pelvic or some kvind then props an acutebacked quadrangle with aslant off ohahnthenth a wenchyoumaycuddler, lying with her royalirish uppershoes among the theeckleaves. [*FW* 608.22-6]

The "wenchyoumaycuddler" incorporates a "whatyoumaycallit" and thus crystallises the shift from an "it" to a "her" which is engineered by the passage as a whole. The "pubicly" in "pubably" is reinforced by the "pelvic," locating a body within the geometry of the "acutebacked quadrangle," and thus recalling the diagram of ALP's sexual parts in II.ii. The "kind of thinglike" as object is also, then, endowed with body, if we insist on finding a pubis in the "pub" of "pubably." But the "thinglike" resembles ("resymbles"?) a "pelvic" and is thus, in its entirety, only part of a larger body. Just as "pubably" also suggests a place of entertainment rendered adverbial, so the "wenchyoumaycuddler" is also an invitation. To whom, one wonders? While the apparent prostration of this figure underlines the sexual nature of the incitement, it is not to be forgotten that she is also a "whatyoumaycallit," that is a verbal blank, marking the absence of another substantive which is unknown or has been forgotten. She, like the "kind of a thinglike," is there but hardly there at all.

When revelation is no longer at stake, the principle of non-contradiction, implicated as it is in the logic of epiphany, lapses into redundancy. Which is not to say that it disappears from view. The property of whatness along with the conceptual substructure it depends on and all narrative and rhetorical forms typical of the epiphanic mode are carried by language beyond the point at which they culminate in that epistemological apotheosis known as claritas, to be taken up by style and played off against each other as textual memories or noumenal traces, items in a totality of cultural forms which no longer know their place. As we have seen above, the *Wake*, alongside its significant penchant for theoretical discourse,[24] constantly mutliplies the properties of the subject and object beyond the law of non-contradiction, acting as if absence were entirely compatible with presence, juxtaposing a logic of representation submissive to the conventions of sequential narrative and its "one great goal of revelation" with a permissive violation of these conventions conceivably inspired by the example of claritas. This may well be its special form of madness and it is served by the capacity of the signifier to enforce its own form of temporality on the transcendent atemporality projected by claritas:

> Signs are on of a mere by token that wills still to be becoming upon this once a here was world. [*FW* 608.26-8]

Presence will always be written over, and the bastardised "thinglike" along with those indefinable half-objectified bodies (or body parts) will play out their existences in the temporal confusion of a preterite-to-be. After the epiphany, whatness is also its own wasness.

---

[24] I am thinking, for example, of the answer to question eleven in I.vi, particularly 149.11-152.03 and 159.24-167.17. The bulk of I.v with its "exegesis" of the "untitled mamafesta" is also representative of this mode.

VALÉRIE BÉNÉJAM
The Reprocessing of Trash in *Ulysses*: Recycling & (Post)Creation

> In woman's womb word is made flesh but in the spirit of the maker all flesh that passes becomes the word that shall not pass away. This is the postcreation. ["Oxen of the Sun," *U* 14.292-4]

The misunderstanding about "Throwaway" is probably the most meaningful focus in *Ulysses* on an object about to be trashed: at the end of "Lotus Eaters," Bloom gives Bantam Lyons an unwitting tip for the Gold Cup race at Ascot Heath, by telling him he can keep the *Freeman* newspaper he is looking at, because he was just about to "throw it away"; and Bantam Lyons, with his mind bent on races, understands this as a subtle hint to bet on the dark horse of the race, called Throwaway. Bloom might have wanted to keep the paper, but he is ready to give it away to get rid of Bantam Lyons:

> Better leave him the paper and get shut of him.
> —You can keep it, Mr Bloom said.
> —Ascot, Gold cup. Wait, Bantam Lyons muttered. Half a mo. Maximum the second.
> —I was just going to throw it away, Mr Bloom said.
> Bantam Lyons raised his eyes suddenly and leered weakly.
> —What's that? his sharp voice said.
> —I said you can keep it, Mr Bloom answered. I was just going to throw it away that moment. Bantam Lyons doubted an instant, leering: then thrust the outspread sheets back on Mr Bloom's arms.
> —I'll risk it, he said. Here, thanks. [*U* 5.529-41]

Bloom wanted Bantam Lyons to disappear, and Bantam Lyons wanted a tip for the race: the transaction is obviously a success, since they both get what they wanted, and Bloom can keep the newspaper. The message, if there is one, could be phrased in the words of a modern advertising campaign: "Don't trash. Recycle. You'll make a profit."

This incident is the introduction to the "throwaway" motif that will run throughout the book, and it is also the high point of the *Freeman*'s career in *Ulysses*.[1] I find this particular item all the more interesting here since a daily paper is by very definition ephemeral and bound for the trashcan (the very opposite of what is defined in "Oxen of the Sun" as literary creation—"the word that shall not pass away," *U* 14.293-4). Further, the *Freeman* paper is here a commodity whose status is almost immediately defined as "throwaway" or trash.

What is exactly the trajectory of this paper in *Ulysses*? Bloom first mentions buying it in "Calypso," in order to find out the time of Paddy Dignam's funeral;[2] we do not actually see him buying it, but we find out he has done so when the newspaper appears in "Lotus Eaters." There Bloom will successively: roll it into a baton to tap against his trouserleg, thus beating time as he walks along;[3] bring it to his nostrils while he is in the postoffice for a pleasant smell of fresh ink;[4] use it for an idle read to give himself composure when M'Coy asks him about his wife,[5] (except this is when he runs into the Plumtree Potted Meat advertisement,[6] which coincides both with his interest in advertising and with his obsession with Molly's impending adultery and Boylan's imminent "potting of his meat"); use it to hide and read Martha's letter unheeded;[7] and employ it to carry the soap he has just bought from the chemist.[8] Obviously, the paper's main function in the episode is to get Bloom rid of Bantam Lyons. Later on, in "Hades," Bloom will quick y glance at the

---

[1] It is picked up in "Lestrygonians" when Bloom is handed the Elijah "throwaway" he will later throw into the Liffey; and the incident with Bantam Lyons only becomes clear retrospectively, with the disparaging comments in "Cyclops" and the definitive result of the race in the *Evening Telegraph* which Bloom reads in "Eumaeus," to be concluded with its exhaustive recapitulation in "Ithaca," which retrospectively gives us the thorough trajectory of the newspaper and of the throwaway theme (*U* 17.327-41). All references to *Ulysses* are to Hans Walter Gabler's edition (New York: Vintage, 1984), with episode number plus line number in parenthesis.

[2] "What time is the funeral? Better find out in the paper" (*U* 4.542-3).

[3] "As he walked he took the folded Freeman from his sidepocket, unfolded it, rolled it lengthwise in a baton and tapped it at each sauntering step against his trouserleg" (*U* 5.48-50).

[4] "While the postmistress searched a pigeonhole he gazed at the recruiting poster with soldiers of all arms on parade: and held the tip of his baton against his nostrils. smelling freshprinted rag paper" (*U* 5.56-58).

[5] "—Wife well, I suppose? M'Coy's changed voice said.
O, yes, Mr Bloom said. Tiptop, thanks.
He unrolled the newspaper baton idly and read idly:..." (*U* 5.141-3).

[6] "What is home without
Plumtree's Potted Meat?
Incomplete.
With it an abode of bliss" (*U* 5.144-7).

[7] "He drew the letter from his pocket and folded it into the newspaper he carried. Might just walk into her here. The lane is safer" (*U* 5.221-2); "He opened the letter within the newspaper" (*U* 5.237-8); "Having read it all he took it from the newspaper and put it back in his sidepocket" (*U* 5.266-7).

[8] Just after Bantam Lyons thrusts the newspaper sheets on Bloom's arms, "Mr Bloom folded the sheets again to a neat square and lodged the soap in it, smiling" (*U* 5.543-4).

obituaries,[9] and remark: "Inked characters fast fading on the frayed breaking paper" (U 6.160), the double meaning of "characters" allowing here for a pun commenting on the common transient nature of both newspapers and human life—"the word that shall [...] pass" and "all flesh that passes" (U 14.293). Finally, the paper will be used in church to protect Bloom's trousers when he kneels at the funeral: as he comes out of the carriage, Bloom takes the soap out of the paper and replaces the paper where he can easily access it, in his hip pocket,[10] then in the chapel he discreetly drops it to the ground before setting his right knee upon it.[11]

In the end, we realize that the *Freeman* is truly a multi-purpose commodity, or rather that this paper, which seemed by its very nature condemned to a short-lived, transitory use as a simple reminder of the schedule for the funeral, is actually not only read or consulted, but also reprocessed as, in turn: walking-stick, deodorizer, professional inspiration and obsession feeder, letter-holder, time-saver (or magic wand to make Bantam Lyons disappear), betting-tip of course, wrapping-paper, and cushion. Not only does the *Freeman* paper not get trashed, its useful life—to use the current terminology—is maximized, and even considerable profit is envisaged. Unsurprisingly, among Bloom's projects listed in "Ithaca," we find a scheme to acquire wealth through "the utilisation of waste paper" (U 17.1701-2).[12]

The manipulation and varied usages of the *Freeman* in "Lotus Eaters" and "Hades" are truly an illustration of Bloom as a model, creative recycler. His innovative way of looking at objects, his capacity to change the habitual, established viewpoints on them, to picture them in different contexts than their natural ones, in different positions, shapes, or uses— in short, Bloom's imaginative viewpoint—make of him a resourceful recycler. His treatment of the *Freeman* paper shows him successively unrolling it and opening it for a read, rolling it lengthwise and turning it into a baton, folding it neatly into a square to put the soap in, unfolding it again to drop it to the ground, each time changing its location, from his hands, to one of his pockets, to the ground, etc. Such careful reconditioning and repackaging are current processes in the recycling industry, allowing one to maximize the useful life of items, and this is all nicely carried out here thanks to Bloom's meticulousness and inventiveness.

---

[9] "Mr Bloom's glance travelled down the edge of the paper, scanning the deaths: Callan, Coleman, Dignam, Fawcett, Lowry, Naumann, Peake, what Peake is that? is it the chap was in Crosbie and Alleyne's? no, Sexton, Urbright" (U 6.157-60).

[10] "Change that soap now. Mr Bloom's hand unbuttoned his hip pocket swiftly and transferred the paperstuck soap to his inner handkerchief pocket. He stepped out of the carriage, replacing the newspaper his other hand still held" (U 6.494-7).

[11] "Mr Bloom stood behind near the font and, when all had knelt, dropped carefully his unfolded newspaper from his pocket and knelt his right knee upon it. He fitted his black hat gently on his left knee and, holding its brim, bent over piously" (6.585-8).

[12] At the end of "Calypso," one may also remember that half of the "Matcham Masterstroke" prize story is recycled as toilet-paper (U 4.537).

Ulysses provides several examples of Bloom's ingenious recycling. Most obviously, there are the references to the second-hand clothes business run by the Blooms.[13] In his work as an ad-canvasser, we also notice—particularly with the House of Keyes example—how he will easily borrow images or slogans and think of reusing them in different contexts.[14] In a way, the very first introduction we get to "Mr Bloom" in "Calypso" ("Mr Bloom ate with relish the inner organs of beasts and fowls." etc.), has prepared us for such a tendency. His taste for kidneys, the pleasure he takes in thus recycling the physiologica trash—or excrement—, are from the start given as his idiosyncratic particularity.[15] Indeed, if we read again Bloom's scheme to make money n "Ithaca," we realize the complete formula runs as follows: "The utilisation of waste paper, fells of sewer rodents, human excrement" (*U* 17.1701-2). Such innovative inversion (or perversion) may very well be at the core of his inventiveness as model recycler.

Speaking of perversions, we might also consider Bloom's sex life as obeying a logic of recycling, when in his resourcefulness he always devises new ways of enjoying that which others would deem out of their reach or lost. This is made possible, for one, by his voyeurism—noticeable as soon as he catches sight of a woman, at the butcher's,[16] or coming out of a jaunting car,[17] but most strikingly exemplified in "Circe," by his fantasy of watching Molly and Boylan's sexual intercourse through a keyhole.[18] Besides, we often see him relishing the sight, or smell, or just the thought, of Molly's discarded underwear, and indeed, fetishism allows him to enjoy the now discarded garments that have first been put on "for him, for..." Boylan. And these two perversions are nicely complemented by masochism, as gradually becomes clear from the correspondance between Bloom's first name, his more than ambivalent obsession with his wife's infidelity, and several allusions to Leopold Sacher-Masoch's *Venus in Furs*.[19] Indeed, fetishism, voyeurism and masochism all make it possible for Bloom to vicariously draw

---

[13] Cf. "the other business" (*U* 11.487). See also the references to clothes in "Penelope," which show Molly easily envisages cutting-up and patching-up operations on her old clothes, and remarks how clothes that seem to be ready to be thrown away may easily come into fashion again. In general, Molly tends to disrupt the traditional hierarchy between trash and new commodities (cf. *U* 18.513-18 about clothes shops).

[14] Cf. the "HOUSE OF KEY(E)S" section at the beginning of "Aeolus" (*U* 7.141-63).

[15] "Most of all he liked grilled mutton kidneys which gave to his palate a fine tang of faintly scented urine" (*U* 4.4-5).

[16] Cf. "the nextdoor girl" (*U* 4.146-190).

[17] Cf. *U* 5.98-140.

[18] Cf. *U* 15.3756-816.

[19] See *U* 15.1046 for an explicit allusion. Also in "Circe," Molly claims she is in her "pelt," meaning both literally that she is naked, and connotatively that she is wearing furs, as in Leopold Sacher-Masoch's *Venus im Pelz*. For a thorough analysis of the allusions to Sacher-Masoch and masochism in *Ulysses*, see Frances L. Restuccia, especially "Molly in Furs," *Novel* 18.2 (Winter 1985).

pleasure from the scraps of his wife's adultery.[20] Instead of considering the relationship wasted or irretrievable, he manages to extend his common life with Molly: his mild, tolerant approach to cuckoldry—especially if you compare it to Odysseus' punishment of the suitors—shows that with a change of perspective, pleasure and sexual energy may be recovered from these wastes.

To speak more crudely, Bloom's capacity to vary the habitual viewpoint and thus to multiply the uses of an object is also at work when he considers sexual objects. Molly's body, for one, is finally contemplated from the back, for when Bloom has completed his spiralling trajectory through Dublin, he will in the end lie down alongside his wife, head to bottom, embracing her from behind, with her "plump melonous hemisphere[s]" his last sight before closing his eyes (U 17.2242). Such fascination for the female posterior may also be noticed when Bloom goes to inspect the Venus of Praxiteles' backside at the museum to check whether there is a hole there. This anal attraction is obviously a way of turning round the sexual object and enjoying it differently, especially since we learn in "Ithaca" that full "carnal intercourse" (with "ejaculation of semen within the natural female organ" [U 17.2283-4]) has been "incomplete" for over ten years between Bloom and his wife. Such maximizing of the sexual object's life through variation of perspectives and positions is perhaps best confirmed in "Sirens," when Bloom plainly states "Three holes, all women" (U 11.1089).

Bloom's careful husbandry—playing here on the double meaning of "husband" as noun and verb—thus allows him to make the most of what others would consider lost, wasted or trashed; and his imaginative, unprejudiced perspective makes him a model recycler both in the economic and in the sexual fields.

The Venus of Praxiteles incident[21] gives us a hint perhaps that Bloom's imaginative recycling may also apply to the aesthetic field.[22] However,

---

[20] Not to mention the "trash" novels, or soft porn, like the infamous Sweets of Sin, which Bloom provides for his wife to fuel the complex economics of their relationship.

[21] Which I have developed elsewhere: "Stephen and the Venus of Praxiteles: The Backside of Aesthetics," Cultural Studies of James Joyce, ed. Brandon Kershner (Amsterdam and New York: Rodopi, 2003) 59-76.

[22] Perhaps this might quickly be explained through an anecdote drawn from art history, one relating to the painters Camille Corot and Gustave Courbet. The anecdote is related in Jean-Jacques Lecercle's The Violence of Language, and used there as a parable with a completely different purpose—to explain his project of describing "the other side of language." I will nevertheless retain Lecercle's narration: "Legend has it that the French painters, Corot and Courbet, used to go on painting expeditions together. Corot, the heir of the Romantic landscape painters, spent hours choosing the place where he would eventually set up his easel: the prospect had to be just right, the landscape must compose itself before he attempted to put it on canvas. When this long and painful process had ended, Courbet, the realist, turned his back on him and started painting whatever was to be seen on the other side." (Jean-Jacques Lecercle's The Violence of Language [London: Routledge, 1990] 52). This U-turn in aesthetics offers a pictorial analogy for what Bloom's reversals of perspective bring in Ulysses: a new kind of realism which, regardless of traditional morals or disgusts, will look at

to appreciate the full extent of the recycling logic at work in the cultural or aesthetic fields in *Ulysses*, we should of course turn to the character of Stephen Dedalus.

Stephen's prodigious memory allows for another form of recycling, one that is less sensible, less down-to-earth or practically oriented than Bloom's, but nevertheless fundamental. If you but look at the first two paragraphs in "Proteus" for instance, or rather, if you but look at Gifford's notes for the first two paragraphs in "Proteus," you find they contain scraps of works by, in turn, Aristotle, Jakob Boehme, Berkeley, Boswell (*Life of Johnson*), Dante, Lessing, Shakespeare (Hamlet), Blake,... and as you know the list needs not be exhaustive.[23] Arguably, this is not as productive or effective as Bloom's recycling; and indeed, Stephen's literary recycling never seems to produce any literary object authored by Stephen—except of course Stephen's erudite stream of consciousness, but this is authored by Joyce. This recycling process is definitely not as potentially profitable as the "Throwaway" tip, but on the other hand its functioning and complexity resemble that of a much more elaborate, modern, and advanced recycling industry. For Stephen's memories of the texts he has read seem to have been broken down, stripped like old cars, the reusable parts have been removed, and fitted again onto new sentences. And at a more minute level, punning and playing with sounds and letters (still quoting from the first two paragraphs in "Proteus": "Diaphane, adiaphane" (*U* 3.7-8); "Crush, crack, crick, crick" (*U* 3.19), you could even say that the words have been shredded, blended, melted down, remixed and recombined with other materials to produce new words and a new text.

Stephen's mind—memory and consciousness together—seems like the crucible where this blending, melting and recombining takes place: his extraordinary memory insures nothing gets wasted, and his stream of consciousness supplies a continual output of reprocessed literature. Needless to say, although Stephen seems incapable of setting pen to paper and writing the books he has dreamt of, Joyce himself did a very good job of repackaging the products of this recycling and reselling them, adequately judging that literary energy could be recovered from these wastes.

Taken together, Bloom and Stephen's complementary methods of recycling may be saying something essential about Joyce's writing itself.[24]

what others tend to discard or throw away, to what otherwise would remain hidden or in the trashcan. This reverse shot at reality may indeed be the idiosyncratic touch of Joycean realism, and Bloom's roundabout way of always looking at the backsides seems to me the best representation of it in *Ulysses*.

[23] Cf. Don Gifford, *Ulysses Annotated* (University of California Press, rev. ed. 1988) 44-5.

[24] If we consider Joyce's choice for his two main male characters, they seem to have been devised in order to allow for the most efficient and thorough recycling, functioning as they are in different fields and using complementary methods. For the picture to be complete, we may add that Molly certainly plays her part in this recycling scheme. On one hand, she cer-

Indeed, it is striking, when considering genetic criticism, how the idea of recycling, or even the word "recycling" itself, frequently pops up,[25] an adequate metaphor perhaps to account for the dialectic of invention and repetition described by Daniel Ferrer.[26] Recently looking at the review section in the Fall 2001 volume of the *James Joyce Quarterly*, I came upon an article by Roland Mchugh about The *"Finnegans Wake Notebooks* at Buffalo,"* edited by Deane, Ferrer and Lernout. A sentence reads as follows:

> *Finnegans Wake* is like a sculpture of great intricacy and beauty, which on closer scrutiny is discovered to be composed of small pieces of rubbish cleverly fitted together.[27]

Further in this issue of the *JJQ*, reviewing a volume of *Essays in Joycean Genetics* edited by Ferrer and Jacquet, Dirk Van Hulle was writing, about a passage from notebook VI.B.9 that eventually had not made it into *Ulysses*:

> Thanks to Joyce's textual economy, however, the words were recycled and incorporated in *Finnegans Wake*.[28]

Which reminded me that at a Joyce conference in Paris in 1999, Dirk had already used the phrase "encyclopaedic recycling" to describe Joyce's writing process.[29]

tainly complements her husband's practical recycling: the second-hand clothes business for instance, is actually presented—at least when Ben Dollard, Simon Dedalus and Father Cowley mention it in "Sirens"—as belonging to her rather than to her husband. And in "Penelope," we find many allusions to old clothes being patched up or worked on or coming back into fashion again, which shows she tends to have that practical, imaginative trend of recycling in her too. But beyond this, in the cultural and literary field, you could say that Molly's all-encompassing flow of contradictions in "Penelope" is a formidable crucible turning and mixing and blending all the possible archetypes and stereotypes about women (woman as holy virgin and great whore of Babylon, woman as inspiring Muse and as debased animal, etc.), and reprocessing them into a definitely new and unusable product—the very mystifying, mythological Molly Bloom, who has already amply proven she could outlive all the theories and criticisms she has triggered.

[25] At the Dublin *Bloomsday100* conference, during Michael Groden's panel entitled "New Research on Joyce at Work on *Ulysses*," Philip Herring, while asking a question to the participants, mentioned that his university course on Joyce used to be entitled "Joyce, The Great Recycler." I find it particularly revealing that this should have come up during a panel about genetic criticism.

[26] *Writing its Own Wrunes For Ever: Essais de Génétique Joycienne / Essays in Joycean Genetics*, edited by Daniel Ferrer and Claude Jacquet (Tusson: Du Lérot, 1998) 48.

[27] Roland McHugh, reviewing The *"Finnegans Wake" Notebooks at Buffalo*, VI.B.3, VI.B.10, VI.B.29, edited by Vincent Deane, Daniel Ferrer, and Geert Lernout (Turnhout, Belgium: Brepols Publishers, 2001)—"A Reader's Guide to the Edition," *JJQ* 39.1 (Fall 2001) 169-70. Italics mine.

[28] Dirk Van Hulle, reviewing *Writing its Own Wrunes For Ever: Essais de Génétique Joycienne / Essays in Joycean Genetics*, edited by Daniel Ferrer and Claude Jacquet (Tusson: Du Lérot, 1998), *JJQ* 39.1 (Fall 2001) 179. Italics mine.

[29] Dirk Van Hulle, "Joyce's Textual Economics: The Encylcopedic Recycling of Wyndham Lewis's Early Joyce Criticism," at the "XXe Colloque James Joyce" (entitled "Cashcash

Indeed, just as an encyclopaedic culture (or Gifford's *Ulysses Anno-tated*) will allow us to understand the recycling process at work in Stephen's mind, the encyclopaedic researches of genetic critics allow us a glimpse into the recycling process at work in Joyce's mind.[30] The notebooks, manuscripts and proofs, thus deciphered and fitted with commentary, stand as so many witnesses to the formidable reprocessing that produced Joyce's text. For when genetic critics look at the *Note-books*, they consider in turn the origin and the finality on one hand, they are concerned with finding the sources Joyce borrowed from, and on the other, with discovering where the quotes have been transferred in Joyce's text. Thus following Joyce's work in progress, the first stage would allow us to compare the notebooks to collection bins, or drop-off centres, where he saved and stored the scraps from his readings. Then the second stage consisted in the treatment of the waste: removing the reusable parts, cutting and shredding bits of sentences, phrases and words. And in a third stage, these parts and scraps were then combined with other material to produce the new text. When the material in a notebook had not been deleted and transferred, it could subsequently be copied into another notebook for later use, thus reducing the volume of the waste after treatment. And the process sometimes required iteration: studying another stage in the recycling, genetic critics have noticed the seemingly never-ending expansion of Joycean proofs, which revealed how often other shreds and scraps were added to an apparently finished recycled product, or even included elsewhere when additions came too late for the printer.[31] In the case of *Finnegans Wake* of course, the recy-cling comes close to nuclear reprocessing, given the thoroughness and the meticulousness of the transformations completed, at the atomic level almost, when the structure of words may be altered beyond recogni-tion.[32] And of course Joyce's consciousness of such recycling appears in the declension, throughout *Finnegans Wake*, of the litter/letter parono-

carackterisccksticks: Joycean Economics") organised by Paris III-Sorbonne Nouvelle and the Institut des Textes et Manuscrits Modernes (ITEM-CNRS). See also by the same author, "Economie textuelle et recyclage chez Proust, Mann et Joyce," *Genesis* 18 (2002).

[30] Reviewing the same *Finnegans Wake Notebooks* edition later in the *JJQ* volume, Finn Fordham used a similar metaphor, from the metal recycling industry this time: "Reading the notebooks in the Archive was like looking into *the linguistic crucible* of somebody's brain" ("A Reader's Guide to the Edition," 173; italics mine).

[31] See Daniel Ferrer's article on Joyce's corrections for the "Circe" proofs ("Reflections on a discarded set of proofs"): he explains how corrections that were sent too late could not be included by Darantiere, so that Joyce then decided to include the additions in the episode on which he was working when the printer returned the proofs, modifying them so that they would fit their new context (in *Probes: Genetic Studies in Joyce*, eds. David Hayman and Sam Slote [Amsterdam and New York: Rodopi, 1995]).

[32] See Dirk Van Hulle, "Dame Plurabelle: Joyce's Art of Decomposition and Recombination" (in *Postcards From Trieste: Risky Readings of Joyce*, eds. Sebastian Knowles, Geert Lernout, and John McCourt [Gainesville: University Press of Florida, 2007] 87-101).

masia: drawing "letter from litter," he gradually produces his own "litter-ingture."[33]

This recycling metaphor also comes in handy to account for the type of literature Joyce chose to recycle. Although *Ulysses* itself could be considered as a gigantic recycling of Homer's *Odyssey* — an exemplum of high culture if there ever was one —, when we look at the detail, at all the bits and scraps that have been quoted, we take the measure of Joyce's predilection for what usually passes as literary "trash." And here I am not only alluding to the kind of softporn literature with which Bloom feeds his wife's fantasy, and his own.[34] Even in terms of Greek mythology and epic literature, Joyce had a preference for alternative versions, of the kind that turned Penelope into an unfaithful wife, mother to the great god Pan. Even in the field of religious studies, Stephen shows himself particularly interested in various heresies — or the trash of Roman Catholic theology. And as far as ephemeral literature bound for the trashcan is concerned, we remember that in *Ulysses*, a whole episode is devoted to journalese and journalism, whilst the first half of "Nausicaa" plagiarizes the cheap kind of female magazines that a girl like Gerty might be reading. The study of the early notebooks of *Finnegans Wake* confirms this fondness for "the trivia of current newspapers and periodicals," which seem to have been the first step in Joyce's project, rather than a later addition.[35] Such fascination with literary throwaways shows how much postcreation may be concerned with the transmutation of "the word that passes" into that which "shall not pass away."

Words pass, or rather are passed on, which brings me back to the tip Bloom passes on, unawares, to Bantam Lyons. Beyond the story of the newspaper as model recycling programme or the coincidental good tip it provides, it is remarkable how Bloom's sentence ("I was just about to throw it away") becomes a linguistic unit ("throwaway"), which will remain in *Ulysses* as a meaningful motif and achieve its own trajectory: after being the name of a horse, it will also refer to the Elijah leaflet Bloom is handed out in the beginning of "Lestrygonians,"[36] and which he will, ironically, throw away to the gulls into the Liffey.[37] Subsequentely, in "Ithaca," Bloom will actually enjoy the title of "distributor of throwaways" (*U* 17.1940), and at that stage, no single or limitative meaning

---

[33] "The litter! The letter!" (*FW* I:93.24), "illiterettes" (*FW* II:284.15), "litterery" (*FW* III:422.35), "artis litterarum" (*FW* III:495.34), "litteringture" (*FW* III:570.18), "letter from litter" (*FW* IV:615.1), etc.

[34] "Do you want another?
—Yes. Get another of Paul de Kock's. Nice name he has" (*U* 4.357-8).

[35] Cf. Roland McHugh, "A Reader's Guide to the Edition," 170.

[36] "A sombre Y.M.C.A. young man, watchful among the warm sweet fumes of Graham Lemon's, placed a throwaway in a hand of Mr Bloom" (*U* 8.5-6).

[37] "He threw down among them a crumpled paper ball. Elijah thritytwo feet per sec is com. Not a bit. The ball bobbed unheeded on the *Wake* of swells, floated under by the bridgepiers" (*U* 8.57-9).

will be given to the word "throwaway."[38] Indeed, by the time we reach "Ithaca," the "throwaway" motif has been made into a veritable leitmotif: presented with meaningful variations each time it appears, it has collected substance and connotations. As we already suspected, the "throwaway" linguistic unit has acquired an independent life of its own, unattached to one single precise signified. Signifiers—as all punsters know—may be recycled.

If you look even closer at what happens during the original dialogue, you perceive that Bantam Lyons, obsessed with races and thus inclined to bad reasoning, has neglected to check whether Bloom's referential context is the same as his own. Ironically, such unscientific interpretation would have allowed him to bet on the right horse, had he risked it: "I'll risk it" are actually his last words as he leaves Bloom with the newspaper sheets on his arms. Except as we learn in "Cyclops," Lenehan talked him out of it. Lenehan must have (scientifically) reflected that Bloom did not know anything about horse races, and therefore should not be trusted as "distributor of throwaways." He may even have surmised that there was nothing but coincidence between Bloom's words and the horse's name. And such scrupulous and methodical interpretation is considered valid... until they find out the results for the race and associate them with what they know—or think they know—about Jews and their talent for making money.[39] As Joyce ceaselessly demonstrates, hermeneutics is a risky affair, and the recycling of signifiers an endless source of irony.

If we look back again on Bantam Lyons's initial misunderstanding, we realize he recognizes, or thinks he recognizes, the name "Throwaway," when Bloom is actually saying "throw *it* away."[40] In other words, in order to recognize the signifier as relating to a horse, he has to effect a linguistic throwing away of his own—that of the pronoun "it." As far as

---

[38] "Ithaca," recapitulative as always, also provides an exhaustive summary of the throwaway trajectory, retrospectively explaining the whereabouts of both the newspaper, the leaflet and the tip: "Where had previous intimations of the result, effected or projected, been received by him? / In Bernard Kiernan's licensed premises 8,9 and 10 Little Britain street: in David Byrne's licensed premises, 14 Duke street: in O'Connell street lower, outside Graham Lemon's when a dark man had placed in his hand a throwaway (subsequently thrown away), advertising Elijah, restorer of the church in Zion: in Lincoln place outside the premises of F.W. Sweny and Co (Limited) dispensing chemists, when, when Frederick M. (Bantam Lyons had rapidly and successively requested, perused and restituted the copy of the current issue of the Freeman's Journal and National Press which he had been about to throw away (subsequently thrown away), he had proceeded to the oriental edifice of the Turkish and Warm Baths, 11 Leinster street, with the light of inspiration shining in his countenance and bearing in his arms the secret of the race, graven in the language of prediction" (*U* 17.327-41).

[39] "He had a few bob on Throwaway and he's gone to gather in the shekels.
—Is it that whiteeyed kaffir? says the citizen, that never backed a horse in anger in his life?
—That's where he's gone, says Lenehan. I met Bantam Lyons going to back that horse only I put him off it and he told me Bloom gave him the tip. Bet you what you like he has a hundred shillings to five on. He's the only man in Dublin has it. A dark horse.
—He's a bloody dark horse himself, says Joe" (*U* 12.1550-58).
Needless to say, on that bet Lenehan should not put on too much either.

[40] Italics mine.

we know, Bantam Lyons is an adept of linguistic throwing away: earlier on in the dialogue, his notable elision in "half a mo" produces a meaning-ful pun. Thus the pronoun "it," once thrown away, might produce profitable meaning. Of course few signifiers are as open to numerous signifieds as a pronoun, and especially this one, which is the vaguest of all, and may be used as a spare part in so many different sentences; so perhaps this is the same pronoun we encounter at the end of the dia-logue, when Bantam Lyons claims "I'll risk *it*."[41] In other words, linguistic waste, if carefully recycled, may produce meaning, and profit-able meaning at that—but only if you are ready to take a risk and invest in it.

Needless to say, it is very tempting to apply these conclusions to Joyce's project. For the recycling of signifiers brings about meaning and, in such recycling, language acquires a life of its own—which may even be endless ("the word that shall not pass away"). What the ironically meaningful misunderstanding between Bloom and Bantam Lyons really teaches us, is that Joyce's predilection for trash and recycling is neither a disinterested, contemplative affair,[42] nor even a question of thrift and good husbandry: if you are ready to risk it, however illogical and far-fetched it may seem, the recycling of trash may bring considerable profit. Who knows? perhaps even immortality.

---

[41] Italics mine.
[42] As Judge Woolsey put it in his decision: "I have not found anything [in *Ulysses*] that I consider to be dirt for dirt's sake" (in *A Centennial Bloomsday at Buffalo*, catalogue by Sam Slote [The Poetry Collection, University at Buffalo, New York, 2004] 26).

JED DEPPMAN
The Problem of Genesis

I. ORIGINATING JOYCE

After reading the fifteen essays in the 2007 *How Joyce Wrote Finnegans Wake: A Chapter-by-Chapter Genetic Guide*, I had no doubt about its value to Joyce scholarship but did wonder how it might impact genetic criticism as a whole—the field has long been something of a soft wax for new scholarship to reshape. New contributions may reinforce its status as either a hermeneutic discipline that develops new protocols of interpretation or a Valéryan one seeking knowledge of immaterialities like the "movements of the creative mind" or the "workings of the writing process." They may follow through on the discipline's philosophical commitments to Baconian empiricism and induction, or else buttress its post-structuralist side by emphasizing the play of signifiers in the text and avant-texte.

Although both sides of these particular divisions find support in the book, insiders will probably agree that the perspective is generally more Iser than Valéry, more Bacon than Barthes, and that the "philological" side received a stronger show of hands. And what will outsiders think? Those who are sympathetic to this kind of criticism—without necessarily wanting to do it—will find much to complement their own thinking on Joyce, but for true skeptics it is harder to say. Will the *Guide* vitiate the discipline's reputation for naïve positivism, blind philology, and mindless draft-dodging? Will there be fewer accusations that genetic scholars pursue quixotic, imitation-science research on the genome of literary creation, that they fatuously fetishize the origins of texts?

"Turn no more aside and brood," I thought as I thought about this, reminding myself that most of these complaints could have been rebutted even before the evidence of the *Wake* book. By and large, genetic scholarship was not pioneered and pursued by wide-eyed visionaries, and one looks in vain through genetic articles for naïve positivism or overblown claims for a new science. (One somewhat misleading exception is Pierre-Marc de Biasi's 1993 essay "Vers une science de la littérature: L'analyse des manuscrits et la genèse de l'œuvre.") In fact only the old aspersion about origins really bothered me. In his tendentious contribution to the 1996 *Yale French Studies* issue *Drafts*, Laurent Jenny made a comment that might still synopsize the problem: "Genetic criticism is searching for a phenomenon that is in effect unobservable,

unobjectifiable: the origin of a literary work."[1] Speaking from a hermeneutic perspective in which the encounter between a (finished) text and
a reader is of utmost importance and alone can justify research in the
humanities, he added with some disgust that the discipline "does not
have as its primary objective the reading of texts but rather the discovery of their origin."[2]

How Joyce wrote Finnegans Wake... Does that "how" include such
questions as "how it all began" or why he wrote it? Together, the essays suggest that as genetic criticism seeks to incorporate a temporal
dimension into the analysis of the literary text, it rarely if ever "searches
for the origin" in any explicit or grand metaphysical sense. In practice
scholars spend more time describing authorial decision-making and,
while respecting the unpredictable mobility of writing, accept that literary composition takes place teleologically. For their part, the editors Sam
Slote and Luca Crispi declare that the book is devoted to something else
entirely: the play between a complicated text and its avant-textes: "The
goal of this volume is to show what might be gained... from reading
Finnegans Wake in the context of its prepublication manuscripts."[3]
Nonetheless, whether or not genetic scholars even postulate that origins
of literary texts are recoverable, their relentless excavation continues to
create for many the expectation that they might shed light on the earliest forms of texts' emergence from the void. In short, however it may
be with the tensions across the discipline's theoretical investments,
which may anyway be constitutive and salutary for it, one thing should
surely have been made available by now, whether through negative or
positive examples: a robust description and interpretation of the possibility and consequences of searching for the origins of literary writing. Has
it?

Well, on the one hand, we know that the form of genetic criticism
that took wing in Paris in the early 1970s drank deeply from structuralist
and post-structuralist notions of textuality. Significant theoretical capital
to theorize the avant-texte was borrowed from figures like Barthes,
Kristeva, and Eco—on such subjects as, respectively, the text rather
than the work, modes of intertextuality, and the "open work." But on
the other hand, and perhaps surprisingly, what might be called in distort-
ing shorthand the postmodern meditation on genesis and origins was,
and has remained, altogether less well integrated into the discipline.
Despite its engagement with avant-textes, teleology, and the whole
calculus of creativity, geneticists have not been much inspired to negotiate texts like Heidegger's The Origin of the Work of Art; Foucault's
Nietzsche, Genealogy, History, and Derrida's work on the concept of

[1] Laurent Jenny, "Genetic Criticism and its Myths," trans. Richard Watts, Yale French Studies
     89: "Drafts" (1996) 10.
[2] Jenny, 11.
[3] Sam Slote, Luca Crispi, eds., How Joyce Wrote Finnegans Wake (Madison: The University of
     Wisconsin Press, 2007) 3.

origin, such as his *Introduction* to Husserl's *Origin of Geometry* or the sections in *Of Grammatology* devoted to Rousseau's *Essay on the Origin of Language*.

Have genetic scholars, in their attention to avant-textes, ignored such basic theoretical questions? In that case the indifference would be due to blindness. Or have they outpaced, overcome, or otherwise seen through such questions thanks to superior knowledge of how texts are constructed? In that case, indifference would be a hard-won philosophical perspective, the result of arduous thought and experience in the archive.

—You see, you have no answer, says Molly Ivors to a flustered Gabriel.

I called for my tablets and began, and begin again now with Nietzsche, who names the thought that hangs like the sword of Damocles over the entire enterprise of genetic criticism: if for a long time "investigators of knowledge sought out the origin of things" in the full belief that "they would discover something of incalculable significance for all later action and judgment," and if they "always *presupposed*... that the *salvation* of man must depend on *insight into the origin of things*," then by the late nineteenth century "the more we advance towards origins, the more our interest diminishes." In fact, he adds in italics, "*The more insight we possess into an origin the less significant does the origin appear...*"[4] Who wants to argue with Nietzsche? What if it were true that going backwards, reading the manuscripts and drafts, the "sources," everything that might expansively be construed as originating or avant-textual material for a literary work, ultimately only demonstrated the "insignificance" of the origin?

"Genealogy" says Foucault drawing upon Nietzsche to oppose more confidently metaphysical forms of historiography, "is gray, meticulous, and patiently documentary. It operates on a field of entangled and confused parchments, on documents that have been scratched over and recopied many times."[5] I am not sure why this famous opening line has not been cited more often by genetic scholars (perhaps they fear the skeptical or "relativist" reputation of the piece?) for it vividly describes a great deal of the work one finds in books like the *Genetic Guide*. "Genealogy..." he continues, "requires patience and a knowledge of details," and "depends on a vast accumulation of source material..."[6]

In fact, to glance like this at the key words of the Foucauldian genealogist is to think not only of genetic critics but of Joyce: meticulous, documentary, entangled and confused parchments, accumulation of source material, pages scratched over and recopied. Whatever may be

4   Friedrich Nietzsche, *Daybreak: Thoughts on the Prejudices of Morality*, trans. R. J. Hollingdale (Cambridge: Cambridge University Press, 1997) 45-6.
5   Michel Foucault, "Nietzsche, Genealogy, History," trans. Donald F. Bouchard and Sherry Simon, in: *The Foucault Reader* (Paul Rabinow, ed. New York: Pantheon Books, 1984) 76.
6   Foucault, 76.

said about the genetic study of authors who leave few avant-textes, the case for Joyce is in part quantitative: the *Guide*'s editors remind us that he left, for his last book alone, a trail of over 25,000 pages, some of which imply the existence of more, e.g. intermediary drafts and lost notebooks. Perhaps then, despite its name, genetic criticism has from its origins and all along been more Joycean or genealogical in the Foucauldian sense than "genetic" in any sense.[7] And yet genealogy, says Foucault, repeatedly and with great conviction, is opposed to the "search for 'origins.'" If genetic scholars are accidental genealogists, wary of or indifferent to the idea of searching for origins, then why do they have the reputation with critics like Jenny of being obsessed with the topic? And what, incidentally, is so philosophically problematic about seeking origins?

These questions can be economically addressed with an example from Joyce.

To ask "what is the origin of *Ulysses*?" or "why did Joyce write it?" is to run the ragged edge between pursuing an important project (practically speaking, this is what many readers would like to know) and floundering in absurdity (such questions are wildly vague and naively presuppose permanent, foundational answers in a hermeneutic field where none can exist.) "The character of *Ulysses* always fascinated me—even when a boy," says Joyce, but such remarks merely place the novel's "origin" in a non-specific "always" as if it were the result of a youthful preference for one kind of hero over others (notably Achilles). "Imagine fifteen years ago I started writing it," he also says, "as a short story for *Dubliners*! For seven years I have been working at this book— blast it!"[8] This gives us two beginnings, one when he "started writing" the book and another when he started "working at" it.

Joyceans, of course, like to think of precise events as originating much of *Ulysses*. September 12, 1904, for example, was the night in the Martello tower when Samuel Chenevix Trench, the model for Haines, dreamed of a black panther and began shooting his pistol at the fire. Or June 22, 1904, the incident in the park when Joyce was helped by Alfred Hunter, the model for Bloom, after being knocked down. Ellmann points out that Joyce's "very lack of acquaintance" with Hunter "was of special interest, since Joyce regarded himself as hemmed in by indifference or hostility, and was the more surprised that someone unfamiliar,

---

[7] Within Foucault's own career trajectory, the genealogy, as a philosophical and historiographical method, represents an approach that includes but transcends his earlier method of the "archeology." (See, for example, *The History of Madness*, an archeology, and *Discipline and Punish*, a genealogy.) Genealogy was intended not only to describe, compare and contrast the contingencies characterizing different periods of history, as did archeology, but also to help understand and analyze the transitions between them. For a more nuanced appraisal, see Gutting, Gary, "Introduction. Michel Foucault: A User's Manual," *The Cambridge Companion to Foucault* (Cambridge: Cambridge University Press, 1994) 1-27.

[8] James Joyce, *Letters I*, ed. Richard Ellmann (New York: Viking Press, new and corrected edition, 1966) 146-7

of temperament and background seemingly opposite, should have cause-lessly befriended him. Here might be one of those 'epiphanies' — sudden, unlooked for turns in experience — which could prove the more momen-tous for being modest."[9] Ellmann's language positions the Joycean epiphany as a genealogical type of artistic origin configured by insignifi-cance, chance, and causelessness.

From a perspective informed by careful analysis of manuscript his-tory, Hans Walter Gabler argues that the writing of *Ulysses* originated in a technical problem of how to rewrite, i.e. how to divide and emplot existing autobiographical material into two different literary works. It is, he says,

> prominently in a mode of rewriting within Joyce's own oeuvre, as well as on the level of concerns about structure that predate the actual writing, that the beginnings of *Ulysses* first manifest themselves. We may dis-cover its earliest formation by evaluating the relation of A Portrait to *Stephen Hero*, and by analyzing the process of rewriting and rethinking of written and unwritten *Stephen Hero* material in the light of Joyce's corre-spondence with his brother Stanislaus.[10]
>
> Together, the tower and library episodes show that the earliest writing for *Ulysses* from the autobiographical fountainhead originated in Joyce's endeavours — approximately between 1912 and 1914 — to define a line of division between A Portrait and *Ulysses*. As for the matter of Dublin, *Ulysses* reaches back to Dubliners, and to a time of conception in 1906.[11]

Here again the origin divides into phases according to topics (autobiog-raphy and Dublin). Beyond these examples, one can obviously increase the play of origins simply by changing the unit: instead of speaking of *Ulysses*, we can ask about the origins of individual chapters, characters, turns of phrase, paragraphs, punctuation marks, styles, etc. each of which, as genetic critics show, has its ramifying genealogy. The famous "schemes" Joyce circulated assigning each *Ulysses* chapter a bodily organ, a technic, a time, etc. can also be seen as devices that scatter and multiply origins, since each textual unit can be interpreted as condi-tioned by — potentially having originated in — almost any category.

To give an even more genealogical example, an origin of many smaller subdivisions of the Joycean text can often be traced to "source material." This is especially true of his last two books, which are so dependent upon and saturated with reading and notetaking that they represent supreme test cases or crises of "influence study." The full range of "originating" powers or modes of these sources has never been easy to describe or define, and the nature and purpose of Joyce's note-

9 Richard Ellmann, *"Ulysses*: A Short History," *James Joyce, Ulysses* (New York: Penguin, 1976) 708.
10 Hans Walter Gabler, "Joyce's Text in Progress," *The Cambridge Companion to James Joyce*, ed. Derek Attridge (Cambridge: Cambridge University Press, 1990) 221.
11 Gabler, "Joyce's Text in Progress," 223.

book material continues to stir controversy. Commenting recently on a source Joyce used for the "Sirens" chapter of *Ulysses*, Susan Brown shows that neither the notes

> nor the source can be fruitfully treated as prescriptive. Joyce, as was his pattern cribbing from esoteric sources, is often inaccurate, sloppy, incomplete, illogical, and impressionistic. Furthermore, even if he understands his own notes (which he often does not), his application of his notes is symbolic and metaphoric—not according to rule. Thus, readers who expect to find in Joyce's texts exact fidelity to a source or concept often miss what is there.[12]

Thus it is that searching for the "origins" of Joyce's texts can become discouragingly idle or endless, a game of suspecting, naming, splitting, narrating, and dissolving influences and possibilities à la the *Wake*an crime plot. But while the elimination of linear narratives might seem, for theorists, to open up the origin to a useless infinity, bland relativism does no justice to a Joyce who devoted too much attention to conceptions, origins, beginnings, and births of all kinds for interpreters to ignore. As for literary genesis in particular, on the simplest level he shows characters writing, thinking about writing, planning to write, reflecting on writing, etc. Genetic critics on Joyce have not explicitly tried to match their methods to these scenes, take their lead from them, or integrate them into their methodological considerations. In short, we have not awarded them any privileged hermeneutic status.

Although there can be no a priori justification for doing so, there are pragmatic reasons for breaking into the hermeneutic circle by examining Joyce's fictional representations of literary genesis. In *Ulysses*, three early scenes in particular seem to form an important local economy or nodal network: first, the scene toward the end of "Proteus" in which Stephen searches for paper to write down a poem—the so-called "vampire" poem—that has come to him during his stroll along Sandymount. Next, Bloom in "Lestrygonians" composes in his mind a poem about a seagull and then revises it, with purposeful irony, later in the same chapter. Finally, Buck Mulligan, in "Scylla and Charybdis," at the end of Stephen's long presentation in the National Library, suddenly shouts out "Eureka!" and begins scribbling down some humorously-intended ideas for a play. As he and Stephen are walking out of the library, he reads from his "tablet."[13]

Together these scenes can be taken as a limited yet serious *étude* by Joyce on emergent writing, its cultural and historical situatedness, and its origins in human character and the Lebenswelt. Each scene also con-

---

[12] Susan Brown, "The Mystery of the Fuga per Canonem Solved," *Genetic Joyce Studies* 7 (Spring 2007).

[13] In one of the many details that link the scenes, his "tablet" is really the free slips of paper from Eglinton's desk at the library; he uses the word with a *Hamlet* resonance, as does Stephen in "Proteus."

tributes to the wider narratives and symbolic movements of *Ulysses*. Stephen's writing in "Proteus," if we except the witticisms and aphorisms of "Telemachus" and "Nestor," represents the origin or first instance of creativity itself in the time-space of the text of *Ulysses*. This, after all, is the first time pencil is creatively put to paper by the character who, through autobiographical identification, will grow up to write the novel we are reading. Bloom's poem contrasts sharply with Stephen's and represents the first clear confirmation of his own advertised identity as a "literary gentleman" (advertised, of course, quite literally: he has placed an ad with that description of himself.) Finally, Buck Mulligan offers a third, uniquely self-stimulating version of literary genesis when he bursts noisily into the complex conversational rhythms of "Scylla and Charybdis" and outlines a parodic play on masturbation.

II. "PROTEUS": STEPHEN'S GENESIS BY THE SEA

One can — perhaps should, to understand "Proteus" — become disoriented by the pullulating metaphors of birth, growth, and death. Not only does the chapter open with Stephen thinking about the originary constraints on every real and possible experience, the "ineluctables" of time and space, he is throughout also concerned with maternity and paternity, as well as with physical, organic, linguistic and other origins. (Joyce designated philology as the "art/science" of this chapter and "primal matter" as the "correspondence" for Homer's "Proteus.") As Murray McArthur has pointed out, the chapter is also saturated with onomatopoiea, the form of language that Vico considered the origin of meaning, the earliest step into signification from sound. Stephen sounds some of these notes when he meditates on the two *Frauenzimmer* he takes to be midwives: "One of her sisterhood lugged me *squealing* into life. Creation from nothing" (*U* 2.35; my italics). Even the fantasy, sometimes attributed to genetic critics, of trying to construe avant-textes as forms of immediate, pre-lapsarian signification is figured by the images, first, of a "navelcord" extending backwards in time all the way to the first parents, and second, of that cord metamorphosed into a telephone line enabling one to call them: "Hello! Kinch here," says Stephen, placing a call to his first parents, "Put me on to Edenville. Aleph, alpha: nought, nought, one" (*U* 2.39-40).[14]

---

[14] In a manner that is problematic and yet typical of genetic criticism, Gabler identifies several structures that control Proteus. There is the Homeric reference point, which helps explain "the chapter's fascinating elusiveness of style and character consciousness." There is also a three-part "fly by the nets" structure, adapted from *A Portrait*: there it was nationality, language, and religion, but here it is family relations (Stephen considers paying a visit to his uncle Richie Goulding and Aunt Sara, but ultimately "flies by" the path to their house), religion (Stephen's iconoclasm comes to the fore), and exile (the sad example of the forgotten wild goose Joseph Casey, fictionalized as Kevin Egan, hangs over the chapter). Finally, Gabler argues that the whole chapter "appears to be retrospectively controlled by Stephen's parting gesture"; he turns and looks back over his shoulder just as Hamlet does as he leaves Ophelia behind and "walks out on his past" (227). Gabler tries neither to harmonize these structures

Stephen's peripatetics on the strand create the expectation that he will give birth to a great piece of writing. By the time he starts scrambling for paper, we have been exhaustively and exhaustingly exposed to the ruminations of this self-styled bard who, equipped with great erudition and several European languages, has been hemorrhaging intelligence and intensity. We understand that he, like the Hamlet to whom he relates so well and so often, is deeply involved in a "lyric" state of grief and melancholy. Now he has time alone, free from the oppressive Mulligans, Haineses, Deasies and schoolboys. Not only that, but he has already accomplished a good deal of difficult preliminary work, most of all by mocking and discarding his earlier self-preening poseur-self:

> Reading two pages apiece of seven books every night, eh? I was young. You bowed to yourself in the mirror, stepping forward to applause earnestly, striking face. Hurray for the Goddamned idiot! Hray! No-one saw: tell no-one. Books you were going to write with letters for titles. Have you read his F? O yes, but I prefer Q. Yes, but W is wonderful. O yes, W. Remember your epiphanies written on green oval leaves, deeply deep, copies to be sent if you died to all the great libraries of the world, including Alexandria? Someone was to read them there after a few thousand years...
> [*U* 3.136-43]

Fully recognizing his former fatuity, surely he will create something better than that villanelle: his own Lycidas perhaps?

So although the narrator gives no specific reason for Stephen to begin writing a poem, we are not surprised when he does. He has been watching a gipsy man and woman, cocklepickers, with their dog on the beach, casting themy in his thoughts as "a ruffian and his strolling mort" and citing a line about the attractions of the woman's body from the gipsy ballad by that name. In the manner of Aquinas's "morose delectation"—the enjoyment of imagining a sin without actually desiring to commit it—he thinks about her exotic blood and sexuality. Then he imagines the moon pulling the tides westward, and her too, and such distant, commanding call-and-response ideas bring vampires to mind:

> Behold the handmaid of the moon. In sleep the wet sign calls her hour, bids her rise. Bridebed, childbed, bed of death, ghostcandled. *Omnis caro ad te veniet*. He comes, pale vampire, through storm his eyes, his bat sails bloodying the sea, mouth to her mouth's kiss.
> Here. Put a pin in that chap, will you? My tablets. Mouth to her kiss. No. Must be two of em. Glue em well. Mouth to her mouth's kiss.
> His lips lipped and mouthed fleshless lips of air: mouth to her moomb. Oomb, allwombing tomb. His mouth moulded issuing breath, unspeeched:

nor to link them to the scene of Stephen's writing; on the contrary he simply suggests that the roaming inspires the writing, as it did Stephen toward the end of *A Portrait* and Joyce himself as he finished *Ulysses*. The disconcerting fact that Gabler does not find any connection between Stephen's poem and the "structures" of the chapter strongly suggests that the scene of literary genesis is somehow problematic or indigestible for Proteus.

ooeeehah: roar of cataractic planets, globed, blazing, roaring wayaway-
awayawayaway. Paper. The banknotes, blast them. Old Deasy's letter.
Here. Thanking you for the hospitality tear the blank end off. Turning his
back to the sun he bent over far to a table of rock and scribbled words.
That's twice I forgot to take slips from the library counter. [*U* 3.395-407]

This brief scene of writing almost does not take place for simple lack of
paper. Stephen's three potential options—Deasy's letter, the banknotes,
and the library slips—broadly represent important material constraints or
spheres of his life as well as his alienation from them. He cannot very
well write on banknotes—"blast them," he says, cursing the physical
incompatibility of art and money—and he is separated from the more
nourishing library by his own forgetfulness. His only option indebts him
to Deasy, and the phrase "Thanking you for your hospitality" therefore
has a double meaning: it is the formula that ends Deasy's letter but
since Stephen appropriates it as he transitions to his own writing he
winds up using both the words and the paper of a man who travels *per
vias rectas* and pays his own way. The tearing of the paper humorously
focuses the irony down to a single moment: we imagine Deasy's response to having his letter mutilated and compare his scene of writing in
"Nestor"—two copies, typewritten, bombastic, self-certain—with
Stephen's hasty scribbling. Having seen snippets of Deasy's prose, we
expect to be able to compare the texts; with our eyes focused on the
torn paper we cannot imagine that Stephen will write a poem that we
will not see, for in *Ulysses* we have had unrestricted access to his mind.
Yet not only are we not given the pleasure of the text, we have it forci-
bly removed from before our eyes: Stephen "lay back at full stretch over
the sharp rocks, cramming the scribbled note and pencil into a pocket"
(3.437-8). In this way the much-heralded work is demoted to the lowest
caste: a "scribbled note" buried and promptly forgotten.

Why does Joyce not show the poem in "Proteus" but instead have
Stephen remember it retrospectively in "Aeolus"? Without a "finished
text" for readers to privilege and interpret, the literary genesis takes on
primary, if mysterious, importance and presents itself as a kind of emblematic or essential proteity. But is the Homeric reference really the
reason the poem is omitted? Is it so simple as being, to borrow the
words Joyce gave to Budgen, "all in the Protean character of the thing"
i.e. somehow more faithfully Protean to emphasize process over product, to show Stephen writing but not what he wrote?[15] If so, is it not
more Platonist than Protean to cleave to illustrating a predetermined
categorical concept, to strive for a "pure" proteity in the first place?
(Later, when the poem appears in "Aeolus," we will have to ask whether
it is not itself a proteiform graph.) At any rate, readers have no recourse
to ideal purity: left with emergent language so inchoate that we can

---

[15] Frank Budgen, *James Joyce and the Making of Ulysses* (Bloomington: Indiana University
Press, 1964) 54.

hardly even recognize it as writing—Tim Martin calls it "proto-poetic"[16]—we are unsure whether there is any stability to the vampire poem at all, on or off the paper.

To appreciate the literary genesis Joyce pursues in "Proteus," the scene must be contrasted with the writing of the villanelle in *A Portrait*. There, genesis takes place as an annunciation in which the supine, passive artist, figured as female, receives the word. Readers hear and see the orgasmic "O!," later so prominent in "Nausicaa," signaling the inseminating moment when the word can become flesh:

> The instant flashed forth like a point of light and now from cloud on cloud of vague circumstance confused form was veiling softly its afterglow. O! In the virgin womb of the imagination the word was made flesh. Gabriel the seraph had come to the virgin's chamber. An afterglow deepened within his spirit, whence the white flame had passed, deepening to a rose and ardent light.
> [...]
> And then? The rhythm died away, ceased, began again to move and beat. And then? Smoke, incense ascending from the altar of the world.
> Above the flame the smoke of praise
> Goes up from ocean rim to rim
> Tell no more of enchanted days.
> [...]
> Fearing to lose all, he raised himself suddenly on his elbow to look for paper and pencil. There was neither on the table; only the soup plate he had eaten the rice from for supper and the candlestick with its tendrils of tallow and its paper socket, singed by the last flame. He stretched his arm wearily towards the foot of the bed, groping with his hand in the pockets of the coat that hung there. His fingers found a pencil and then a cigarette packet. He lay back and, tearing open the packet, placed the last cigarette on the window ledge and began to write out the stanzas of the villanelle in small neat letters on the rough cardboard surface. [*P* 219-21]

The amniotic prose nourishes the poem, and vice versa, the scene so patiently and rhythmically written that it remains a high point of romanticism in modernism. There are obvious differences with "Proteus": the matutinal Stephen of *A Portrait* rises with the world and wakes to its rhythms, but the "Proteus" Stephen is mired in the languid noon of the Mallarméan faun. The villanelle emerges from the real relationship between Stephen and Emma Clery; in "Proteus," the poem-process (seemingly) originates in a hazy thinking about the relationship between two passersby, disconnected (at least in Aquinas's terms) from Stephen's real desire. Since both geneses involve a tearing of paper and reappropriation of a surface, one must also compare the rich connotative force of the pack of cigarettes—its portentous *one last cigarette* and

---

16 See Timothy P. Martin, "Joyce and Wagner's Pale Vampire," *JJQ* 23 (1986): 491-96.

intoxicating incense—to the torn last scrap of Deasy's letter to the editor about foot and mouth disease.

In *A Portrait*, the sensitive and precise artist-priest preserves the majesty of a lyric annunciation expressed in Christian terms: Stephen overcomes the rough (but sturdy) cardboard surface with a writing technique that resembles engraving, so "small" and "neat" that it pays attention to each individual letter. The villanelle, we see, is meant to last forever unchanged. By contrast, in "Proteus," the cosmic profundity signaled through words like "behold," "bids," and "cataractic planets," clashes sharply with the reality of the writing process. Stephen turns "his back to the sun" and bends "over far to a table of rock and scribble[s] words." Hunched, self-occluding, and scribbling in darkness, he is no priest of the eternal imagination but a distracted Bartleby.

The main difference in the representations of genesis is that in "Proteus" the poetics of birth is replaced by a poetics of excretion. In both books, the urge to write a poem comes upon Stephen the way a bowel movement or a sexual urge might, and he writes to satisfy himself, but while the passive, involuntary artist in *A Portrait* goes on to give birth, and we watch the baby being born tercet by tercet, in "Proteus," just after Stephen writes, he urinates and picks his nose.[17] The plot sequence cuts off any lingering, Shelleyan "afterglow" of form and deromanticizingly realigns poetry-writing with human waste, the delivery of words to the world taking place as an evacuation or ejaculation instead of a culminating, deliberative event in Stephen's aesthetic consciousness. There is no ethereal ascension beyond the constraints of time and circumstance: urine, snot, and Stephen's note are not only waste products but quickly biodegradable ones that begin to lose their integrity the moment they mingle with the external world. From this perspective, the scene of literary genesis reminds us that the chapter's striking proteity belongs to products as much as to processes, to decomposition as well as composition.

That the poetics of excretion is a studied feature of this particular genesis is made clear by the language Joyce chooses to register the sound of the "unspeeched," pre-linguistic, "issuing breath:" "ooeeehah." Budgen is wrong to speak of Stephen's "inspiration" before writing the poem for there is neither a sudden spiritual manifestation nor any physical breathing in that might resemble an annunciation or fertilization. The sound of the air leaving Stephen's body is unintelligible and pre-

[17] Building on three passages from *Finnegans Wake*, Andrew Mitchell argues that Joyce transcends traditional satirical and naturalist scatology and instead turns to excrement in order to satisfy the totalizing demand of his own aesthetic of self-creation: "Were Joyce to leave excrement out of this artistic vision, something of this life would remain outside of it, too. There would be an outside. Joyce seizes upon excrement in order to reintegrate it with the created life in the quest for a whole life." Mitchell's argument can be adapted to *Ulysses* if we agree to interpret Stephen's unsatisfying excretory genesis as a small part of a differential economy of creativity including, among others, Bloom, Mulligan, and Joyce himself.

onomatopoietic; it enacts, signifies and sounds like nothing.[18] Within a couple of pages, however, the noise takes on meaning when we hear the "fourworded wavespeech" of Stephen's urine: "seesoo, hrs, rssee-iss, ooos" (2.455-6). If we remove the "s" sounds that express the meeting of waters then we have a close graphic and sonorous match with the gaseous origins of Stephen's poem. Later, all of this will be driven home when Stephen delivers Deasy's letter to newspaper editor Myles Crawford in "Aeolus." Crawford asks: "who tore it? Was he short taken?" (i.e. did he have an urgent need to wipe himself?) The reader can see what the editor cannot, that the remark has hit upon the truth: in "Proteus" Stephen is short taken and does use the scrap as toilet paper to wipe his mind. In fact he is caught twice in rapid succession, once without paper and once without his handkerchief, and just as he wonders who will eventually read his poem, so he muses over who might see his snot-monument.

It is therefore a mistake to think that craftsmanship or creativity guide the genesis of Stephen's "note." The proto-poem's meaning is not explicable in traditional aesthetic terms because it is chiefly that of a waste product, a composite residue of binge-thinking and binge-reading that Stephen's body and mind expulses and that he keeps out of reten-tive habit. At first the profound, music-of-the-spheres setting for his lyric activity may seem to recall the intense emotional backdrop to the villa-nelle, but the "Proteus" genesis actually owes much more to morose, mediated, constipated delectations of reading and memory than to any immediate experience.

This becomes still more clear if we consider one of the seemingly in-finite sources or origins for the poem, the 1898 *Book of Images* by W. T. Horton,[19] in which there is a sequence of three entitled "The Path to the Moon," "Diana," and "All Thy Waves are Gone Over Me." Each of these resonates with Stephen's proto-poem: the last, in particular, shows a "pale vampire" "through storm his eyes" with "bat sails bloody-ing the sea." In his introduction to the volume, Yeats comments that this particular image reveals "a kind of humorous piety like that of the medi-aeval miracle-plays and moralities" and treats the drawings generally as artifacts of symbolist thought experiments (14). This further suggests that we not be fooled by the fact that attention to process usually heightens the aura surrounding an artwork; to the contrary, Stephen's literary genesis on the strand has as much in common with Bloom's visit to the outhouse as it does with the writing of the villanelle.

In fact the no-nonsense attention to process in the Proteus scene of literary genesis makes it all but impossible to maintain the idea, fre-quently asserted by critics, that Stephen is gripped by grief or his psyche tortured by demonic visions. The way he talks to himself is clear, care-

[18] Budgen, *James Joyce and the Making of Ulysses*, 55.
[19] *A Book of Images Drawn by W.T. Horton & Introduced by W.B. Yeats* (London: Unicorn Press, 1898).

ful, and unemotional, reminiscent not of the villanelle but of the rhetoric of self-control and release Bloom used for his defecation. "Put a pin in that chap" says Stephen, before adding a mental note to edit to two mouths: "Must be two of em" "Glue em well." (Incidentally, this little discussion Stephen has with himself about how to compose this line is at odds with critics' claims that it is simply plagiarized).[20] And even as he is scribbling the words, at precisely the moment of (what should be) his greatest rapture and concentration, he muses detachedly, in a complete, quiet sentence, "That's twice I forgot to take slips from the library counter." Bloom manifests the same "yielding but resisting" attitude as he simultaneously reads and allows "his bowels quietly to ease themselves": "No great hurry. Keep it a bit" (*U* 4.501-7). Neither of them is composing in a species of fine frenzy.[21]

Ultimately, in the transition between the *Portrait* and "Proteus" Stephens, the shift from genesis as royal birth to genesis as excretion, we can glimpse the onset of a Nietzschean-Foucauldian attitude toward the origin:

> History also teaches how to laugh at the solemnities of the origin. The lofty origin is no more than "a metaphysical extension which arises from the belief that things are most precious and essential at the moment of birth." We tend to think that this is the moment of their greatest perfection, when they emerged dazzling from the hands of a creator or in the shadowless light of a first morning. The origin always precedes the Fall. It comes before the body, before the world and time; it is associated with the gods, and its story is always sung as a theogony. But historical beginnings are lowly: not in the sense of modest or discreet like the steps of a dove, but derisive and ironic, capable of undoing every infatuation.[22]

III. STEPHEN IN "AEOLUS": THE VAMPIRE OF THE SON

In "Aeolus," characters like O'Madden Burke, Myles Crawford, Professor MacHugh, and Lenehan are all so loud that they destroy the possibility of quiet conversation, much less meditative or lyric thought.[23] Stephen is subdued and overblown, and when his "Proteus" poem returns to his mind—set aside in italics—it is in a typically windy moment with many open and competing dialogic frames, beginning with Lenehan's riddle:

---

[20] For a genetic analysis of Proteus and of this passage that takes into account the manuscripts acquired in 2002 by the National Library of Ireland, see Sam Slote's "Epiphanic Proteus."

[21] If Stephen's exertions recall Bloom's defecations, they also adumbrate the scene in "Nausicaa" when, nine hours later in precisely the same place, Bloom will ejaculate and produce another work-in-progress destined to dissolve and go unread.

[22] Foucault, "Nietzsche, Genealogy, History," 79.

[23] By contrast with Stephen, Bloom's attitude toward poetry is partly informed by the efficient and prosaic genetic conditions of the newspaper business that we glimpse early in *Aeolus*. In an exchange with Bloom about the Alexander Keyes advertisement, Red Murray, with a "pen behind his ear," tells him: "Of course, if he wants a par... we can do him one" (*U* 7.34-5). Amid all the mental and mechanical processes involved in turning out a great organ, Murray's smaller organ is always already out.

—Silence! What opera resembles a railwayline? Reflect, ponder, excogitate,reply.
Stephen handed over the typed sheets, pointing to the title and signature.
—Who? the editor asked.
Bit torn off.
—Mr Garrett Deasy, Stephen said.
—That old pelters, the editor said. Who tore it? Was he short taken?

On swift sail flaming
From storm and south
He comes, pale vampire,
Mouth to my mouth.

—Good day, Stephen, the professor said, coming to peer over their shoulders. Foot and mouth? Are you turned...?
Bullockbefriending bard.

SHINDY IN WELLKNOWN RESTAURANT
—Good day, sir, Stephen answered blushing. The letter is not mine. Mr Garrett Deasy asked me to... [*U* 7.513-41]

Despite many confident pronouncements, every critic who has given this scene and the poem any attention has had trouble with it, usually struggling in one way or another with the problem of its origins. These include Robert Day, David Hayman, Robert Martin Adams, Stanley Sultan, Murray McArthur, Michael Murphy, Tim Martin, Sam Slote, Fritz Senn, and Hans Walter Gabler. A good portion of the debate has been about the quality of the poem, a key point of contention being the way it seems to echo the last stanza of the poem "Grief on the Sea" from the Gaelic Leaguer and Irish folklorist Douglas Hyde's *Love Songs of Connacht*:

And my love came behind me—
He came from the South;
His breast to my bosom,
His mouth to my mouth.

Thus one reason Stephen blushes as he recalls his poem may be that he knows he has incorporated a line from Hyde's book, precisely the book that the insufferable Haines is so excited about. (Stephen could also be embarrassed to do Deasy's bidding, embarrassed about his poem, embarrassed that he was in fact "short taken.") Best later explains in "Scylla and Charybdis" that Haines is "quite enthusiastic, don't you know, about Hyde's *Lovesongs of Connacht*. I couldn't bring him in to hear the discussion. He's gone to Gill's to buy it" (*U* 9.93-5). Eglinton comments that the "peatsmoke is going to his head," and there is room to believe it may also have gone to Stephen's (*U* 9.100). Some critics see Stephen's borrowing or plagiarism—there are many potential sources besides the ones so far mentioned—as Joyce's critique of his former self; others argue that the poem, in the best traditions of folklore, is of mixed heritage and represents something like a distilled version of the relentlessly intertextual *Ulysses*, a miniature experiment in Bakhtinian dialogicity.[24]

The nutrients in Stephen's piece of shit have often been analyzed, but rarely has the awkward dynamic of the poem's suppression and return been addressed. The problem is acute because the poem's radical distance from its origins—e.g. its origins in many other texts, in Stephen's body and mind, or in the Proteus chapter of *Ulysses*—makes it virtually unreadable and uninterpretable. The surfeit of visible intertexts may suggest just the opposite—that the poem is bursting with a postmodern semantic plenitude—and so might the existence of so many critical interpretations, but before we can even describe those intertextual relationships the problem is to know where the poem is, to what it attaches or refers, and these are virtually unsolvable problems.[25] To take but one example: to whom does "He" refer in the third line? Putting the poem back in "Proteus," we might assign it to the enDraculated "ruffian," as if the poem were voiced by the female gipsy cocklepicker, or else (despite the gender of the pronoun) to Stephen's mother, mutating the vampire theme prominent in "Nestor" (e.g. Stephen's identification with the blood-sucking student Cyril Sargent) and elsewhere (e.g. "Circe" where Stephen sees his mother as a ghoulish chewer of corpses.) Stanley Sultan addresses the protean pronoun problem by

---

[24] McArthur is one of the most enthusiastic: "In Stephen's writing, we don't see a second-rate poet plagiarizing a rather inferior source, but the process of intertextuality itself, in which one text develops out of another and larger field of texts (*Dracula*, *A Book of Images*, etc.). Stephen, after all, does on a very small scale what Joyce does in borrowing and transforming the Odyssey and many other texts to produce *Ulysses*. Stephen's spontaneous inscription also fulfills the prophecy at the end of *A Portrait*: "I go to encounter for the millionth time the reality of experience and to forge in the smithy of my soul the uncreated conscience of my race." Borrowed from the speech of the folk, Stephen's poem is a perfect example of the "uncreated conscience of my race." In "Proteus," we are also given a direct representation of the process of literary creation in the "smithy of my soul," and that process does not produce an original work of art, but a copy of other copies. Although Stephen changes and adapts his copy, just as Joyce adapted his copy of the *Odyssey*, it is still a copy" (Murray McArthur, "'Signs on a White Field': Semiotics and Forgery in the 'Proteus' Chapter of *Ulysses*," *ELH* 53.3 [Autumn, 1986]: 633-652; 650). Gifford's annotations describe the poem more dismissively as "a souped-up (Canting Academy) version of the last stanza of "My Grief on the Sea." Gifford also glosses the bat as a medieval symbol: "in the Middle Ages the bat was symbolic of black magic, darkness, and rapacity and was a portent of peril or torment" (Don Gifford with Robert J. Seidman, *Ulysses Annotated: Notes for James Joyce's Ulysses* [Berkeley: University of California Press, 1988] 62).

[25] A related problem is whether the poem on the page is the same as the poem in the pocket. *Does* Stephen remember it? Does he reproduce it exactly, or does he alter it to suit the circumstances in which he finds himself? This second option is precisely what Bloom does in "Lestrygonians." Fritz Senn notes that "we cannot tell whether the version given in typographical arrangement (suitable for a chapter dealing with printing and newspapers) is what Stephen wrote down on the beach. For all we know, he could have transformed the four lines several times in Protean perpetuation. We only know that selective and compositional changes were being made in between. Without the later passage, the earlier one would remain highly opaque... Hindsight discloses a major narrative omission" (Fritz Senn, *Inductive Scrutinies: Focus on Joyce*, ed. Christine O'Neill [Baltimore, MD: The Johns Hopkins University Press, 1995] 86).

interpreting the vampire as neither Stephen nor his mother: he sees Stephen composing a "crude quatrain about the coming of a personified death to his mother" and argues that it is "far more polished" by the time we see it in "Aeolus."[26]

If we attach the poem to "Aeolus," then the choices are just as numerous: "He" might be Deasy—a pale vampire sucking Stephen's artistic lifeblood—or, oddly, Professor MacHugh, who is a candidate because the poem says "He comes" at precisely the moment that he does. MacHugh may seem like an unlikely vampire, but the detail of his noisily flossing his teeth a few pages earlier is suggestive. Or maybe the idea is the one suggested to me by Terence Killeen, that Stephen has been called from a distance and is moving unknowingly but inexorably toward the more kindly vampire Bloom.

There are other options. The point is that by the time we read this vampire poem it has been decontextualized but not meaningfully recontextualized, brought back to Stephen's (Protean? Aeolian?) consciousness not by any sequence of ideas or images (he is not thinking about vampires or kisses or mouths or south) but by its materiality: the paper befouled by the poem. Thus it is an error to analyze it either New Critically as a free-standing lyric or poststructurally as a play with signifiers and intertexts; it is best understood as a failed genesis expressed through a poetics of excretion. Exiled, it appears in Aeolus not as a delayed presence or a connection across time to a primordial Edenville atelier, but as a deracinated anachronism, a Kevin Egan, a wince-inducing memory, and an autobiographico-archeological discovery of a poorly wrought urn. Its status in *Ulysses* becomes clearer when we compare it to Bloom's and Mulligan's literary geneses.

IV. "LESTRYGONIANS": THREE QUARKS FOR MR. BLOOM

The advertisement to which Martha Clifford and many other women responded was from a man who, just like Stephen, styles himself as "literary." In the outhouse Bloom thinks of writing a collaborative piece with Molly, a short story to illustrate a proverb—"Which?" he asks himself as if this were the main creative problem to solve—and another time tries, in a quasi-programmatic epiphanic mode, jotting down on his cuff what she says while dressing. In "Sirens" he will actually put pen to paper to compose a letter to Clifford, in "Nausicaa" he will start a message in the sand to Gertie McDowell, and in "Ithaca" the narrator recalls some poems he had written at the ages of 11 and 22.

But early in "Lestrygonians," Bloom momentarily becomes a poet again at the age of 38. He is thinking of food, of rats in vats of porter (the homonymy strikes him), of throwing himself in the river, of the example of Reuben J.'s son who nearly drowned, and of seagulls. He

---

[26] Stanley Sultan, *The Argument of Ulysses* (Columbus, OH: Ohio State University Press, 1964) 58.

throws down a ball of paper—a crumpled-up throwaway ad for the coming of Elijah—and thinks to himself: Elijah is coming at 32 feet per second per second. But the birds are not fooled: they think neither that the paper is food nor that Elijah is coming. They just wheel about, flapping. Then we read:

> The hungry famished gull
> Flaps o'er the waters dull.
> That is how poets write, the similar sounds. But then Shakespeare has no rhymes: blank verse. The flow of the language it is. The thoughts. Solemn.
> Hamlet, I am thy father's spirit Doomed for a certain time to walk the earth. [U 8.62-8]

Bloom's poem is a different kind of Joycean experiment on deracinated or un-originated poetics, for it is in print before or outside of any process of composition. Even to call it "Bloom's" poem is loose, for it is "his" only by virtue of the fact that it occurs in his consciousness, in the conventional poetic language (e.g. "o'er") he has inherited from his cultural milieu, and not because he lays claim to artistic agency. There are just the words arranged, instantly and unproblematically—one must say unthinkingly and unpoetically. No calling for tablets, no tortured intensity, no rapture, no mixtures of intertexts, no pre-proto-primordial onomatopoiea—in short, no genetic event.

Nor, although it would have supplied him with paper, does Bloom regret throwing away his throwaway. He dispenses happily with the supplement of material inscription, and his insouciance toward *écriture* raises the uncomfortable question of why Stephen and Buck are so desperate to write things down. Does Joyce betray here an attraction for the fatherless text, the epiphanic product of a thought that is free of literary erudition and thoughtlessly true to the essence of what is observed and no more? Bloom speaks the whatness of gullness of allgull, and, however dull, the poem's dullness is the dullness of truth. And he does so instantaneously, in thought represented as "thought" or "writing" or "creation" only *ex post facto*. The poem becomes a "poem" only when a genesis is invented for and retroactively applied to it. In fact, taken alone, Bloom's paperless poem seems to admit no interpretation, no hermeneutic depth, no symbolism—it seems able to become complex only when placed in a dialectic with others.

While Stephen has his identity wrapped up in his status as a bard— painfully, since he is a *poète manqué*—Bloom announces himself as a non-poet and sees his couplet only as the kind of thing others do. His thought is that poets pay attention to "similar sounds"; in his example the gull-dull rhyme stands out along, perhaps, with the subtler assonance and consonance of "famished" and "Flaps." But maybe Lenehan is right that there is "a touch of the artist about old Bloom," for although his poem has not sent critics scrambling backwards to famous verses on skylarks, nightingales, and albatrosses or uses of the gull / dull rhyme, the six feet do scan perfectly as iambic trimeters or, run together, as a single hexameter (the meter of the Homeric epic), i.e. an alexandrine with an internal rhyme and a conventional caesura (*U* 10.582-3). And on second thought, perhaps the poem does require some interpretation: does the "hungry famished" sequence represent thoughtless repetition? Or intensification? Or revision within the poem? Does Bloom violate a principle of lyric economy or capture the extra-hungry hunger of gulls?

This poem-without-or-before-genesis postulates not automatic writing (the poem's form is too conventional) but the furthest possible radicalization of the idea of the passive artist. For this is a portrait of art without artistry or artist, of epiphanic illuminations that need no sensitive soul to receive and record them with great care. For all its pragmatism and simplicity, the poem therefore represents a limit case or unreachable asymptote in Joycean composition: gloriously, Bloom will not leave 25,000+ pages of avant-texte. He'll leave none, and no text either.

Perhaps most importantly, the straightforward couplet reflects the poetics of the *homme moyen sensuel* and joins the *Ulyssean* project of contrapuntally reframing, perhaps even redeeming, the youthful, aestheticizing, omphalos-observing Stephen. Readers are invited to compare the two poems and scenes of genesis not only because they share basic situations (a bat and a bird flying over water) and stylistic features (present-tense verbs in third person singular, masculine rhymes) but also because Stephen's poem appears suddenly in his mind in "Aeolus" and Bloom's in *his* right at the beginning of the next chapter, "Lestrygonians." But while the vampire that Stephen complicatedly imagines and outsources comes across the water on batwings as a restless, miscegenated, bilious composite of immediate experience, memory, and many texts carrying a welter of associations, Bloom's gull is just hungry, very hungry, and right there in front of him. His poem belongs to him not because he composes it but because its empathetic and realist poetics originate in his character.

The differences between the two literary geneses and their products are striking, but we might ask whether it is really fair to see Bloom's unheroic-heroic couplet—as well, perhaps, as the modes of human being and creativity it reflects—as initiating a dialectic with Stephen. It is if we accept that, for the reader of *Ulysses*, it is not an innocent example when Bloom cites Shakespeare's *"Hamlet, I am thy father's spirit,"* but rather a way for Bloom to announce himself (unconsciously) as a spirit-father, or benevolent vampire, to Stephen. (The rest of the quotation is obviously appropriate to Bloom, too, for he is doomed to walk the earth: he is a Jew, a cuckold who cannot return home, and a canvasser for ads.) Bloom's actions also prepare for the way he will treat and be treated by Stephen. Where Stephen excretes his poem, stretches out on the rocks, urinates, and picks his nose, Bloom continues to worry about the welfare of the seagulls he has lyricized, even though (in another detail that links the scenes) "they spread foot and mouth disease" (*U* 8.84-5). He buys them two Banbury cakes for a penny and feeds them, just as he will take such pains to feed Stephen in "Eumaeus," finally noting, with characteristic equanimity, how ungrateful the gulls seem to be: "Lot of thanks I get. Not even a caw" (*U* 8.84).

Later in "Lestrygonians," Bloom sees George Russell, the mystic, with a young woman; he remembers the language of the personal ad that he placed—"To aid gentleman in literary work"—then wonders what Russell is saying to her; he assumes it is "something occult: symbolism" (*U* 8.530). Russell's beard, bicycle, and vegetarianism come together in his mind, and he thinks:

> Her stockings are loose over her ankles. I detest that: so tasteless. Those literary etherial people they are all. Dreamy, cloudy, symbolistic. Esthetes they are. I wouldn't be surprised if it was that kind of food you see pro-duces the like waves of the brain the poetical. For example one of those policemen sweating Irish stew into their shirts; you couldn't squeeze a line of poetry out of him. Don't know what poetry is even. Must be in a cer-tain mood.
> *The dreamy cloudy gull Waves o'er the waters dull* [*U* 8.542-550].

Like an engaged anthropologist or ethnographer, Bloom tries his hand at writing like one of these strange vegetarians and dreamy, cloudy es-thetes. He falsifies reality (gulls are hungry, not dreamy) and fleetingly proposes a broad explanation for literary genesis: poetry results from mood, and mood from food. Out goes the "hungry famished" gull and in comes the "dreamy cloudy" one; out goes the realist "Flaps" and in comes the oneiric "Waves." Irish stew could never produce such writing, but that may not be a bad thing; Bloom remains sympathetically equidis-tant from both gassy mystics and sweaty policemen. His genetic logic seems meant in part for Stephen, whose fecal vampire poem he would probably trace to overreading.

V. "SCYLLA & CHARYBDIS": BUCK MULLIGAN'S PEN ISOLATES HIM

Finally, Buck Mulligan's moment of literary genesis occurs at the end of Stephen's dialogue in *Scylla and Charybdis*. Stephen's long last sentence ends:

> ...in the economy of heaven, foretold by Hamlet, there are no more mar-riages, glorified man, an androgynous angel, being a wife unto himself.
> — Eureka! Buck Mulligan cried. *Eureka!*
> Suddenly happied he jumped up and reached in a stride John Eglinton's desk.
> — May I? he said. The Lord has spoken to Malachi.
> He began to scribble on a slip of paper.
> Take some slips from the counter going out. [*U* 9.1051-8]

Instead of being something to think about seriously, the promise of a permanent state of self-sustaining androgyny in the economy of heaven represents for Mulligan a chance to mock the unmarried men in the library. He performs his grandiose literary genesis while Stephen, Eglinton, and Best continue their conversation, awkwardly negotiating the competing demands of silently writing and attracting attention: at one point he stands "up from his laughing scribbling, laughing" (*U* 9.1086). When he and Stephen are leaving the library together, he performs:

> I have conceived a play for the mummers, he said solemnly.
> The pillared Moorish hall, shadows entwined. Gone the nine men's morrice with caps of indices.
> In sweetly varying voices Buck Mulligan read his tablet:
> —Everyman His Own Wife
> or
> A Honeymoon in the Hand
> (a national immorality in three orgasms)
> by
> Ballocky Mulligan
> He turned a happy patch's smirk to Stephen, saying:
> —The disguise, I fear, is thin. But listen.
> He read, marcato...
> He laughed, lolling a to and fro head, walking on, followed by Stephen:
> and mirthfully he told the shadows, souls of men... [*U* 9.1167-91]

Appearing shortly after Stephen's critique of the literary talent of the God of *Genesis*—"The playwright who wrote the folio of this world and wrote it badly (He gave us light first and the sun two days later)..."— Mulligan's composition is clearly a masturbation; he is the only person pleased by it (*U* 9.1046-8). His self-satisfying performance in front of Stephen recalls Deasy's journalistic genesis in "Nestor"—"I don't mince words, do I?" was his rhetorical question—but at least Deasy had a public issue in mind (2.331). As the ironic play on the word "conception" suggests—"I have conceived a play for the mummers"—Mulligan's various voices, smirking, laughing, and lolling head reveal too much pleasure taken in a puerile and sterile production.

Stephen has performed in the arena of the "nine men's morrice" dance, Mulligan only on the side. Twice, once before and once after his composition, we hear that he speaks to "shadows" rather than to real people. Because his creativity is so ostentatiously public but his creation audible only to an audience of one (Stephen, who does not acknowledge it) Mulligan's scene represents the limit point of a prestidigitative artist and an artistry without any art: the opposite, then, of the Bloomian genesis.

If Stephen's literary shit has the potential to become fertilizer—it is a very rich composite, if repugnant in its present form—and Bloom's poem has the force of honesty and humility, then Mulligan's obnoxious play is so much spilled seed,[27] all the more clearly a failure because it arrives third in this little economy, i.e. in the Hegelian position of synthesis. Coming off as a juvenile failure and missed opportunity, Mulligan lacks the strengths visible, sketchily but unmistakeably, in Stephen (serious-ness, erudition, experimentalism) and Bloom (integrity, empathy, directness). His literary genesis reveals mainly that he has removed him-self from the valuable, if still largely symbolic, human dialectic developing between the other two.

VI. CONCLUSION

What does this brief study suggest about the hermeneutic conse-quences, for genetic critics and others, of Joyce's fictionalized scenes of literary genesis? The lengthy and absolute genesis enshrined, with what-ever degree of irony, in the villanelle scene in *A Portrait* has in *Ulysses* been fragmented into shorter, more individualized ones. There is no pre-tense to a single poetics of genesis, no aesthetic vocabulary or metaphorical system from Aquinas or the book of *Genesis* to underpin the various scenes of writing. On the contrary, the conceptual and metaphorical frameworks that guide our understanding of the genetic processes examined above—Stephen's excretion, Bloom's default to cultural norms, Mulligan's masturbation—are all presented as obviously partial and insufficient.

Of a piece with this detranscendentalizing, genealogical attitude to-ward literary genesis in *Ulysses* is the way Joyce pursues a *via negativa* instead of a heroic model, algebraically manipulating unsuccessful scenes of genesis with larger, more positive goals in mind. The genetic economy of Stephen, Bloom, and Mulligan recalls that of *Dubliners* in which Joyce used figures like Little Chandler, Ignatius Gallaher, Joe Hynes, and Gabriel Conroy to show the kinds of writers he did not wish to become, all without depicting ones he did. But while the *Dubliners* authors were essentially beyond hope, somewhere in the abstract for-mula "Stephen plus Bloom minus Mulligan" lies a more promising origin myth for the text of *Ulysses*.

Taken together, the foregoing scenes suggest that scholars of the profoundly genealogical author Joyce might look more synoptically and simultaneously at the poetics of genesis in play in different units of his texts and avant-textes. Looking at the published text of *Ulysses* is al-ready enough to encourage us to continue developing the field of differential or comparative genetics, for example by examining and com-paring more partial, localized, abortive, or otherwise unheroic and

---

[27] It is therefore ironic that in his conversation with Haines in "Wandering Rocks," Mulligan claims that Stephen will never be a poet because he cannot understand creation, birth, and death. The Jesuits drove Stephen's "wits astray" with "visions of hell," Mulligan opines, and so preempted the "note of Swinburne, of all poets, the white death and the ruddy birth." That, he concludes, is Stephen's "tragedy. He can never be a poet. The joy of creation" (*U* 10.1072-5).

unconsummated genetic events. Ultimately, the book also suggests that it can itself be interpreted as a retrospective commentary on its own genesis, and on genesis itself. Like every other piece of new genetic scholarship, it has the potential to put its stamp on the soft wax of genetic theory and criticism.

ALEXANDRA DUMITRESCU
Mapping Networking Universes, or, Bootstrapping *Finnegans Wake* in Search of Truth

1. PRELUDE

Speaking to the Polish writer Jan Parandowski, James Joyce illuminated his technique and vision in a way which supports the increasingly well-spread assumption with regards to the enhanced accessibility of the *Wake* as a vocalised, rather than a read, text:

> the few fragments [of *Finnegans Wake*] which I have published have been enough to convince many critics that I have finally lost my mind, which, by the way, they have been predicting faithfully for many years. And perhaps it is madness to grind up words in order to extract their substance, to create crossbreeds and unknown variants, to open up unsuspected possibilities for these words, to marry sounds which were not usually joined before although they were meant for one another, to allow water to speak like water, birds to chirp in the words of birds, to liberate all sounds from their servile, contemptible role and to attach them to the feelers of expressions which grope for definitions of the undefined.... With this hash of sounds I am building the great myth of everyday life.[1]

Thus, there is no doubt that the *Wake* world is meant to be listened to. The author himself entreats us to lend our ears to its music:

> Lissom! Lissom! I am doing it. Hark, the corne entreats! And the larpnotes prittle. [*FW* 21.2-4]

Sounds do not structure hierarchically. Unlike written words which relate hierarchically, there is no precedence of one sound over another: the initial fiat, Joyce seems to suggest is as present as any sound or word ever pronounced. Sounds accumulate and interrelate, storm into one another and depart creating whirlwords that mirror "whirlworlds":

> Countless of livestories have netherfallen by this plage, flick as flowflakes, litters from aloft, like a waast wizard all of whirlworlds. [*FW* 17.26-9]

[1] Quoted in Armand and Pilný, eds., *Night Joyce of a Thousand Tiers. Petr Škrabánek: Studies in Finnegans Wake* (Prague: Litteraria Pragensia, 2002) 2.

2. ABSTRACT

The vortex-like succession of words and sounds, evocative of concepts, ideas, or whole paradigms of thought in James Joyce's *Finnegans Wake* may be interpreted as suggestive of the fact that human experience does not structure itself hierarchically in meaningful categories. This is further reinforced by the free associations—that the notebooks, in conjunction with the finished text often reveal—between images, concepts, narratives. When read parallel with Joyce's notebooks, *Finnegans Wake* expounds a theory of knowledge and of literature that can be understood in the light of the latest discoveries and scientific results. Re-defining the concept of bootstrap and applying it to cultural paradigms and literary texts, the paper will address the question whether the bootstrap model may and can be fruitfully employed in trying to understand the complex world of *Finnegans Wake*.

In the Preface to the second edition of *The Cambridge Companion to James Joyce*, Derek Attridge notes that 'in *Finnegans Wake*, [Joyce] attempted to embrace the languages and cultures of the entire human community' (xii). By associating non-hierarchical items of information, Joyce seems to suggest that no significant barriers separate epistemes as diverse as mythology, science and literature, pre-Christianity, Christianity and atheism or *libre pensée*. The bootstrap model will help to interpret these domains as representing structured agglomerations of concepts that stand for nodes in epistemic networks. The sum of these networks comprises the entire human knowledge and all vocalised achievements as invoked in *Finnegans Wake* and presumably made somewhat more accessible and comprehensible by the notebooks.

3. DEFINING BOOTSTRAPPING

As a philosophical term, bootstrapping refers to a conception of the material world as an interconnected web of relations.[2] The bootstrap philosophy is potentially appealing to postmodern theorists, as it 'not only abandons the idea of fundamental building blocks of matter, but accepts no fundamental entities whatsoever—no fundamental constants, laws or equations.' The bootstrapping model regards "the universe [...] as a dynamic web of interrelated events. None of the properties of any part of this web is fundamental; they all follow from the properties of the other parts, and the overall consistency of their interrelations determines the structure of the entire web."[3]

[2] Fritjof Capra, *The Turning Point: Science, Society, and the Rising Culture* (London: Wildwood House 1982).
[3] Capra, *The Turning Point*, 39.

3.1. BOOTSTRAPPING & THEORY

If a text can be construed as a network made up of nodes and links between them, bootstrapping refers to the dynamics of the network. Its defining function is the emergence of meaning as a result of this dynamism. Because it signifies the dynamism of a network, bootstrapping allows for the simultaneous co-existence and applicability of different models (or paradigms of understanding) that may emerge from one and explain and complete one another. Thus, paradigms of thought as diverse as postmodernism and metamodernism[4] are not seen as mutually exclusive, but as completing and defining each other. Moreover, their explanatory relevance emerges from their interrelation. To give just an example relating to one aspect of the two paradigms: only after dissatisfied with the ethics of proximity will one understand the need for a kind of ethics that govern human relationship worldwide. This means that one is aware of the existence of a previous pattern of thought, but is able to see its limitations, and, preserving its functional aspects, is capable of integrating it.[5]

3.2. BOOTSTRAPPING TEXTS

Contrary to regressive genetic analysis (that would read earlier versions of a text in the light—blinding, more often than not—of the final text[6]), and refining the radical progressive readers' approach (that might regard all versions as having been created equal) bootstrapping stands for a model that attempts to pin down the interconnectivity between different versions of a text, between the text and the mind of the reader, and between the text and the world.

In this essay, however, I will not rest at length upon bootstrapping the text of *Finnegans Wake* as such, but rather on pinpointing the important part that interconnectivity and networking play in structuring the world of a final version of the text (2 February 1939).[7] And in order to do that I need to cast a glance at the ways in which Joyce organises his world in the *Wake*.

---

[4] As we cannot ponder at length upon it at this stage, suffice it to say that the concept of metamodernism may be employed to describe a paradigm of thought subsequent to the postmodern one. For further clarifications regarding metamodernism, see Alexandra Dumitrescu, "Innocence and Experience in Arundhati Roy's *The God of Small Things*," *Rites of Passage in Postcolonial Women's Writing*, eds. Pauline Dodgson and Gina Wisker (Amsterdam and New York: Rodopi, forthcoming) and "Interconnections in Blakean and Metamodern Space," *Double Dialogues* 7/2007.

[5] To give just an example relating to one aspect of the two paradigms: it is only after one is dissatisfied with the ethics of proximity that s/he will understand the need for a kind of ethics that govern human relationship worldwide. This comes down to saying that an ethic of proximity— characteristic of postmodernism and the ages before— coexists, in a metamodern age, with the imperative for a global type of ethics. And it is in relation with the former that the latter is being shaped.

[6] In many genetic accounts, though, the "final text" is but part of a process rather than an end.

[7] The 2 February 1939 limited edition was by no means *the* final one, as it was closely followed by a trade edition on 4 May 1939, which included some corrections. The two 1939 editions were the only anthumous ones.

4. THE MODERN IMPERATIVE: "MAKE IT NEW!" CONSEQUENCES & IMPLICATIONS

Traditional pre-modernist narratives would be organised as hierarchical orderly structures with identifiable beginning, content and conclusion. Against the grain of such a tradition and faithful to the modern imperative voiced by Ezra Pound to "make it new!," Joyce replaces the monolithic structure of narratives with repetitive spiral-like patterns that, through successively circular movements aspire to englobe the world's cultural inheritance, every-day experience and life itself, with its cross breeding and errors, changes and noises, meaningless(ness) or meaningful(ness).

4.1. CROSSBREEDS & NETWORKS

Paraphrasing his conversation with Jan Parandowski quoted above, it can be said that Joyce attempted to crush words in order to sublimate their essence and create new unexpected ones from fragments of the old. He allowed words to associate freely—as images and memories do in dreams—as if submitting to the forces of attraction for one another, in the hope of freeing them of their loathsome role as mere signifiers, as pointers to a reality other than their own.

Following in the footsteps of William Blake, his Romantic predecessor who attempted to create a whole mythology of political and spiritual resurrection with a view to implement a politics of awakening by means of his artistic work, James Joyce takes pains to outline a kosmos in which the different ontological levels exist inasmuch as they are rendered in linguistic form, a world that stands for its own immanence and transcendence, a mythological universe that contains its own text and interpretation.

Although tantalizing, the well-spread assumption that *Finnegans Wake* "manages to deconstruct the very conditions that make it possible to speak or write about literature" will not arrest our attention here. I will resist the temptation to read it as "a paradigm of the fundamental conditions of literature and of language per se,"[8] and I will argue a slightly different point, namely that the *Wake* provides us with a (theoretical/linguistic) model of the world as an un-hierarchical structure of interconnected elements.

4.2. "A WAAST WIZARD ALL OF WHIRLWORLDS": MELTING POT OR STRUCTURED ORGANIZATION?

Finnegans Wake contains numerous instances of hierarchies being levelled down, all merging in the all-encompassing melting pot of human experience, countless life-stories governed by rules as simple and as

---

[8] Geert Lernout, "Further Notes Toward a Reading Proposal: *Work In Progress* and *Finnegans Wake*," *Papers on Joyce* 2 (1996) 35.

indomitable as death and love. These stories stretch the span of existence, human or not, from the first *fiat* to individual instances of death:

> Countless of livestories have netherfallen by this plage, flick as flowflakes,
> litters from aloft, like a waast wizard all of whirlworlds. Now are all
> tombed to the mound, isges to isges, erde from erde. Pride, O pride, thy
> prize! [*FW* 17.26-30]

The paradigmatic image is that of *babylone*, ostensibly unordered, un-
hierarchical, accumulation, characterized by *coincidentia opositorum*. In
this universe of ontological mirroring and linguistic mimicry, contrasts
and contraries co-exist: large and small, equal and unequal, inasmuch as
and inaslittle as:

> Fiatfuit! Hereinunder lythey. Llarge by the small an' everynight life olso
> th'estrange, babylone the greatgrandhotelled with tit tit tittlehouse, alp on
> earwig, drunk on ild, likeas equal to anequal in this sound seemetery
> which is leebez luv. [*FW* 17.32-6]

Echoing the Ecclesiastes' *vanitas vanitatum* Joyce's *erde*.[9] coupled with
the descending image of snow flakes accumulating: "flick as flowflakes,
litters from aloft," twirling in whirlwinds, or rather wirlworlds, as Joyce
puts it, reinforce the idea of a world image in which up and down, high
and low coexist as interchangeable coordinates. There is no privileged
topos. This world evinces not just a reversal of hierarchies—as in Blake,
for whom high is low and low is high, the elect are doomed and the
sinners ingratiated, hell takes on all energy and liveliness, whereas
heaven is stuck in motionless self-absorption and self righteousness—but
also a thorough cancellation of hierarchies that adumbrate postmodernism. For Joyce there seem to be no sublime and trite acts, no high and
low when it comes to lived experience: urinating seems as significant as
meditating in Ecclesiastes' terms on the *vanitas* of any undertaking.

4.3. UNHIERARCHICAL READS UNSTRUCTURED?
Perceived by critics as a labyrinth made up of seemingly senseless con-
catenations, this Babylonic image of the world that *Finnegans Wake*
displays is a view much in agreement with the non-hierarchical perception favoured in this paper. But are these accumulations in the *Wake* un-
hierarchical as well as unstructured?

The obvious answer would be *no*: there is structure displayed as re-
versibility. The very shape traced by the river Liffey is a paradigmatic
image as it indicates a return if not to, at least close to the point of origin. Similarly, the *Wake* world is mapped by returns perhaps not to the
spring, but somewhere to a stage that would re-enact the origin. This

---

[9] Erde derives from Erd, the Old English for earth.

stands for a recursive pattern that Joyce can identify not only in life, but also in stories and mythologies.

Finnegans Wake, with its unhierarchical textual organization affords a vision of the world crystallized alongside principles of interconnectivity: a universe perceived as made up of networks whose cultural, political, economical, historical or human nodes or hubs determine and explain each other. More significantly, *Finnegans Wake* advocates a vision of truth and meaning that unfold as a result of interconnections. Vortices — metaphoric correlatives of network hubs — map the world of the *Wake* as they do that of Blake's.

Joyce's narrative about HCE and his wife Anna Livia Plurabelle contains Everyman's and woman's story. HCE stands for the common, trite, devoid of sublimity post-lapsarian human, who seems to thrive in the precariousness of his fallen condition. Yet, the story of HCE's encounter with the king and his acquiring the Earwicker title may read as suggestive of the fact that even the tritest of stories may have a share in romance, that the most common of human beings is the descendant of someone who walked in the garden of Eden and communed with God(s). Everyone can be saved by a story, for everyone has a story to tell:

> The movibles are scrawling into motions, marching, all of them ago, in pitpat and zingzang for every busy eerie whig's a bit of a torytale to tell. One's upon a thyme and two's behind their lettice leap and three's among the shrubbery beds. [*FW* 20.21-3]

As opposed to the mind of the poetic genius which is distinguished by superior ways of organizing reality,[10] stories co-exist in the mind of everyman as units linked by free association, much in the way Joyce's words freely combine and merge. They develop meander-like patters that accommodate contraries:

> What a meanderthalltale to unfurl and with what end in view of squator and anntisquattor and postproneauntisquattor! [*FW* 19.25-7]

Joyce never tires of reinforcing the idea that the kosmos he creates, as the world he sees (and listens to), defies ranking not only when it comes to the sounds and words used to describe it and its dynamism, but also in terms of the non-linguistic constitutive elements it evokes:

> To sa too us to be very tim, nick and larry of us, sons of the sod, sons, littlesons, yea and lealittlesons, when uses not to be, every sue, siss and sally of us, daughters of Nan! [*FW* 19.27-30]

Interrelated stories map the history of humankind and of individuals: phylogeny and ontogeny interrelate and define one another:

[10] Frank Kermode, *Romantic Image* (London: Fontana, 1971).

For then was the age when hoops[11] ran high. Of a noarch and a chopwife; of a pomme full grave and a fammy of levity; or of golden youths that wanted gelding; or of what the mischievmiss made a man do...But lay it easy, gentle mien, we are in rearing of a norewhig. So weenybeenyveenyteeny. Comsy see! Het wis if ee newt. [*FW* 20.28-31, 21.2-4]

4.4. MAPPING JOYCE'S UNIVERSE

As we have seen, Joyce's world structures as multiple-centred network organised around what we can call vortices: agglomeratiors of meanings around which segments of text gravitate, describing recursive movements.

Circularity maps Joyce's universe not only structurally, but also in its thematic idiosyncrasies. Early critics such as Clive Hart would take at face value reports such as that of Adaline Glasheen; apparently Dr. O'Brien, a friend of Joyce's, informed her that Joyce had 'told him 'that *Finnegans Wake* was "about" Finn lying dying by the river Liffey with the history of Ireland and the world cycling through his head." Consequently, Hart thought he could identify "three consecutive four-part cycles in I.6, forming a microcosm of Books I-III."[12]

Moreover, the circular, or rather spiral-like movement from innocence to experience, and then to regained innocence—a favourite with Blake, Joyce's literary model for a while—finds its reflection in Joyce's concept of the *Wake* with its ambivalent meaning (as in "awakening" and as funeral "wake"). Associating presumably spiritual "awakening"— as the quintessential lived experience understood as an attempt at approximating the pre-lapsarian innocence—with the death of the body comes as no surprise when one thinks of Joyce as an author well-read in theological literature.[13]

Further impetus towards cyclical movement in *Finnegans Wake* is given by the "dream-representations of Finn-Earwicker at different stages of his career."[14] The phases of this movement are three, as with Blake: "first, the youthful vigour Finn is allotted two hundred years of full power (equivalent to the Earwicker of Book I)." Second, Finn lives through the decline and decrepitude of his last thirty years (the windy but effete Earwicker of Book II). And finally, the "moment of death, the 'auctual futule pretering unstant' of transition from one world to the next" stands for a state of "suspensive exanimation"[15] bringing together the ideas of re-animation, that is, new life—supposedly of a spiritual nature, as in Christ's resurrection —, and examination as a prerequisite for awareness. Thus, although apparently divergent, the cyclical patterns

---

[11] another circular suggestion.
[12] Clive Hart, *Structure and Motif in Finnegans Wake* (London: Faber and Faber, 1962) 81.
[13] Most Christian literature considers bodily annihilation as prerequisite for spiritual resurrection.
[14] Hart, *Structure and Motif*, 81.
[15] Hart, *Structure and Motif*, 81.

through which Blake's[16] and Joyce's characters live may be seen as converging in their overall outline, that is, in the movement from an initial moment of potentiality, to a stage in which energies are used to the full, then to a point where experience is examined and ascribed meaning.

6. NETWORKS & UNASHAMED TEARS

The very title of one of the major guides to understanding James Joyce's *Finnegans Wake* cannot fail to draw attention to the idea of linking and interconnectivity. Published in 1939, "A Symposium: Our Exagmination round his factification for incamination of Work in Progress," brings together in one title two possible keys to understanding *Finnegans Wake*: circularity (evoked by "round") and networking (suggested by "incamination"). "Incamination," in its turn, reminds of Italian *cammino* (way, road, path), and invokes "incatenation" or "incameration." These reinforce the fact that James Joyce himself and those who were the closest to him regarded his work as best understood both in its interconnectivity and circularity, as significance emerging from revisiting several hallmarks along the progression of the text. Moreover, the *Wake* reminds us once again that meaning emerges at the intersection between the text and reader's perception, cultural background, and aesthetic education, as a dynamic process that everyone experiences differently (which take us back to Lernout's position mentioned previously).

An example underscoring the connection between notebook entries and Joyce's overall frame of mind, his earlier preoccupation and constant concerns is provided by VI.C.1-64,[17] where a notebook entry in Joyce's own handwriting reads:

> mark my use of
> you—notice how I [1st 2 lines crossed over]
> God bless the prince
> of Wales
> sociable [line crossed over]
> physical hind ____
> in time
> waste time
> temporal
> con____ry
> contemporary
> Fr. Livingstone cf. I.M. north

---

[16] Blake's Albion, in *Jerusalem* is but one such example.
[17] James Joyce, *Finnegans Wake: A Facsimile of Buffalo Notebooks VI.C,* ed. Danis Rose (New York: Garland, 1978) 18. * Editorial Note: Notebook VI.C.1:64 is an amanuensis copy of what Joyce himself wrote in VI.B.16.132-33, the latter being available in the *Notebook Edition* published in Oct 2003. In a regressive perspective, Joyce took those notes from Pierre Key's *John McCormack: His Own Life Story* (1918).

G Wash and J. C
wept honest unashamed tears

The last line of the manuscript notebook echoes Blake's "voice of honest indignation"[18] especially if linked to one of Joyce's Padua notes. Joyce transcribes and translates from Italian into English a fragment by Pietro Colleta, in which the latter attempts to account for his persuasiveness. In a Blakean note, Coletta (1775-1831) invokes honesty as the justification of his charisma and creativity:

> Everyone who has known me has granted me a talent for persuading others: and I myself [...] have experience it on more than one occasion. The cause of this is not eloquence [...] for I am quite lacking in the art of oratory and in the wisdom on which oratory is based.[19]

Not eloquence, but heartfelt conviction lends persuasiveness to Coletta's charismatic discourse and texts: "I have always [...] I have always spoken in good faith."[20] Surprisingly, the sincerity of the one who never speaks "except at the bidding of conscience," the feeling of whom "is plainly legible in [his] eyes and gestures, in the logical consequences of the ideas"—fails to impress as heartfelt. Instead, he passes "in the world for a shrewd man, that is to say, a pretender, a liar and a sly deceiver."[21] Joyce's transcribing and translating the whole quote marks an act of appropriation and identification: Like Coletta and Blake, Joyce would construe the persuasive power springing from sincerity as the axis of his personality.

Despite tempting considerations regarding the possible theatricality of such remarks, i.e. the likelihood of Joyce's putting on a mask that may or may not become him, which may or may not express his position, we can sense here a certain uneasiness of Joyce's with not being read as he would be read. And a willingness on his part to have his texts be taken at their word and, what is more, to have the audience open towards receiving, understanding and appropriating the truth in defense of which he has taken up the pen.

In the Cornell notes Joyce praises Blake for "il coragio di portare nella strada il berretto rosso, emblema della nuova era."[22] It is this very courage to express one's position in spite of likely retaliation on the part of the authorities that constitutes much of the substance and concentrates much of the energy of Joyce's work, as well as Blake's.

---

[18] Blake, *The Marriage of Heaven and Hell*, Plate 12: "the voice of honest indignation is the voice of God."
[19] James Joyce, *Notes, Criticism, Translations, & Miscellaneous Writings* (New York and London: Garland, 1978) 273.
[20] Joyce, *Notes*, 274.
[21] Joyce, *Notes*, 274-5.
[22] Joyce, *Notes*, 215.

Thus, the appeal of Joyce to the intelligentsia of all nations has to do, perhaps, not only with a certain fascination exercised by the incomprehensible (or the difficult to understand) that requires clarification or disentanglement—which may or may not be one of the motivations behind several Blakean and Joycean studies—but also with a certain relentless vehemence of the artist's voice that oftentimes led him to assume positions that are quite shocking. A desire to raise their audience into awareness, to make readers vibrate to the truth that triggered the artist's vision, may well be the prime mover of Coletta's, Blake's and Joyce's discourses. When he ends his notebook entry VI.C-64[23] with "wept honest unashamed tears," following closely after the name of Livingstone, Joyce reiterates the quality and the duty of true visionaries to enlarge the knowledge and awareness of their contemporaries and posterity.

Danis Rose regards the materials for *Finnegans Wake* as mere importations from other sources.[24] Unsurprisingly, Joyce does what writers have always done: he sublimates and interprets, establishes new connections and ascribes novel meanings. But this he does to words, as opposed to other writers who may seem to be doing it with ideas, themes, stories, events, or characters. Moreover, the transformation undergone by words—from their sources (either bookish or vocalised experience) to the text of the *Wake*—is marked by series of intermediate steps, the notebooks being the first interpretive filters that words pass through in their way to the finite text. It is true that the entries in the notebooks seem to be direct or indirect quotations from sources that Joyceans are so keen to identify, but these serve as hallmarks—interpreted hallmarks, to be sure—that are far from being raw quotations thrown randomly in the river overflowing with words that the *Wake* is.

As many critics have noticed, Joyce's method is one that deepens the implications and the suggestive power of words by merging them (by marrying them, as a Blakean would put it), thus establishing unexpected connexions between words as entities, and between words as semantic fields, epistemes or paradigms of thought. In spite of warnings against searching for a key, a "scheme beyond the scheme," in the manuscripts, the bootstrapping model provides a useful tool. Defined as the dynamics of a network, bootstrapping allows for the coexistence of conflicting interpretations of the text, and, within the text itself, it focuses on meanings as emerging from the interaction between words and the various levels of the text, between notebooks, earlier versions and the final text. To 'bootstrap', in this context, would mean to consider the text, the manuscripts and biographical anecdotes as making up a whole that allows for a plurality of interpretations, none of which can be deemed to be 'false' or 'the only true.' Considering the interplay of many

---

[23] James Joyce, *Finnegans Wake. A Facsimile of Buffalo Notebooks*, VI.1,2,3,4,5,7, prefaced and arranged by Danis Rose (New York and London: Garland, 1978) 8.
[24] Danis Rose, *The Textual Diaries of James Joyce* (Dublin: The Lilliput Press, 1995) 332.

systems or cultural levels (such as the historical, mystical, theological, literary, etc), deeming none superior to another, what Joyce actually does is to "bootstrap" these, that is, he integrates them in a network within which they communicate and fertilise one another. Their meaning is thus developed and deepened as they interrelate. In an epistemological context, bootstrapping means the negation of a single absolute truth in favour of truths that interrelate and thus define themselves in the process.

Although likely to be equated with Blake's 'the same old dull round,' Giambattista Vico's image of the rebirth of the cycle of history, which Joyce certainly shared, encapsulates an inherently optimistic mood. In ages—such as his and ours—marred by the catastrophic result of apparently reasonable ideologies that would, on the level of collective psyche, proclaim the resurgence of the aggressive ego (masculine or otherwise), Joyce's *Finnegans Wake* advents an age of a contrasting movement towards the collective unconscious evoked by his feminine character Anna Livia Plurabelle and the Liffey river. As if dominated by a mother's perspective, which would be always impartial in her showering of attention to those within her reach, *Finnegans Wake*'s is a world undivided by hierarchies between ideas, words, worlds or concepts. Joyce leads the reader towards the realm beyond reasoned experience, where concepts and myths take form, and the fundamental unity of all linguistic and lived experience is revealed.

Thus, the bootstrap model affords an intuitive all-encompassing approach to and reading of *Finnegans Wake*, which yields a vision— traditionally associated with the waters of *materia prima* in alchemical texts—characterised by a feminine-like totalizing perspective, as opposed to the scintillating, yet limited, soundness of reason.

JOHN MARVIN
Finnegans Wake III.3 & the Third Millennium: The Ghost of Modernisms Yet to Come

A way a lone a last a loved a long the...
[... wren, the wren, the king of all birds.]

"The Third Watch of Shaun" traces an archeological expedition. On the surface rests the sublimely schizophrenic Yawn. In the deepest strata lurk the polyvalent gospelers who may hearken back to the four tormenters of Job, or even to the original tormenter trying to lure the wild man from Borneo back into a numbingly comfortable zoological garden.

The characters include a hillock and a variety of spectral phenomena such as might be evoked at a séance or an experiment in physics. How such characters interact may provide insight into art for life's sake; art as the means by which we can read all signs. This is the perspective of transmodernism extrapolated from Nietzschean critical theory brought to life in the latter (ladder) episodes of Ulysses and especially in the litter (letter) of the *Wake* where it adumbrates a possible cultural paradigm for the 21st century: "it is only as an *aesthetic phenomenon* that existence and the world are eternally *justified.*" [1]

Breadcrumbs scattered through the *Wake* show the reader how to "rede [...] its world" (*FW* 18.18-9). For example:

> (Stoop) if you are abcedminded, to this claybook, what curios of signs (please stoop), in this allaphbed! Can you rede [...] its world? It is the same told of all. Many. Miscegenations on miscegenations. Tieckle. They lived und laughed ant loved end left. Forsin. [*FW* 18.17-21]

To read *Finnegans Wake* one must stop and stoop—get down to earth, appreciate the moment at this space in time. A stoop can be as humble as a bow and as ferocious as the attack of a peregrine falcon. The letter that may be the *Wake* was scratched up by Biddy the hen, distant, humble cousin of the falcon, stooping by the stoop. The "allaphbed" might remind one of the olive bed, the secret by means of which Pene-

---

[1] Friedrich Nietzsche, *The Birth of Tragedy* trans. Douglas Smith (Oxford New York: Oxford University Press, 2000) 52.

lope finally reads through disguises and recognises Odysseus so it becomes a sign of return, reunion and a suggestion that Joyce was aiming
at synthesis, the reconciliation of opposites.

A-b-ce-d-minded—is alphabet minded, interacting with the world by
means of symbols, gestures, facial expressions, and postures. Along the
evolutionary way sounds (generated by gestures of the lungs, throat,
and mouth) combined with, then distanced themselves from, the external gestures to become the primary means of representation. The a-b-ce-
d-minded reader must be able to operate on the level of the fun-
damnmental particles of signing and recombining so as to see the many
faces of every word and the many worlds each represents.

Joyce provides a lecture on the history of communication from gestures, to sounds, to written symbols. Since God is dead, it is the
handwriting of nature that inscribes the world, then the walls of caves,
then the pages of books. Each step of the way handwriting becomes
more alienated from gestures and sounds, more arbitrary. Although
"mene, mene, tekel upharsin" means that nature qua nature writes its
own story which is interpreted by living things as part of the art of survival, humans seem to have evolved the ability to re-(or over-)write
nature's story. The extent to which this revision enhances survival remains to be seen. Perhaps we would have been better off with just a
"claybook," a book of earth, of the Earth, a book of the music (clef) of
the sphere. We seem to have chosen a wrenching change of key and it
is evidently too late to tune back.

> But the world, mind, is, was and will be writing its own wrunes for ever,
> man, on all matters that fall under the ban of our infraratioral senses fore
> the last milch-camel. [*FW* 19.35-20.2]

The world will write its own history until judgement day, but days of
judgement arrived when humans learned to reason and decided to recognise no limits to their ability to read. Joyce enjoys this belief and tests
its boundaries in the form of a hallucination or dream in which all of the
characters are the dreamer. Anthropomorphising the self, including the
author who is then murdered, is balanced by paramimesis—self parody
and mime from within. Postmodernism's murder-suicide has been overcome preemptively in Joyce by showing through parody, mime, and the
auto-ironic that the essential homunculus can be reborn as Übermensch.
Joyce's version of the handwriting on the wall is "many tickle foreskin."
It suggests that there is only one person generating the intracourse of
this chapter.

"What regnans raised the rains have leveled" (*FW* 56.36-57.1). The
hill was once a mountain, perhaps a volcano raining ash and smoke.
"Before he fell hill he filled heaven," mingled with the rain and formed
rivers "a stream, alplapping streamlet, coyly coiled um, cool of her curls"

(*FW* 57.10-12). Later, the rugged mountain has worn down to a rounded hill, perhaps the Hill of Howth or Uisneach.

"Pure Yawn lay low. On the mead of the hillock lay" (*FW* 474.1-2). Yawn breathes a hummed song. It is a deep, pure tone with harmonic overtones, and not so much a song as a moan, but rhythmic, throbbing with the possibility of meaning. It is earthy because Yawn is Earth, at least the living, historic, cultural infestations seething across the world. The intonation is reverie, perhaps drunkenness from the honey wine flowing from the hillock, fermented in the little hill or midden. Hills in all their forms form waves of seas and airs and granite outcroppings and limestone formations and the debris of oscillating ice sheets, rubble covered with growth as well as the Viconean waves of the cultures of the Occident also leaving behind artifacts, rubble upon which new growth can occur.

While Joyce was writing, Einstein was grappling with the relationship between the world of things we sense, and the uncertain, chaotic world view that emerges from quantum mechanics and the inexorable laws of chance. The four waves are lapping against the hill the hill the king of all hills because it is the human mountain that keeps on growing. Its limits cannot be determined because it doesn't make sense, there are no theories for it. It is that which is left over from the primordial chaos. In Joyce's time, as in our own, there was no theory that explained the universe. Relativity explained activity on a large scale and quantum mechanics explained the subatomic world, but the two are irreconcilable. Neils Bohr's followers say it doesn't matter. We can never know the thing in itself. All we can do is read meters and gauges and try to derive our understandings from experimental results. We are nothing more than "stenoggers" (*FW* 476.12) scribbling notes dictated by apparatus. We are inquisitors torturing the moaning mounds of cyclotrons, asking again and again, "What are you saying?"

HCE and Shaun become everybody by inheritance and through intrigue, allegation, rumor, rebirth, and the mystery of the text's boundless overlapping identities. It is not a difficult step from there to imagine him (them) as every place and every time, that is, the entire universe as understood by relativity, quantum mechanics, and soon by the forthcoming theory of everything that the physicists have been promising for at least a century.

The family is already associated with hills, rivers, rocks, trees, and clouds. The tale of Yawn is a "drama parapolylogic" (*FW* 474.5). It is beside and side by side as parallel paragraphs. It is beyond, past, a parodic, paranoid paradox. It is many parallel words and worlds all in the same place at the same time. Yawn is the hill upon which he is lying. He is the land upon which the hill rests. He is the world of which the land is an integral part.

These truths can be confirmed by an astrophysical lightshow of trails in a cloud chamber recorded as crackles of quanta interacting with a certain degree of violence. Such encounters in the sky result in trails of fireworks like the northern lights, or trails of sparks like burning meteors.

> Phopho!! The meteor pulp of him, the seamless rainbowpeel. Aggala!!!! His bellyvoid of nebulose with his neverstop navel. Paloola!!!!!! And his veins shooting melanite phosphor, his creamtocustard cometshair and his asteroid knuckles, ribs and members. Ooridiminy!!!!!!! His electrolatiginous twisted entrails belt. [*FW* 475.12-17]

Cosmic rays rain down from the hum of the musical universe. Larger litter, debris of supernovas, "nebulose," condensed to 'meteor pulp," constitute the stuff of which planets and all the life upon them is composed. Without knowing the process by which solar systems are made and the elements of life spilled upon the planets, Joyce intuitively wrote the poetry of creation into his text.

The gracehoper's song ends, "Your genus its worldwide, your spacest sublime!/But, Holy Saltmartin, why can't you beat time?" (*FW* 419.7-8). Music is a time art. Melody and rhythm, like logos, sweep songs inexorably along the temporal axis, the illusory narrative, the arrow that never turns back. Epic, drama, lyric, and all prose, left to their own devices, are confined to this one dimension. Writers have always sought ways to beat time, with occasional limited success. But Joyce realised that harmony is the means to beat the one dimensional world of the time axis and fly freely through the Einsteinian continuum. The 20th century project of physics has been to spatialise time by means of geometry. *Finnegans Wake* does the same thing by means of harmony, the spatial aspect of music, simulated by means of word play. Spatial dimensions in combination allow freedom of motion back and forth along and among three axes. Harmonic motion beats time, at least in any particular moment.

Common time, in Western music, is four-four time. The four, therefore, are not to be taken lightly. In spite of their apparent bumbling and grumbling they are the four dimensions that harmonise our perception of everything. On the other hand they are to be taken lightly. They represent, as light, the four forces of the universe: gravity, electromagnetism, and the two nuclear forces. Physicists have sought to achieve scientifically what Joyce achieved artistically: the unification of the four forces. He does so by blurring the boundaries among characters until all become one.

Mark claims that "yav hace not one pronouncable teerm [...] to signify majestate, [...] or mooner's plankgang there to lead us to hopenhaven" (*FW* 478.11-6). He emphasises Max Planck's quanta and the Copenhagen interpretation of quantum mechanics that has dominated particle physics since the 1920s. Its uncertainty principle is the perennial rape victim of postmodernism. Mark seems to be saying that there is no way to pin things down. The possible roads a particle can follow can only be guessed at according to the laws of chance. The problem is that the more completely it's examined the more uncertain it seems to become.

Yawn, in a wonderful parody, suggests it may be a linguistic problem.

—How? C'est mal prononsable, tartagliano, perfrances. Vous n'avez pas d'o dans votre boche provenciale, mousoo. Je m'incline mais Moy jay trouvay la clee dang les champs. Hay sham nap poddy velour, come on! [*FW* 478.19-22]

Yawn takes Einstein's side. He says that whatever difficulty the four are having understanding is only an artefact of the language being mispronounced. The key is the fields. Quantum mechanics harmonises the music of the spheres by means of force fields. Thus, in part, the interrogation of Yawn by the four is an argument about the fundamental nature of reality. Does it consist of hard little lumps that fly around according to the mechanistic laws of classical physics or of energy fields that collapse into matter as a result of certain interactions according to the probabilistic laws of quantum mechanics? These questions, like the phenomena about which they inquire, are suggested indirectly.

The many subjects of III.3 are disparate to communicate among themselves. How can such creatures, locked inside id entities, make contract. It's a long trope. "The Song of the Trees" (*FW* 503.26-506.8) provides an example of how the process might work if it can work. Yawn: "The flagstone. By tombs, deep and heavy. To the unaveiling memory of. Peacer the grave" (*FW* 503.26-7). The beginning is etched in stone. The *Wake* is constantly arcing between being and becoming. Joyce made philosophy with Thor's hammer. Yawn fears that the "flagstone" is stone cold death. Joyce explodes this thought with the dynamite word, "unaveiling." His particle accelerator bombards "v-a-i-l" with ε [epsilon] energy, and the cloud chamber lights up with vapor trails. Suddenly the veil that obscured the undiscovered country is pushed aside.

Being, by itself, is the rock of death that robs life of meaning. Life becomes unavailing in the entropic universe that was the world of classical mechanics. The replacement of the "a" with an "e" releases the ghosts from the machine. Now, perhaps, one can see "un-navel-ing," breaking the link with the creative mother described in "Proteus." It is vile to think of death as an absolute break, a quantum leap into oblivion. The middle of "unaveil" is "ave," a fond farewell, not just to things and appearances, but even to the "memory of." Peace or the grave means the only hope for availing is the reconciliation of opposites. The rock and the tree must somehow reach across the river.

The opposite of the rock is "An overlisting eshtree?" The tree is the "I" (subject), or "eye" (organ) of vision which on the opposite shore will be becoming. The tree, we soon learn, is related to Yggdrasil of Norse mythology, called "eggdrazzles" (FW 504.35), a combination of creation, the fall, and razzle-dazzle; the flashy magic show of lexical and rhetorical pyrotechnics. Out of the word comes the world, this time the world of science beginning with the science of becoming, biology, and its fundamental theory, evolution by means of natural processes. The "origin of spices" was met "with silk blue askmes chattering in dissent [...] guelfing and ghiberring proferring praydews to their anatolies and blighting findblasts on their catastripes" (FW 504.28-31).

The red state of death, the only door to heaven, is preferred by some to the blue state of life. To join the rock and the tree stranded on opposite banks, Joyce had them jump in the river with a "Splanck!" (FW 505.28). Supersymmetry is a special extension of the fie d theories that describe the behavior of fundamental particles and forces. A "Splanck" is a supersymmetrical Planck. Joyce's version of supersymmetry is supersynthesis achieved by means of the superconductirg supercollider word play, his own alchemy. In this segment of III.3 he synthesises the scientific way of telling "The Story" with the mythological one. "Upfellbowm" (FW 505.29) is the rise and fall of the arrow (contra Zeno), another version of the Norse Yggdrasil, the bows of the family tree, the branches of life, the apple that revealed the laws of gravity, and the rainbow that revealed the pot of gold, quantum mechanics. "Splanck!" Knowledge and myth combine and exeunt from the hinder garden into the real world.

Thus the Bible lies. Humans were not expelled from Paradise, the spin word for ignorance. After Eve, the first scientist, discovered thought they left of their own violition, and in the process flipped Yahweh the king of all birds.

ALAN R. ROUGHLEY
Feigning Dublin: Joyce's Repositioning of His Readers

But who is it that is addressing you? Since it is not an "author," "narrator," or a "deus ex machina," it is an "I" that is both part of the spectacle
and part of the audience; an "I" that, a bit like "you," attends (undergoes)
its own violent reinscription within the arithmetical machinery; an "I" that,
functioning as a pure passageway for operations of substitution, is not
some singular and irreplaceable existence, some subject or "life," but
only, moving between life and death, reality and fiction, etc., a mere function or phantom.[1]

In defining "Joyce's Uncertainty Principle," Phillip Herring mapped out
some of the problems of reading Joyce with which Joyce's current
readers must still contend. According to Herring, this uncertainty principle has several effects: "to make readers think harder, to question what
is missing, and with absence in mind to interpret what is present in the
text."[2] Before the publication of Herring's study in 1987, uncertainty
and the indeterminacy which it produces were recognized by critics like
Jacques Derrida as a powerful force in the aesthetic and philosophical
play of Joyce's texts as well as in the play of writing in general. Derrida
approaches uncertainty through the metaphor of the roll of dice and the
"hymen," the space where inscription takes place and is itself inscribed.
This hymen, "composed of chance and necessity," is a writing which
"prepares to receive the seminal spurt of a throw of dice."[3] Herring's
view of uncertainty is more limited than Derrida's, and his assertion that
Joyce's uncertainty principle is primarily "responsible for obfuscation"
seems restrictive, to say the least, but his exploration of Joyce's incor-
poration of uncertainty as a heuristic device for his readers offers
insights into the effects of Joyce's writing that remain useful tools for
investigating the reader–text relationships and for identifying important
textual patterns in writing.

---

[1] Jacques Derrida, *Dissemination* (Chicago: University of Chicago Press, 1981) 325.
[2] Phillip Herring, *Joyce's Uncertainty Principle* (Princeton: Princeton University Press, 1987)
203.
[3] Derrida, *Dissemination*, 285.

In spite of the vast amount of theoretical work that has been done on the nature and the role of the reader in the reading process, the relationships between texts and their readers remain highly problematic, and the various theories about these relationships have done little to resolve the essentially philosophical difficulties of trying to establish how a text can help to create a narrative space in which an innumerable series of different readers can situate themselves. Some of the difficulties of exploring the nature and the role of the reader, as that reader is created by the text or at least provided with a narrative space in which he or she can situate themselves as readers within the text, are explored by Jacques Derrida's interrogation of the "voice" "that is addressing you."

The traditional approaches to the problems of the author–reader and text–reader relationships within criticisms of literature focusing primarily upon texts written in, or translated into, English have tended to focus upon the status of the reader as a constructed reader. Ruth Anne Reese explores these constructed readers in her work on *Writing Jude*, and she summarizes these constructed readers and their creators. Exploring what these constructed readers "should look like," she uses Elizabeth Freund's reassessment of the reader-response criticism to demonstrate how "each theorist has christened the reader with his or her unique name. Thus the constructed reader bears the following titles: 'the implied reader' (Booth, Iser), 'the model reader' (Eco), 'the super-reader' (Riffaterre), [...] 'the narratee' (Prince), 'the ideal reader' (Culler), [...] 'the actual reader' (Jauss), 'the informed reader' or 'the interpretative community' (Fish)."[4] The fact that these models are still extensively used in criticism reveals that many critics and readers still find them as valuable ways of approaching the problematic nature of the reader and his or her roles in creating the text, but for a writer like Joyce, who, particularly in *Finnegans Wake*, interrogates the nature and the roles of the reader from a philosophical as well as a literary perspective, Derrida's more philosophical investigation of the reader–text relationships offers a valuable, alternative way of opening up an engagement with these relationships.

Investigating Joyce's first work, Herring considers the function of the term "gnomon" which occurs on the first page of "The Sisters" in *Dubliners*. He argues that Joyce used the term to evade censorship by controlling "perspectives" on the text so that "a maximum of political and moral impact could be attained with a minimum of censorship." Herring argues the term gnomon can "also be seen as an early endorsement of a kind of reader response theory that assumes that readers will bring to the text a range of perspectives": "readers brought their perspectives, but they confused mysteries with problems, mostly believing that mysteries were simply more complicated problems having real solutions."[5] What Herring cannot consider is that the term triggers off a

4 Elizabeth Freund, *The Return of the Reader: Reader-Response Criticism* (London: Methuen, 1987) 7.
5 Herring, *Joyce´s Uncertainty Principle*, 203.

more detailed account of the reader–text relationship for Joyce's readers than he could have accounted for at the time he wrote his study. The concept of gnomon offers a model of the relationships between the individual stories in *Dubliners* and the collection as whole, and it also provides a model which can also be used to investigate the relationships between Joyce's writings and his readers as those relationships are established in those writings.

Herring uses the term "gnomon" to signify "an incomplete geometrical structure." This reveals that he considers a gnomon as an incomplete parallelogram. Without this so-called incompletion, however, the gnomon would not exist for it is the removal of the smaller, similar parallelogram from the corner of the large one that creates the gnomon. In terms of the geometrical creation of a gnomon, one can in fact argue that a complete parallelogram is an incomplete gnomon, and that the removal of the corner from the parallelogram is the completion of the gnomon.

There are also at least two other semantic values for the term which are relevant to its function in "The Sisters." In addition to its etymological and semantic relationship to the Greek term, *gnosis*, or knowledge, gnomon also signifies the "pin or triangular plate in an ordinary sun-dial" "which by its shadow indicates the time of day." In geometry the gnomon is "that part of a parallelogram which remains after a similar parallelogram is taken away from one of its corners." (OED) The practical function of the gnomon on a sun-dial is inextricably linked with the concept of time, and in Joyce's short story, the nameless young narrator identifies the death of Father Flynn with the time of the stroke that kills him: "There was no hope for him *this time*: it was the third stroke" (*D* 1, emphasis added). The first part of the story is also structured between the poles of light and dark which symbolize the boy's life and the priest's death and the poles of the boy's attempts to understand language and to make sense of his relationship with Father Flynn. These poles of light and dark are also signified by the shadow and light with which a gnomon indicates time on a sun dial. With a regular temporal pattern ("Night after night") the boy "had passed the *lighted* square of window: and *night* after *night* I had found it *lightened* in the same way, faintly and evenly" (*D* 1, emphasis added). Father Flynn's death exists in the narrator's mind as a possibility defined by light and darkness: "If he was dead, I thought, I would see the reflection of *candles* on the darkened *blind* for I knew that two *candles* must be set at the head of a corpse" (*D* 1, emphasis added). Temporality, light and darkness structure the narrative at both a thematic and narrative level, but these signifiers also regulate the play of the text as an interplay between the time of inscription and the operations of the white, blank spaces and the dark ink of inscription or impression.

The relationship between the boy and Father Flynn is thematically and semiotically constructed around the polarities of light and darkness. The boy visits the priest in "the little dark room behind the shop" where he empties snuff into the priest's "black snuff-box" (D 4, emphasis added). The source of the oppression which darkens the boy's outlook is of course never revealed in the story, but it is linked with the ambivalence of his attitude towards the priest's paralysis and his death. The word, paralysis, "sounded to me like the name of some maleficent and sinful being. It filled me with fear, and yet I longed to be nearer and to look upon its deadly work" (D 1). The power that the priest exerts over the boy is linked with the latter's inability to understand and interpret language. When he first hears of the priest's death, the boy is unable to decipher the words of his uncle's acquaintance, old Cotter, when he discusses the priest as "one of those [...] peculiar cases" (D 2). The boy has to "puzzle [his] head to extract meaning" (D 3) from old Cotter's words. His reaction to the priest's death is marked by a sense of liberation: "Neither I nor the day seemed in a mourning mood and I felt even annoyed at discovering in myself a sensation of freedom as if I had been freed from something by his death" (D 4). This sensation of liberty is linked to the boy's ability to read and interpret language. When he first hears of the priest's death he must try and "puzzle" the meaning of old Cotter's words, and he has difficulty deciphering the priest's "murmured" words. It is reading the card announcing the priest's death that persuades the boy that the priest is dead and as he walks "away slowly along the sunny side of the street," he is able to read "all of the theatrical advertisements in the shopwindows as [he] went" (D 4).

Herring views Joyce's use of the term, "gnomon," as an "early endorsement of a kind of reader response theory that assumes that readers will bring to the text a range of perspectives," but the term also offers a valuable model of the relationship between the position of fictional readers in Joyce's writing and the positions that Joyce's real readers must adopt in reading his texts. The boy's position as a naive reader who must "puzzle [his] head to extract meaning" from old Cotter's "unfinished sentences" parallels the positions of the readers who tries to decipher Joyce's writings, and the image of the gnomon as that part of a parallelogram which remains after a similar parallelogram has been removed from one of its corners provides a parallel between the boy's reading of language and the multiple readings produced by Joyce's readers. The boy literally introduces the term into Joyce's writing, and the reader adopts a similar position to the boy in trying to follow the boy's attempts at extracting meaning from Joyce's texts. The gnomon can also function as a signifier of the relationships between "The Sisters" and the rest of the stories in *Dubliners*. "The Sisters" can be read as a smaller parallelogram that can be isolated and temporarily removed from the other stories for critical isolation, leaving the rest of the collection as the gnomon to which the story is reconnected when the reader is finished with temporarily isolating it for critical attention.

The important but difficult processes of deciphering language play a small but significant part in "The Sisters" that finds parallels in several other stories in the collection. These marginal linguistic encounters operate at the mimetic language of the narrative while simultaneously leaving gaps for which the reader can try to account. Mahony's desire to know why boys "couldn't read" "some of Lord Lytton's works" "agitated and pained" the narrator of "An Encounter" (*D* 17) and leaves the mature reader to supply an answer that the narrator can never know. Shortly before her failed attempt to leave home, Eveline sits with letters addressed to her father and brother, but as the "evening deepened in the avenue," the "white of [these] two letters grew indistinct" so that they cannot be read in the growing darkness (*D* 32). Eveline cannot share the reader's awareness of the fear that paralyses her; the reader who knows or finds access to the Maria's song recognizes the inability to remember language which is the cause of Maria's embarrassment in "Clay" (*D* 102). The reader is aware of the combination of fear, loneliness and insecurity that James Duffy strives to hide with his attempts to be an educated reader and writer in "A Painful Case," but Duffy cannot understand the cause of the revulsion he feels upon reading the account of Emily Simco's death in the fictional newspaper report that provides the title for the story (*D* 111). Gabriel Conroy's journalism for *The Daily Express* incurs the scorn of Miss Ivors, who taunts him for being a "West Briton" (*D* 190), and it is Gabriel's ability to decipher and "read" Gretta's narrative about Michael Furey, as well as Gretta's grief, that provides him with the painful epiphany that he has never loved Gretta with anything like Michael's passion. In each case, the reading and deciphering process is never fully complete, or if it is, it lacks the sense of completion or satisfaction which is frequently associated with finishing a narrative. In "A Little Cloud," Little Chandler wants to "write a book and get it published," but his attempts to read Byron while holding his son results in the recognition: "It was useless. He couldn't read. He couldn't do anything" (*D* 79).

In the bricolage of styles and narrative modes of *A Portrait of the Artist as Young Man* Joyce's writing test the limits of the novelistic genre. Operating on the border between the sub-generic distinctions of the kunstleroman and bildungsroman, *A Portrait* challenges its reader's assumptions about traditional novelistic patterns. The styles in the group of textual narratives are well known and intimate: catechism, children's poetry, confession, philosophical dialectic, epistles, oratory, nursery tales, prayer, prose fiction, poetry and song. The text incorporates both realist and symbolist modes of representation, and its narrative structure is also sustained by metaphors like the table, the net, the bird, the tower, the old sow and a variety of religious symbols. These metaphors are all supported by the chain of metonymy that supports the metaphors and provides the reader with an alternative network of paths for traversing the text. Joyce's alter-ego and artist manqué provides the primary model of a subject–language relationship that might be investigated in terms of the relationships between the writing reader and the text.

Dedalus might not provide us with many examples of the writer–text relationship, but his role as a subject with a continually changing relationship to language dominates the text's narrative modes.

There are few examples of Stephen Dedalus as a writer in Joyce's narrative, but there are enough to undermine a reading of the text solely as a portrait of a young man who has yet to become an artist. Yet apart from the flyleaf inscription in his geography (*P* 14), the essay for which Mr Tate accuses him of heresy (*P* 72), the villanelle he writes to EC (*P* 197) and the "foul long letters" that he imagines "some girl might come upon" (*P* 107), Stephen Dedalus writes very little until he commences his journal towards the conclusion of the text. At this point, where Joyce breaks with the earlier, third-person points of view sustained in his various narratives, Dedalus does begin to write, and his writing coincides with Joyce's break from the traditional, conclusive closure of a novelist formal ending. The narratives of *A Portrait* terminate with Stephen's present-tense assertions of "I go" and "stand me now" (*P* 228). Stephen's first assertion holds open the end of *A Portrait* as it looks forward to his departure to Paris. The second is the direct address to Dedalus which transgresses the border between the inside and the outside of the text. Addressed simultaneously to Dedalus as his symbolic "Old father" (*P* 228) and to the pronominal referent in the extra-textual citation from Ovid ("Et ignotas animum dimittit in artes"), Stephen's invocation operates on the very border between the text's internal narrative and the external epigram printed on the blank page preceding the first words of the text proper.

In *Ulysses*, Joyce's writing is structured in part by the paronomasian link between representing Dublin and a writing that is continually "doubling" its subject. This punning on *doubling* operates extensively in *Finnegans Wake*, but it is also foregrounded in the well-known doubling of Bloom with Odysseus, Stephen with Telemachus and Molly with Penelope. There are at least two distinct endings to *Ulysses*: the first, which could be crudely categorized as male ending, is marked by Stephen departing from 7 Eccles Street (and, as a significant character, from Joyce's writing) and Bloom retiring to the bed from which he picks "some flakes of potted meat" (*U* 17.2125). A variety of textual clues suggest that Molly and Blazes Boylan ate the potted meat together in the bed earlier in the day and trigger off another signifying chain from the signifiers, "potted meat." The second ending is provided by the conclusion of Molly's meditative memories of the day, her life with Bloom and her childhood in Gibraltar. Molly's discourse provides the most sustained relationship between the linguistic subject and language in the text. Read from the fold of a mimetic reading, the character of Molly exemplifies the split that occurs in the speaking subject explored by Julia Kristeva in

Desire in Language. Molly is simultaneously the enunciating subject and the "subject of utterance."[6]

Because Joyce imitates, parodies and appropriates an encyclopaedia of writing (and not only so-called "literary") styles in his description of a day in the life of Dublin, the text continually overwhelms its readers, allowing them to experience both a desire to understand and comprehend Joyce's writing while simultaneously experiencing an abjection, or at least estrangement, from that writing. The alternating experience of attraction and estrangement are linked to the two phases of Joyce's modernity. It is the tension between mimesis and the unrepresentable in language or what Jean-François Lyotard terms the sublime of the modern. The name "Plumtree's potted meat" feigns to reassure us with its mimesis of aesthetic solidity. It is, after all, no more than the name of a jar of meat like those one can purchase at a grocery store. Joyce humorously disrupts this reassurance by placing the advertisement beneath a newspaper's "obituary notices," where other, metaphoric occurrences of meat being potted are recorded. He then employs metathesis to destroy the representation of this "proper" name Plumtree and subverts any mimetic reading of it that attempts to move beyond a simple phonetic signification: "Trumplee. Montpat. Plamtroo" (*U* 17.604-5). As Joyce's writing withdraws from mimetic representation to simple linguistic inscription, it allows the reader to experience the "sublime relation between the presentable and the unpresentable."[7]

Among the numerous models of the relationships between the linguistic subject and language several articulate the essential linguistic constitution of the major characters. Molly attempts to conceal her possible sexual activity by hiding Boylan's letter beneath her pillow, but the personified envelope in which his letter was delivered betrays her: "A strip of torn envelope peeped from under the dimpled pillow" (*U* 4.308). This simultaneous concealment of the letter and the revelation of it by the "peeping" "strip of torn envelope" feigns to mimetically represent the letter from Boylan to Molly that makes Bloom's "quick heart slow [...] at once" (*U* 4.244) while withdrawing from representing it. The reader can only adopt the position of Bloom. Bloom fears what he does not know: the content of the letter. When he asks Molly, "Who was the letter from?" he seeks an answer that he already fears he knows. Molly reveals only that Boylan is "bringing the programme" for the concert at which, ironically, she is to sing *Love's Old Sweet Song* (*U* 4.312). The reader may, like Bloom, suspect that Love's Old Sweet Song is also on the programme for the Boylan's visit to Molly, but the visit itself is never directly represented. Joyce's writing keeps it hidden, and the reader, like Bloom, must piece together the textual clues about the series of events

---

[6] Julia Kristeva, *Desire in Language*, ed. Leon S. Roudiez (New York: Columbia University Press, 1980) 74.

[7] Jean-François Lyotard, *The Postmodern Condition: A Report on Knowledge* (Manchester: University of Manchester Press, 1984) 79.

that end with Bloom picking pieces of potted meat from the bed that he and Molly share.

The polysemous signifying play triggered off by the advertising slogan, "What is home without Plumtree's Potted Meat? Incomplete. With it an abode of bliss" (*U* 17.597-9) has been explored elsewhere, but as a guide to the reader and caveat about a solely mimetic reading of *Ulysses*, the text also uses it to "allude to something which does not allow itself to be made present."[8] The reader experiences Bloom meditating on the slogan as he eats his infamous gorgonzola sandwich at Davy Byrnes, but after the ironic catechism of the "Ithaca" episode asks about what had "stimulated [Bloom] in his cogitations" during the course of the day, it asks for an example of something that "never" stimulated Bloom (*U* 17.596). Bloom has been trying to forget about the foolish placement of an advertisement for potted meat below "obituary notices," and he has been trying to suppress his thoughts about Boylan's visit to Molly. Nevertheless, he has thought about these events, so the answer to the question of what had "never" stimulated Bloom in his cogitations is ironic:

What is home without Plumtree's Potted Meat?
Incomplete.
With it an abode of bliss.
Manufactured by George Plumtree, 23 Merchant's quay, Dublin, put up in 4 oz. pots, and inserted by Councillor Joseph P. Nannetti, M.P., Rotunda Ward: 19 Hardwicke Street, under the obituary notices and anniversaries of deceases. The name on the label is Plumtree. A plumtree in a meatpot, registered trade mark. Beware of imitations. Peatmot. Trumplee. Montpat. Plamtroo. [*U* 17.597-605]

Bloom's subsequent discovery of flakes or potted meat in his bed and the links this establishes between potted meat and Boylan's visit to Molly doubles the ironic force of the answer.

In terms of its positioning of the reader, the description of the insertion of the advertisement in the newspaper demonstrates the impossibility of fully bridging the gap between non-linguistic objects and the words used to represent them or position them in language. The parallel between the adjectival past participles "manufactured" (modifying the pot of meat) and "inserted" (modifying the advertisement) precisely marks the gap between the "manufactured" physical object of the jar of potted meat and the linguistic signifier of it which can be "inserted" into the language of a newspaper. Opening up this gap, the passage warns the reader against relying solely on mimesis as a mode for reading Joyce's writing: "Beware of imitations." The warning is a useful tool for the reader to employ in a reading of Joyce's final text.

---

[8] Lyotard, *The Postmodern Condition*, 80.

It is now more than twenty years since Stephen Heath remarked on the impossibility of concluding a reading of *Finnegans Wake*. In "Ambiviolences: Notes for Reading Joyce," Heath contends that "there is no conclusion to be reached in a reading of Joyce's text.[9] In the same collection of essays, Jacques Derrida articulates the impossibility of concluding a reading of the text by using the *Wake*'s own metaphor of its language as a flowing and continually changing river or language, or a "languo of flows" (*FW* 621.22). He argues that even after "twenty-five or thirty years" of trying to read the *Wake*, the reader remains on the bank of Joyce's river of language. He or she must "stay on the edge of reading Joyce [...] and the endless plunge throws you back onto the river-bank, on the brink of another possible immersion, ad infinitum."[10]

In trying to describe the endless circularity of reading Joyce's text and the ways in which it forces its readers to accept the impossibility of finishing or concluding a reading of it, *Finnegans Wake* demands that we consider the tools with which we try to read it. In one of the multiple narratives wherein the *Wake* creates a metaphor for itself, the text of the *Wake* is identified as an "original document" (*FW* 123.32-3) that was "pierced butnot punctured (in the university sense of the term) by numerous stabs and foliated gashes made by a pronged instrument" (*FW* 124.1-3). At least two possibilities are offered about how the text came to be pierced. A possibility to which we will later return is that the manuscript was pierced by the beak of the hen who uncovers it while scratching for food in a midden heap. Another possibility is that the manuscript was accidentally pierced by the fork of an academic while he was eating his breakfast. The feigned report of a detective explains: "Yard inquiries pointed out→that they ad bîn provoked" or made by "the fork of a grave Brofesor: àth és Brèak—fast—table" (*FW* 124.8-10).

Because of the spatial temporal disruptions and distortions of the author as a "presence" (the author ceases to be present with, or identical to, his or her thoughts and the language in which they are inscribed as soon as inscription commences) to whom the reader might have had access (but this access can be little more than a dream or an illusion once the process of writing has begun), the interrogation of the force addressing the reader from within the text needs to be carried out within what Derrida terms the "arithmetical machinery" of the text. Within this machinery, the narrative spaces created by pronominal positions become textual passage ways in which the reader can situate him- or herself. The position of the "I" which the author occupies in inscribing the text ceases to be a signifier of any unique presence in the same way that the

[9] Stephen Heath, "Ambiviolence: Notes for Reading Joyce," *Post-structuralist Joyce: Essays from the French*, eds. Derek Attridge and Daniel Ferrer (Cambridge: Cambridge University Press, 1984) 61.
[10] Jacques Derrida, "Two Words for Joyce," trans. G. Bennington, *Poststructuralist Joyce: Essays from the French*, 148.

"you" or "I" occupied by the reader loses its value as a signifier of the so-called "real" identity of the reader (no author, obviously, can "know" in advance all of the identities of each reader who might read her or his text) and becomes a shared textual position that can be occupied by the author and reader alike.

In Derrida's terms, the "I" that addresses the reader becomes "both part of the spectacle and part of the audience." It operates within the textual machine as a position which can simultaneously operate in the staging of the spectacle (whether as part of the plot or within the *mise en scene* of character, scenery and properties) and as a position a little like the chair within the theatrical chair which the reader as a member of the audience witnessing the spectacle occupies. Both the author and the reader occupy an "I" that can become a "you" in the dialogue of reading, and this "'I' [...] a bit like 'you,' attends (undergoes) its own violent reinscription within the arithmetical machinery."

Drawing on Althusser's concept of interpellation as the call of ideology to the individual, Pam Morris adapts the term to signify the "process by which texts, as it were, hollow out a linguistic space for the reader to occupy." She argues that by "assuming that place we assume also the viewpoint and attitudes that go with it."[11] This interpellation by which the listening or reading subject ("you") is positioned within spoken or writing discourse operates in all writing, but in Joyce's writings interpellation is fore grounded with a frequent articulation and remarking of the readers' ("our"?) positions within certain folds within those writings. This interpellation is not simply an ideological call from the text (or from an imaginary "I" positioned within that text) to the reader, nor only a textual space in which the reader can position him- or herself within the text. It is more like an intertextual space in which the reader as a linguistically-constructed subject encounters and engages the text as another linguistically-constructed subject and experiences the effects of reading the text as well as those which his or her reconstruction of the text produce. Amongst all of Joyce's writings, it is *Finnegans Wake* in which the reader-text relationship finds its most explicit articulation.

Jonathan Culler's term "ideal reader" is one that is taken from *Finnegans Wake*. Among the many simulacra of direct addresses to "that ideal reader suffering from an ideal insomnia" (*FW* 120.13-4), we find the *Wake* staging questions about our roles as readers of that text. In so doing it creates textual and linguistic spaces in which its readers can position themselves in Joyce's writing through the interpellation which helps to make an engagement with that writing possible. Reflecting upon the relationships between speech and writing, the *Wake* aligns the potential sound of its language as spoken language with "Irish sense" and the typography of its printed characters with "seen" "English": "Behove this sound of Irish sense. Really? Here English might be seen. Royally?"

[11] Pam Morris, *Literature and Feminism* (London: Blackwell, 1998) 28.

(*FW* 12.36-13.2). Sustaining, and sustained by, the semantic links and the paronomasian play with O'Reilly (and hence with the French term for 'earwig' or 'ear piercer'), the passage shifts from 'Really' to 'Royally' to 'Regally' before pronouncing on the relationship between silent, written and printed language and the spoken recreation of imaginative spaces by speech: "The silence speaks the scene" (*FW* 13.2-3). The text remarks this feigning of a relationship between silence and speaking within writing as a feint and creates the fold in which the feigning is remarked as false, or a "Fake." (*FW* 13.3) The *Wake* then directly questions its reader about his or her position within this "scene" spoken by "silence," asking if she or he belongs in the text: "So This Is Dyoublong?" (*FW* 13.4).

Of course "Dyoublong" is also a punning variation on the name of Dublin, so the question 'do you belong?' is articulated simultaneously with the assertive declaration 'so this is Dublin,' and the declarative statement is simultaneously a question. Such double, "doublin" (*FW* 3.8) doubling is characteristic of the logic of the *Wake*'s writing and of the puns on which that writing is grounded for the mechanism of the pun requires a phonetic similarity between at least two terms. In *Finnegans Wake*, the proper name of Joyce's home city is articulated in a writing practice that continually threatens that proper name. This is one way in which Joyce's exploitation of the pun reveals its simultaneously radical and conservative character. Where literary studies frequently treat the pun as a linguistic trope and an adorning supplement to the themes developed with literary and poetic styles, Joyce's writing of the *Wake* draws upon the fundamentally radical function of paronomasia as a writing against ('para') the name ('nomos') and the logic and laws with which the proper name is used to shore up the capital of certain forms of historical language governed by the model of the line. As writers like Derrida and Hillis Miller have shown us, this model of the line is one of the ways in which logocentrism governs writing and suppresses its polysemous play. As Hillis Miller explains in "Line": "The linearity of the written or printed book is a puissant support of logocentrism."[12]

Derrida notes the necessity of reading and rereading in the *Wake* of previous writers as the "mark[ing] out and read[ing of] a text simultaneously almost identical and entirely other."[13] Rereading Joyce's *Wake* and reading in the wake of Joyce—and there is little else we can do when confronted with the demands of Joyce's writings—requires that we situate ourselves in a text where our confusion becomes fused with, or "(con)fused" with the confusion programmed in that text. The reader's confusion becomes doubled and "(con)fused" with the reading and rewriting of the confusion pre-programmed by Joyce[14]: "You is feeling like

[12] J. Hillis Miller, "Line." *The Narrative Reader*, ed. M. Mcquillan (London: Routledge, 2000) 231.
[13] Derrida, *Dissemination*, 4.
[14] Jacques Derrida, *Positions* (London: The Athlone Press, 1981).

you was lost in the bush, boy?" (*FW* 112.3). In the very process of articulating the question which asks the reader if he or she feels confused or "lost" in this textual thicket, the text intensifies the notion of being lost by confusing a simple subject–verb agreement and substituting 'is' for 'are' and 'was' for 'were' or 'are.' The substitution of "You is feeling like you was lost" for the more standard grammatical sequence of 'you are feeling like you were [or are] lost' remarks the singularity of being lost. The feeling of being lost can be the same in any number of situations for it entails a similar lack of basic knowledge about the environment (be it textual, physical, urban, rural, arboreal, etc.) in which one finds oneself lost. At the same time that the sequence states that the reader "is" feeling like he or she "was" lost, it moves the feeling from the present ('is') to the past ('was'), thus marking the passage from the present to the past which characterizes the temporal dimension of all reading and writing.

After programming the reader's possible sense of feeling lost with the metaphor of the text's language as a thick bush or undergrowth, the *Wake* proffers a possible exclamation of confusion on the part of its readers, enlarging and doubling the metaphor of the "bush" to those of a "jungle" and a forest or "farest" in order to imitate a correlative growth in the reader's sense of being lost and confuse: "You says: it is a puling sample jungle of woods. You most shouts out: Bethicket me a stump of a beech if I have the poultriest notions what the farest he all means." (*FW* 112.3–6). The "puling sample" exemplifies the 'whimper' ('pule') or plaintive cry of the reader lost in the text, but it is also puns on that textual whimper as a part of a text that is a "pure and simple jumble of words."[15] As well a punning on the surname of Samuel Beckett, "Bethicket me" draws together the pronoun 'me,' which situates the ideal reader in the text, with the 'be' which sustains the metaphor of the text-as-vegetation. The 'me' of the reader is co-inscribed with the being of the text-as-thicket, "(con)fusing" the reader's position in the text with the textual articulation of that position.

Finnegans Wake is a democratic text which invites its readers to share in a recreation which is, literally, a re-creation, and there is little evidence to suggest that it ensnares its readers or draws them into its dense textual thickets only to leave them wandering lost in the middle of its woods. The text feigns to calm and reassure its readers, providing them with advice on the quality needed to survive their traversing of its textual meanderings: "Now, patience; and remember patience is the great thing, and all things else we must avoid anything like being or becoming our of patience" (*FW* 108.8-10). Although the *Wake* subverts all attempts to clearly identify its genre, there is a comic impulse frequently reminding its readers that there is "fun for all at Finnegan's

[15] Roland McHugh, *Annotations to 'Finnegans Wake'* (Baltimore: Johns Hopkins University Press, 1980) 112.

Wake." This comic impulse is detectable in the text's description of the reader as an "ordinary man with that large big nonobli head" on whom the text is playing a joke by pulling the reader's leg: "Your machelar's mutton leg's getting musclebound from being too pulled" (*FW* 64.32-3). The transition from the metaphor of the text as a wood or forest in which the reader gets lost to that of the sheet of paper which Biddy Doran discovers buried in a midden heap is inscribed in the tale of the hen. As "Belinda of the Dorans," this hen scratches in the midden heap where she discovers the document with which the text identifies itself, providing readers with a position that feigns to give them more control in terms of reading the text.

As the "missive" (*FW* 111.31) uncovered by the "lookmelittle, likemelong hen" (*FW* 111.33), the text has "features" (*FW* 111.35) some of which have become unclear and difficult to decipher. The *Wake* informs us that the "farther back we manage to wiggle [it] the more we need the loan of a lens." This lens, which will enable us to "see as much as the hen saw" is provided by the metaphor of the hen who discovers the text. The passage narrating Biddy's discovery of the text is punctuated by the repetition of "Tip" (*FW* 111.30; 112.2). These two "Tip[s]" signify the full stops punctuating the sentences concluded by each "Tip"; the two "selfsame [...] spots naturally selected for her perforations by Dame Partlet on her dungheap" (*FW* 124.22-3); and 'tips,' or hints, to the reader about the nature of the lens "we need the loan of" in order to better understand the text itself. The doubling of this "Tip" sustains the doubling, "doublin'" bifurcation of the *Wake* as it moves between its poles of night and day, life and death, death and resurrection, beginning and ending, ending and restarting, male and female, war and peace, creation and destruction, speech and writing, model and copy, etc.

The transition from the position of a passive reader as a babe lost in the woods of the *Wake*'s words to that of an active reader who participates in remarking the meaning and play of the text is marked by the shift from 'paltry' notions of what the "farest he all means" to a 'poultry' notion of the *Wake*'s textual operations. These 'paltry' and 'poultry' notions are brought together and "(con)fused" in the pun, "poultriest notions" (*FW* 112.5-6), and the feigned address to the reader shifts from male to female (from "boy" to "Gee up, girly!" (*FW* 112.3 and 6, emphasis added) and interrogative to exclamation before the text announces that "The quad gospellers may own the targum but any of the Zingari shoolerim may pick a peck of kindlings yet from the sack of old hensyne" (*FW* 112.6-9). Textual "authorities," like the authors of the four biblical gospels, may possess "authentic" documents like the "targum," or "each of [the] Aramaic translations and interpretations of parts of the Old Testament,"[16] but even "Zingari shoolerim," or 'vagrant', 'gypsy' 'scholars' can interpret and mark meaning in the text of the

---

[16] McHugh, *Annotations*, 112.

Wake as a letter discovered by the hen, Biddy Doran, in a midden heap. If Biddy Doran can discover the letter and punctuate it with her beak, then human readers can read and interpret the *Wake* in order to make sense of it: "What bird has done yesterday man may do next year" (*FW* 112.9-10). Questions of origins and of a concomitant originality guaranteed by authorial authority recede when one realizes that the metaphor of the *Wake* as a letter found in a "mudmound" (*FW* 111.34) by a hen who was "kind of born to lay and love eggs" (*FW* 112.13-4) restages the "at once trivial and philosophical question of 'the chicken or the egg,' of the logical, chronological, or ontological priority of the cause over effect."[17]

The creation of textual positions within which the reader can textually situate him- or herself is only one of the numerous strategies by which the *Wake* assists its readers, and its use of pronouns for the interpellation of its readers is inscribed in a writing that identifies itself as "prepronominal" (*FW* 120.9). Although the *Wake* proffers pronouns with which its readers can identify in order to situate themselves in the text, these pronouns provide only temporary and unstable positions of identity. The impossibility of establishing stable and unchanging identity is frequently reiterated. Identifying itself with a charade and the collection *A Thousand and One Nights*, the *Wake* declares "in this scherzarade of one's thousand one nightinesses that sword of certainty which identifide the body never falls" (*FW* 51.4-6).

---

17 Jacques Derrida, *Dissemination*, 87-8.

Contributors

LOUIS ARMAND is director of the Centre of Critical and Cultural Theory in the Philosophy Faculty of Charles University, Prague. His books include *Literate Technologies* (2006), *Incendiary Devices: Discourses of the Other* (2006), *Technē: James Joyce, Hypertext and Technology* (2006) and *Event States: Discourse, Time, Mediality* (2007). He is the editor of *Contemporary Poetics* (2007), *Joycemedia* (2005) and, with Clare Wallace, *Giacomo Joyce: Discourses of the Other* (2002). He was founding editor of *Hypermedia Joyce Studies*.

VALÉRIE BÉNÉJAM is *Maître de Conférences* in English Literature at the University of Nantes. A former student of the Ecole Normale Supérieure, she has written many articles about Joyce's work, which have appeared in *European Joyce Studies*, in various French journals, or have been published online (*Genetic Joyce Studies*, *Hypermedia Joyce Studies*). She is currently writing a monograph about *Ulysses* (*All About Molly*, forthcoming), as well as co-editing a collection of articles on the issue of Joyce's representations, across his work, of spatiality and space (*Making Space in the Works of James Joyce*).

JED DEPPMAN is Irvin E. Houck Associate Professor in the Humanities at Oberlin College and has published widely on 19th- and 20th-century literature and philosophy. He is the translator and, with Michael Groden and Daniel Ferrer, the coeditor of *Genetic Criticism: Texts and Avant-Textes* (University of Pennsylvania Press, 2004) as well as the author of *Trying to Think with Emily Dickonson* (University of Massachusetts Press, 2008).

ALEXANDRA DUMITRESCU is a lecturer in English at Babes-Bolyai University of Cluj-Napoca, Romania. Her Ph.D. thesis (conducted at the University of Otago, New Zealand) argues for and illustrates the shift from a (post)modern to a metamodern paradigm in culture and literature. She is the author of several academic articles, book reviews and encyclopedia entries. Her research interests include early modern literature and romaniticism, postcolonial literature, alchemy in literature and film, and trends in contemporary literature (metamodernism).

JOHN MARVIN is a poet whose work has been published in journals throughout the U.S. He is best known in the Western New York poetry scene for his readings. Having retired from teaching he earned his Ph.D. in literature and has published and presented papers on Joyce, Nietzsche, Kubrick, Asimov, and poetic theory often examining interfaces between science and art.

LAURENT MILESI is a Reader in 20th-Century British/American Literature and Critical Theory at Cardiff University (Centre for Critical and Cultural Theory) and a member of the ITEM-CNRS Research Group on James Joyce's manuscripts in Paris. He wrote numerous essays on Joyce and related aspects of modernism, 19-th and 20th-century (American) poetry, postmodernism and poststructural sm, with a particular emphasis on Jacques Derrida and Hélène Cixous. His edited collection, *James Joyce and the Diference of Larguage*, was published by Cambridge University Press in 2003 (digitally reprinted in 2007), and his annotated translation of Jacques Derrida's *H. C. pour la vie, c'est à dire...* appeared at Stanford University Press in 2006.

ANDREW NORRIS completed a doctorate on *Finnegans Wake* at the University of Leeds in 1992. A poet and musician, he lives in Brussels and teaches at the Insitut supérieur des traducteurs et interprètes. He is co-author (with Michel Delville) of *Frank Zappa, Captain Beefheart and the Secret History of Maximalism* (Salt 2005) and is currently working on a manuskript entitled *James Joyce: Subject, Object, Style*.

ALAN R. ROUGHLEY is a Canadian currently teaching in the UK. He is Associate Professor at Liverpool Hope University and the C.E. of the International Anthony Burgess Foundation. His major research area is the relationships between James Joyce and Jacques Derrida. Alan has recently published chapters on Burgess, Derrida and Joyce and edited books on Burgess and Liminalities. He hopes to retire back to Canada in 2010 and resume his creative writing and musical studies. He is formerly an editor of *Hypermedia Joyce Studies*.

DONALD F. THEALL (1928-2008) published widely on communication theory, virtual reality (VR), cyberspace, Marshall McLuhan, poetic theory and James Joyce. His books include *The Virtual Marshall McLuhan* (McGill-Queen's University Press, 2001), *James Joyce's Techno-Poetics* (University of Toronto Press, 1997), or *Beyond the Word: Reconstructing Sense in the Joyce Era of Technology, Culture, and Communication* (1995). A pioneer in computing in the humanities, Donald Theall made an extraordinary contribution to literature online with his Web version of James Joyce's *Finnegans Wake* and *Ulysses*.

DARREN TOFTS is Associate Professor of Media and Communications, Swinburne University of Technology, Melbourne. His publications include: *Memory Trade: A Prehistory of Cyberculture* (1997), *Parallax: Essays on Art, Culture and Technology* (1998), *Prefiguring Cyberculture: An Intellectual History* (2003), *Interzone: Media Arts in Australia* and *Illogic of Sense: The Gregory L. Ulmer Remix* (2007).

DAVID VICHNAR is the author of *Joyce Against Theory* (forthcoming with Litteraria Pragensia) and the current editor (since 2007) of *Hypermedia Joyce Studies*. A Ph.D. student in the cotutelle programme of Charles University, Prague, and Université Sorbonne-Nouvelle, Paris, he is currently at work on his thesis devoted to Joyce, the avant-garde, and postmodernism.

CLINTON CAHILL (frontispiece) is a Senior Lecturer in Design in the School of Art, Manchester Metropolitan University, England, and has taught art and design since 1981. His practice-based research is primarily concerned with relationships between images and text, with particular reference to acts of drawing, illustration and narrative. He has a longstanding interest in *Finnegans Wake*. His work has been exhibited in the UK, China, USA, Mexico, Costa Rica, and Holland.

IAN HAYS (cover art) has been a University Lecturer since 1989 after completing a BA (Hons) with a 1st Painting at Coventry University; an MA and M.Phil. in Art History and Theory at the University of Essex in 1989 and 1992 respectively. He has been working steadily and with an ever-increasing fascination on his project of *Reading Joyce Reading Duchamp*. He has given papers and shown most of his visuals at James Joyce Symposia in Dublin 2004, Budapest 2006, and Tours 2008.